The Flower Chronicles

A Radical Approach to Systems and Organizational Development

Pravir Malik

Dedicated to the ubiquitous Flower
Simply embodying a great secret

ISBN-13: 978-0-9903574-0-7

I have been meaning to make available the initial 2013 digital edition of this book in paperback format for many years. But it is only now, in 2021, that I am able to do so. In part this has been due to the Cosmology of Light book series that I have been involved in creating since 2015. There are ten books to that combined series that thankfully I did finish in 2020.

As I reflect on the book writing journey over the last 15 years, The Flower Chronicles perhaps becomes an apt metaphor to connect the grounded Fractal Series of books to the larger more contextual Cosmology of Light series. For it is the flower itself, emerging from a complex fractal root system, seeks always the light. But I would not have known this before I completed the light-focused series.

This book is the third in a series. Perhaps it is fair to say that the series is a quadrilogy.

The first book "Connecting Inner Power with Global Change: The Fractal Ladder" introduced a fractal model that offered a deeper analyses and framework for change for organizations and systems, regardless of size and complexity.

The second book "Redesigning the Stock Market: A Fractal Approach" utilized the fractal model and analyzed key aspects of our global financial system and the resulting crises, and suggested a way to redesign the stock market to make business and our financial system more sustainable.

This book "The Flower Chronicles: A Radical Approach to Systems and Organizational Development" looks at many categories of organizational and system problems from the local to the global, and suggests ways to reinterpret and address these based on the ubiquitous fractal for progress that was identified in Connecting Inner Power with Global Change. This ubiquitous fractal for progress is simply represented by the growth of a flower.

As such, this book highlights practical applications to the more complex model introduced in Connecting Inner Power with Global Change, and puts into simpler language and more practical terms solutions to complex organizational problems. I was propelled to write this book for a few reasons.

First, was the feedback I received when the initial book went into print, that it was too complex. The publisher themselves indicated to me that while "the book was a jewel and they were therefore obliged to publish it, it would never be a bestseller". Given this I wanted to summarize the complex model into its essence in a simple way.

Second, I wanted to indicate its vast applicability in a range of areas. Hence in this book I have applied the Flower model to a diverse range of areas such as individual development, organizational development, political development, country development, market development, amongst other areas.

In my estimation this book is in general a far easier read than the previous ones in the quadrilogy. If there is a difficult section it is only in the first few pages where I translate the more complex fractal model into its essence, as captured by the growth of a flower. But the reader will quickly find that the basic idea is reinforced again and again and again in many different areas that are subsequently considered through the rest of the book. Hence any initial complexity is quickly diffused and progressively will become second nature as one continues with the reading.

Albert Einstein has stated – "When the Solution is Simple, God is Answering." There is in fact a simple answer staring at us from all facets and corners of life, regardless of the question, regardless of the problem. This answer is summarized by a flower and captured in the journey that a seed makes in becoming a flower.

In this journey there are 3 stages – the seed or physical state, the stalk or vital state, and the flower or mental state. Any sustainable organization or system will be found to have traversed these stages. Any organization or system that is floundering or facing challenges, will be found to be stuck in one of these stages.

Hence, the state of an organization or system can be understood by chronicling the stages of the flower journey it may have gone through. Its road to fulfillment can be envisaged by foreseeing the stages of the flower journey it has yet to go through.

This simple truth is true regardless of the scale or complexity of the organization or system. Hence it is true of the person, of a team, of a corporation, of a market, of a country, or of a global system.

The Flower Chronicles will elaborate this simple approach through reflecting on many classes of practical organizational and system problems we are confronted with daily. These reflections will be from the realms of personal development, organizational development, industry development, market and financial development, political development, and global development.

The book consists of 8 parts.

In Part 1 – The Flower Philosophy, the radical approach to organization and system development will be simply laid out. In Part 2 – Individual Development, the key role that an individual has in bringing about ground-breaking change will be explored. In Part 3, Organizational Design & Development, some organizational basics will be laid out, an interesting case-study on the 500-yr old architectural masterpiece, Machu Picchu, will be explored, and some experiments over the course of three years in the application of the Flower Chronicles conducted by the author at Stanford University Medical Center will be discussed.

Part 4, Industry Development, will explore the future of key industries such as Food & Agriculture, Energy, Retail, Internet, Software, Healthcare, and Consulting, from a Flower Chronicles perspective. Part 5, Financial Rebirth, will look at how to shift our global financial environment by changing the way markets function, again by the application of the Flower Chronicles paradigm.

Part 6, Global Political Development, will in look at some global lessons from the 2012 Presidential Election in the USA, and study some of the issues discussed from a Flower Chronicles perspective. Suggestions for creating a safer, more peaceful world will naturally emerge from also looking at macro- and micro-level developments that need to take place in various regions of the world. Part 7, The Nth + 1 Wave of Sustainability, will examine the deepest drivers of sustainability and provide some insight into how to promote these. The role that Human Resources can play in making this real will be examined. Finally, Part 8, Paradigms for the Future, will examine a flower-based framework of future development, some paradigms to move us along the phases of this framework, and a possible future were the journey to the heart of the flower to be successfully completed.

The answers are simple, and are always staring at us in the face. The real issue is whether we have the courage and will to execute what is being suggested. This too is a certainty, but like every other journey, has to go through stages before it culminates in the reality of a flower.

PART I – The Flower Philosophy

When I was a child I used to have a recurring experience during episodes of high fever. Perhaps it was that during such times the veil between the material and other realms thins, and therefore the experience became possible. But whatever the reason, it left its impact in my consciousness.

The experience was the following: I would see myself looking at a drop of falling water. In the drop I would again see myself looking at a drop of falling water. In that drop the same thing would happen, and this seemed to repeat itself many times over. Therefore, there was a fractal reality to the experience. Further, the passage of time would change. Everything seemed to slow down. The end result of this space-time modification was that I would come 'out of myself', and it seemed that consciousness was being repeated on smaller and smaller scale. Interestingly, this coming out of myself would cause me to sweat, and my fever would break with the release of many, many drops of 'water'.

So when I was introduced to the concept of a fractal - a pattern that repeats itself on different scale - about a decade ago, there was an immediate resonance with it. While fractals were being abundantly used to understand the geometry of irregular objects on the physical plane, I was predisposed to seeing it as describing repeating dynamics and phenomena in complex behavioral systems. Perhaps in addition to the "drop" experience, this impulse has definitely derived from studying a magnificent piece of work by Sri Aurobindo, Savitri, in which the very structure of existence is laid out in a comprehensive poetry. To me, Savitri also represents the most comprehensive end of a gradation in the use of fractals. Definitely the seed, or root, or overarching consciousness of which all other phenomena are diminished reflections as in drops within a drop, within a drop.

At the other end of this gradation is the very work of Mandelbrot, who coined the term fractal, and who formulated the Mandelbrot Set, which has been termed by Arthur C. Clarke, as "the thumb-print of God" because of the possibility of a vast array of objects, plants, and animals, as being potential offshoots and images of the underlying Mandelbrot Set (Lesmoir-Gordon 2004). The Mandelbrot Set looks like a turtle of sorts, and the logical next question is, what could possibly give this pervasive spherical-like structure the stability that allows all the shapes we see around us to persist?

This takes us to a deeper level in the gradation, and to the work of Nassim Haramein whose use of fractals describes the very structure of space (Haramein 2008). Haramein leverages the most stable geometrical structures known, and abundantly used and popularized by Buckminster Fuller in his own comprehensive work, the tetrahedron and the octahedron (Fuller 1982). Haramein proposes a unified theory connecting atomic-level structure with stellar and larger-level structure where the tetrahedron, octahedron and a 64-tetrahedron grid emerge, as it were, from the density of vacuum, to form dynamic structures that possess equilibrium at the micro and the macro level.

The octahedron, comprised of 8 tetrahedrons pointing inward, is balanced by the star-tetrahedron comprised of 8 tetrahedron's pointing outward, and symbolize the basic polarity inherent in any unit of space. The 64-tetrahedron grid provides the dynamic structure with which the energy streaming out of a singularity or mini black-hole in the vacuum 'clothes' itself. Rotational movement, caused by the bending of space-time in the vicinity, gives a boundary to the rotating grid that then appears as the spherical-like structures of Mandelbrot's Set. Space-time torque, the result of the rotating object, streams back in to the black hole, and a sustainable source of energy results.

But then, the next logical question is where does all the possibility and tremendous scheme of things inherent in the vacuum come from? This leads us right into Savitri and I quote a few lines from this 24,000-line poem (Aurobindo, 1950, p 100 – 101):

"At first was laid a strange anomalous base,
A void, a cipher of some secret Whole,
Where zero held infinity in its sum
And All and Nothing were a single term,
An eternal negative, a matrix Nought:
Into its forms the Child is ever born
Who lives for ever in the vasts of God.
A slow reversal's movement then took place:
A gas belched out from some Invisible Fire,
Of its dense rings were formed these million stars;
Upon earth's new-born soil God's tread was heard."

My use of fractals, attempting to follow the source of its inspiration, is therefore more comprehensive, also exceeding its common use of describing physical-level structure and phenomena only. I have used a dynamic fractal, comprised of fundamental elements, that will cause events to precipitate in a certain way depending on the combination of elements active in the fractal. Further, there is a disposition in the fractal itself to tend toward a certain combination of elements, that in fact is defined by a universal pattern of progress observable regardless of scale. These dynamics and the accompanying overarching framework have been described in detail in my book Connecting Inner Power with Global Change (Malik 2009).

But simply put, the elements can be thought of as the parts of a flower. We have the seed or physical state, the stalk or vital state, and the flower or mental state. A sustainable outcome implies the seed or physical state, yielding to the stalk or vital state, yielding to the flower or mental state. This in fact is the natural direction embedded in all circumstance. Moving against this direction causes pain and suffering, and therefore forces a reexamination of circumstance.

In the gradation just described, we start from the Mandelbrot Set – the visible structure before us. This represents the physical or seed state in a ubiquitous journey. We then enter into the dynamics upholding the visible structure as elaborated by Buckminster Fuller and Nassim Haramein's – the vital or stalk state. We then enter into the cause behind, that which seeks to clothe itself in the dynamic structure of space – the flower or mental state. And hence we experience a version of the flower in this very consideration.

To me such a structuring of phenomena is a practical matter. Links between the micro and the macro in complex behavioral systems become clear. The logic of consciousness repeating itself on different scale becomes apparent. So too therefore does the set of actions required to reverse seemingly irreversible macro situations.

This is what will be explored in subsequent chapters.

In this chapter we examine some of the basics of the Flower Chronicles philosophy. We will start from a consideration of its simple and ubiquitous existence, to its answer to problems, to the deeper order behind it. We will look at some of its possibilities, basics, and the necessity of considering it when trying to address practical problems. These considerations will set the basis for approaching the rest of the book.

"When the Solution is Simple, God is Answering"

When considered from a fractal point of view, there are some simple structures that provide a lot of insight into the dynamics of life. The geometric 'point' is one such structure.

If a 'point' is repeated or replicated on different scale it can result in a vast variety of shapes. For example, if a point is replicated to the left and to the right of itself for some time, it results in a simple line. The line can then be replicated in different planes to result in a vast variety of 2-D and 3-D shapes: squares, triangles, cubes, tetrahedrons, and so on, to mention a few. If the same line is then bent to form an arc, and similar arcs are brought together this will result in a circle. If the circle is spun on its own axis it results in a sphere. If a number of spheres are brought together in different arrangements all molecular structures can be replicated. Hence all of the physical structure, including galaxies and universes, can be thought of as the child of a point.

Another such structure is that of the growth of a flower. The flower goes through 3 stages in arriving at itself. It starts as a seed – an inert, isolated entity – seeking to maintain the status quo forever. When germinated, a second stage may be experienced, manifest as a stalk and a root system, which seeks to grow, often uncontrollably. In the right conditions a third stage may result, where the intent resident in the seed may manifest as a flower.

Both these simple structures have much deeper significance. The point is a representation of the here-and-now, of living utterly in the moment. Doing so deconstructs all filters, connects simply to that which is the all, and each point becomes equal to every other point. Equality, liberty, fraternity can be revealed in an instant.

The flower is a representation of the DNA embedded in circumstance, regardless of scale. All life that progresses does so along the 3-fold pattern embodied by the growth of a flower. All life that chooses to progress must shift its orientation from the seed-view (or physical) to the stalk-view (or vital) to the flower-view (or mental): exceeding of the status quo through adventure and experimentation allows the insight embedded in the seed to flower.

Rightly perhaps has it been said time and time again that the most complex things are the simplest. As Albert Einstein has succinctly stated: "When the solution is simple, God is answering."

Applying Mandelbrot...And More

The creator of Fractal Geometry, Benoit Mandelbrot, passed away on October 14, 2010. Mandelbrot's unique contribution was to establish an approach to understanding 'roughness' – a term he used to summarize the incredible variability and irregularity of phenomena. Nature is created from anything but straight lines, circles, and triangles (the stuff of Euclidean Geometry). As he said "Clouds are not spheres, mountains are not cones, coastlines are not circles, and bark is not smooth, nor does lightning travel in a straight line" (Mandelbrot 1982).

However, what he did discover was that Nature employed incredible order in the design of her many constructs, using self-similar patterns that repeat themselves on varying scales. The Mandelbrot Set is an epitome of this self-similarity repeating itself on different scales, and in an insightful book – The Colours of Infinity – is even portrayed as being the "Thumb-Print of God" (Lesmoir-Gordon, 2004). That is, the Mandelbrot Set is seen as influencing, or existing behind much of physical creation. All constructs of Nature are almost as if outcomes or emanations or parts of the underlying Mandelbrot Set. That this should be has almost a poetic sense to it in that the essence of Mandelbrot's work seems to be about unifying the phenomena of variability and irregularity, of "roughness", into a meaningful framework.

Fractal Geometry has today been applied to a host of areas. Some of these include – image and information compression, mechanical design, music and art creation, medical analyses, stock market analyses, amongst others. The notion of "roughness" after all, appears to be a universal phenomena regardless of the area we look at. At the physical level this is obvious. As Mandelbrot implies - spheres, cones, circles, planes, lines do not show up as these in constructs of nature. Instead they seem to show up as some combination of these base shapes to create a "seed pattern" that then repeats itself in fractal manner to create the familiar rough shapes we see all around us.

Even at a level beyond or above the physical, this notion of roughness seems to intuitively apply. Complex phenomena are not generally the outcome of some neat theory, such as the Efficient Market Hypotheses as applied to global markets, but more a competing of different possibilities of even a different order, that in that competition for expression create the phenomena of roughness. Here though, that is at the physical level, is where I would place the limits of Mandelbrot's work.

Fractal Geometry is all about physical patterns – patterns that exist at the level of material manifestation. But when we cross into realms of emotion and thought, key constituents of complex behavioral systems – whether markets, corporations, collectivities, teams, or individuals - the fractal framework has to be expanded to include those kinds of dynamics. In my book, Connecting Inner Power with Global Change I sought to explore such a practical fractal framework that may exist behind, or be the system context for complex behavioral systems such as individuals, teams, collectivities, corporations, and markets. While this book leveraged the notion of fractal as Mandelbrot had envisioned it, it further expanded it to include emotion and thought components.

The idea that complex macro phenomenon such as Climate Change and the Global Financial Crises can be explained by fractal patterns of the expanded type mentioned, is I believe not only a critical departure and development from the purist view of fractal geometry, (Wikipedia 2013a) but a necessity in truly understanding how to address these formidable global problems. Without such a framing of the problem any solution we arrive at will by definition be incomplete. In fact, Mandelbrot himself applied the notion of chaos theory and fractals to understand stock market movements. Conventionally, stock markets have been modeled according to a random Gaussian distribution. This is a "smooth" as opposed to a "rough" model. Mandelbrot proposed that instead of following a strict random walk, stock price variations executed a Lévy flight - a random walk that is occasionally disrupted by large movements. While this is a 'physical' rendering of a complex phenomenon, that is, a rendering based on shifts of observable stock value, and if it had been followed would already have reduced the gravity of the global financial crisis, the reality is that the stock market itself is also the result of various collective emotion- and thought-dynamics, and itself a symbol of smaller and larger fractal patterns that of course repeat themselves on varying scales. That is, it not only requires an extended fractal also comprised of emotion and thought components, but a fractal analyses of human and market psychology, to shed more lasting insight into its truer nature. I have analyzed this in detail in, Redesigning the Stock Market (Malik 2011).

In this vein, I believe that to do justice to the life of Mandelbrot, to embody the visionary aspect of his life's work, the interpretation of Fractal Geometry has also to be expanded, beyond its current recognizably ground-breaking insights of physical phenomena, to begin to address a larger set of problems using a larger framework than one just based on physical or observable values.

The Flower Chronicles, describing examples of the physical or seed state, the vital or stalk state, and the mental or flower state, and their connection and interactions, is one such expansion of Fractal Geometry.

Connecting Inner Power With Global Change: The Fractal Ladder

Connecting Inner Power with Global Change proposed that we live in a conscious, purposeful, progressive, fractal-based world-system.

This proposal has been developed through observation of progress across many distinct organizational entities, ranging from an idea, to a person, to a corporation, to a market, to planet earth herself, each an instance of a more complex organizational entity. The trajectory of progress that in the end is found to be inevitable, regardless of the type of organization being considered, is one and the same across organization. Hence, the same trajectory or pattern, repeating itself on different scale, from the micro to the macro, suggests that it may be a fractal. The book explores this possibility to conclude that this is indeed the case.

Further, through analyzing the components of the fractal it isolates building-blocks, that like DNA, when combined together in certain sequences, creates the reality of the resultant organization. The book proposes that there is one particular sequence, however, that results in progress, and that this sequence is the same regardless of type or complexity of organization.

The book suggests that the ubiquitous fractal for progress is an essential shift in orientation from a primarily physical-vital to a primarily mental-intuitional way of being captured succinctly by the journey from a seed to a flower. The journey through a primarily physical to vital to mental way of being is observed in many different kinds of organizations, in spite of tremendous opposition to this passage, and in many instances, almost even automatically. The fact that there is the progress in spite of such opposition, that progress of this nature is observed all over the world in every kind of field, that it happens through leveraging the right circumstances and instruments - hence implying incredible awareness, that the opportunity for progress even exists in the first place as opposed to an as real alternative of uncaring aloofness, in other words, that the nature of progress is almost as though 'omnipotent', 'omnipresent', 'omniscient', and 'omnnicaring' or 'omniloving' in the scheme of things, points to a possible fourfold reality that seems to be the abiding context of our world-system. In fact, in this analysis a personified Progress with which it may even be possible to enter into relationship, seems to emerge

But none of this can be even remotely perceived so long as the anchor of consciousness is at the physical-vital side of the awareness. Such perception requires a shift to the mental-intuitional phase of the ubiquitous journey.

Our definitions and the meaning we have ascribed to common institutions of our life, whether of business, money, self, organization, world, amongst others, receive their stamp from the physical-vital orientation. When we shift to the mental-intuitional orientation however, marked by the possible reality of a fourfold abiding context, a personified Progress, and the existence of a ubiquitous fractal for progress, the definitions and meanings of these common institutions prove vastly inadequate and fall apart.

In a revised definition and meaning, the fourfold context, the personified Progress, the ubiquitous fractal for progress, and the very different ways to live in a world characterized by such reality, become part of the common institutions, whether of business, money, self, organization, world, amongst others. Hence the way we need to manage these institutions, and even address global symptoms, whether of financial crises, or climate change, needs to change radically. In the final analysis, hence, this book proposes nothing less than a sea-change in our definitions and notions of business, money, self, organization, and world. In so doing, it attempts to close the gap between the meaning we have ascribed to common institutions of our life, and the meaning that the truth of our reality seems to demand.

In The Flower Chronicles, we take the theoretical framework that was elaborated in Connecting Inner Power With Global Change: The Fractal Ladder, and see how it is actually playing out in many, many practical fields of life.

The Possibilities of the Flower Chronicles

The Flower Chronicles can be thought of as a process by which we can more clearly come to see more of the reality in which we live. The completest view of reality will always be the province of a Seer, a Rishi, a Sage. Such a person transcends the limits of their physical, vital, and mental instrumentation to become one with the reality of the underlying system. Many ways of becoming One exist, and consistent with achieving the prize of such a nature, the price one pays can supposedly be high in that the path is detailed and arduous, and ultimately its successful traversal is the gift of the larger system to its construct that aspires to reflect its own reality.

The Flower Chronicles on the other hand, is an approach employing reason and observation of facts around us to free us from some common assumptions that may limit our view, to allow us thereby to glimpse something of the reality that the Seer may have come to know by native sight and therefore right. As a result insights into the underlying system come to the surface and a new relationship of organization with underlying system more easily comes into focus.

In this developing relationship new possibilities unfold. First, is the possibility of a larger synthesis of knowledge in which the fractal links between the micro and the macro becomes clear. Second, is the resultant access to bold insight, which is also the seed of the third possibility, that of deeper transformation of both the organization under consideration, and larger sub-systems within the underlying or environing system.

Such transformation is the goal of many groups today. The most common efforts of the times focus on removing the environmental and social costs of business action. But there are so many other efforts that ultimately seek to create truly more sustainable enterprise. Such enterprise scans the range from society building to the education of a child. These and other efforts can only be profoundly assisted by the vaster knowledge, bolder insight, and access to possibility of more lasting transformation that the Flower Chronicles, that wisdom journey made by the ubiquitous flower provides.

Many structures at the physical or material level have been created using a fractal approach. Common examples include broccoli and fern where base-patterns repeat themselves on different scale to create the entire structure. Unusual insight into the broccoli-system can be gained through understanding its fractal make-up. When it comes to more complex behaviorally-related systems, my research (refer to Connecting Inner Power with Global Change: The Fractal Ladder) has indicated that self-similar patterns similarly animates these, and as in the case of broccoli, understanding its fractal make-up also provides unusual insight into these complex systems.

Assuming that a complex system is built from layers of sub-organization and that the complex system indeed exhibits fractal make-up, each such sub-organization would need to be comprised of self-similar and repeating patterns from the micro to the macro within that sub-organization. In analyses such patterns indeed exist and are created from common building-blocks arranged in different ways. Ability to perceive these patterns provides an entirely different understanding of the system: what it is, what is driving its development, and what it is tending to become.

We can refer to these common building-blocks as the physical-state, the vital-state, and the mental-state. The physical-state can be thought of as reality as defined by what the eye can see. The vital-state can be thought of as reality as defined by the play of different and often competing energies. The mental-state can be thought of as reality as defined by the play of ideas. These three states are like DNA, and the active dynamics and rules of being at any particular level of sub-organization will be entirely determined by the active relationship between these fundamental building-blocks, or the way that they combine with each other.

Patterns that exist at a base level of sub-organization tend to replicate in subsequent layers of sub-organization to the limits of the complex system under consideration. Hence the nature of the complex system is strongly influenced and often determined by the nature of the pattern at the base level in that system.

It has also been found that the bases of progress, regardless of the type or organization under consideration, can be tied back to the stringing together of the common building-blocks in a particular sequence. This sequence is a physical-vital-mental sequence so that a physical orientation tends to yield to a vital orientation, which tends to yield to a mental orientation over time. Since this fractal for progress or progress-fractal is ubiquitous it gives insight into the underlying-system. Such insight surfaces, particularly because progress happens inspite of all the other fractals in existence, the random-fractals, which are often of a contrary nature to the fractal for progress.

Understanding this play of random-fractals, the progress-fractal, and the contextual or underlying-system within which all this play takes place is essentially what Flower Chronicling is about. The flower's component parts are the physical (seed), the vital (stalk), the mental (flower). The fractal for progress is summarized in the journey that culminates as a flower. Remaining in the seed or stalk state epitomizes the anchoring in a contrary-fractal. The flower itself is a unique expression and houses seeds for myriad other journeys.

Flower Chronicling allows organizations to reconfigure themselves to generate inherently system-aligned lines of progress that will allow deeper, more sustainable and powerful acts of creativity to come to the surface. The repetition of such creativity will progressively alter the basic dynamics of the organization to push it into another way of being. The dawning of this other way of being is particularly relevant in times of great transition such as we are experiencing now, because the wisdom of the system whose knowing is beyond our knowing, is being leveraged in normal acts of operation.

The Necessity of Flower Chronicling

The root problem of many economic, social, and other issues we face, regardless of field and regardless of scope, is that we continue to ascribe a meaning to key components of the field that is vastly out of sync with the meaning that the truth of reality demands.

Flower Chronicling is about more accurately perceiving the truth of reality, and about more accurately repurposing and realigning the operation of key components based on that reality. In other words Flower Chronicling is about understanding and more fruitfully relating to the system that we are a part of. Such insight can make all the difference between a life lived in smallness or one lived with sustainable purpose and an on-going sense of success, whether at the individual, corporate, market, or societal level.

Research indicates that the nature of the environing system is fractal (Malik 2009). That is, it is comprised of patterns that repeat themselves on different scale from the micro to the macro. Proof for this is evident in the material field through the works of mathematicians and scientists such as Mandelbrot. Proof for this will be self-evident in more complex fields involving people, organizations, and societies, once one makes the effort to perceive this.

There is therefore the necessity of a new profession – that of a Flower Chronicler. This is in no small measure spurred by the range of crises we face today. Such a Chronicler will:

1. Help others see the fractal reality of our contextual systems. Such a seeing will awaken the sense that we exist in a fully integrated, purposeful, conscious world.
2. Help others expand their notion of self to logically see how the micro is a reflection of the macro and the macro is a reflection of the micro.
3. Help others expand their notion of corporation, or market, of system, so that these are perceived as instances of conscious world-purpose in process of being worked out.
4. Help others more accurately perceive the tight inter-relationship between the 'layers' of the world-system, starting from the person, moving through the corporation, market, system, and culminating in the world itself.
5. Help others perceive the true meaning of crises as an opportunity offered by the world-system to once more align with world-purpose.
6. Build awareness of non-linear techniques to take action in a fractal-based world.

Through facilitating such redefinition a Flower Chronicler will also facilitate understanding its impact on all aspects of organizational operation. Such redefinition may involve visioning and setting strategy, reinterpreting internal organizational and external market and system dynamics, and guiding and coaching leadership in light of a differently perceived or realized playing-field.

The price we pay for not syncing with the reality we are a part of is increasing in magnitude every day. The cost of our inaction has now exceeded the cost of change. It has therefore become an imperative to engage in the change. Flower Chronicling is a way to facilitate the needed changes by addressing the root causes.

A Vesica Piscis: Becoming Vessels of the New Seeking to Manifest

Recently as I climbed to the lookout at Peace Grove in Berkeley Hills I witnessed a natural display of a vesica piscis. In this case the Vesica piscis was formed by the large 2-dimensional circles of equal radius emanating from the Sun and the Moon.

The vesica piscis is an ancient symbol that has reoccurred through the Ages in different mystical traditions, and in sacred geometry is considered to be the womb from which all else manifests. Many fundamental shapes we experience in life – the triangle, the square, the pentagon, the pentagram, the hexagon, and so on - which are considered to be the bases for all other shapes, find their birth in the vesica piscis. Some would even say that it is a gateway or opening into the invisible, and that its natural occurrence signals new birth.

But let us take a look at it from the viewpoint of flower chronicler. In flower chronicling a universal fractal of progress is found to be the movement from a physical orientation to a vital orientation to a mental orientation. In my book Connecting Inner Power with Global Change (Malik 2009), I call this fundamental and universal fractal the Physical-Vital-Mental Fractal (or fully the Sun-Marked Physical-Vital-Mental Fractal), and it signifies the fundamental progressive DNA that exists in all circumstance, regardless of scale. The left circle I witnessed summarizes this fundamental pattern that connects the Earth with the Sun.

When organizational psychology, regardless of scale, is such the physical-vital-mental fractal is completed at every opportunity, that opens the consciousness to a fourth state – that of Intuition, which in many systems of thought and experience, is represented by the Moon. The circle on the right that I witnessed connects the Earth to the Moon and can hence be thought of as a continual presence or action of Intuition, and in fact is represented by the more complete physical-vital-mental-intuitional fractal.

The intersection of these two circles, one with its radius defined by the connection between Earth and the Sun, and the second with its radius of equal length defined by the connection between the Earth and the Moon, hence defines a new vesica piscis. This vesica piscis exists because of a fundamental change in psychology where common limits are continually broken to allow a fundamentally different orientation, that of Intuition, to effectively come into being. Intuition is the fruit of this limit-breaking orientation.

The shapes that emanate from this vesica piscis are therefore of a fundamentally different nature in which the psychology has already been fundamentally altered. Such shapes – whether of thought, feeling, will, action, sensation, etc - are brought into being to expedite the movement of sustainable progress. New energies, new movements, new models, new orientations, new possibilities, that shatter and build anew are the norms of this way.

Let us therefore recreate this vesica piscis within us, and become vessels of the New seeking to manifest.

Summary

There is a simple answer staring at us from all aspect of life. This answer is summarized by the growth of a flower. Though appearing deceptively simple this answer is an instance of a ubiquitous pattern of sustainable progress. The change in orientation that the flower makes in becoming itself parallels changes in orientation required by any organization, regardless of scale, if it is to remain sustainable. These changes are summarized by the seed-state (physical), the stalk-state (vital), and the flower-state (mental).

Mandelbrot's work suggested that all structure and shape that appears in physical life is the result of repeating patterns or fractals. In Connecting Inner Power with Global Change I suggest that all complex organizational structures and dynamics are also instances of repeating patterns or a fractal, and that there is one particular fractal, summarized by the flower-pattern that is the pattern of sustainable progress.

There are many insights that arise when this view of reality comes into focus. There is a potential sea-change to the notion of the world we live in, and our possible relations with it. The flower chronicler is a new class of a systems analyst that helps organizations understand, see, and act from the insights that arise with this new focus.

Much or practical life can change in a more holistic way, with a larger and more natural balance, through the efforts of such flower chroniclers. Such change in individual development, organizational development, industry development, financial development, political development, and global development will be explored in subsequent chapters.

Part 2 - Individual Development

The flower-journey at the individual level is the first amongst all journeys to be made, and the successful basis for every other journey that will be considered in this book. We will consider different aspects of this journey and the true power each of us has when we operate in this manner.

Embracing the Flower

We are entering into a radically different space. There are no short-cuts. There are no quick fixes. A new mood arises. We turn from the outer to the inner. The times demand this.

To pronounce that we are done with recession is to not see the true demands of the time. The true leader would say - "Listen. Quieten down and hear the footsteps of the future. They lead us into a space of wealth where all shines with native light. Not the light of false sources, of money made by deceit, manipulation, greed, and fear, but made by the light of inner strength unveiling its face in the depths of our heart. Hear its voice and the call of its song. It beckons us to abandon our attachments to the small and the petty, and to arise as conquerors of our own nature. It beckons us to become who we really are and in that manner open the floodgates of inner wealth."

Imagination? Then quieten down more and with objective eye see the hand of strength that in an instant has cleared the path toward the future. It says, "The apparent keepers of wealth are being toppled. And this is only the beginning. The fury of my breath grows in tornado and storm and the heat of my insistence is felt in the rising temperature around the globe. The blind demands of the selfish has created a facade. And now I am about to rip it down."

Resource constraints and a reality of overshoot, signifying that the demand for earth's resources has exceeded the supply, have bounded the possibility of unending growth as it has been understood for centuries. Yes, wealth will still increase, but rather than that barbaric notion of wealth by which we have driven activities over the last couple of centuries, we are now entering a phase of increasing inner wealth.

It is inner wealth that must become the driver of future development. It is that possibility peeking out, or felt silently behind the inner facades and acts of constant and pervasive prostitution, that must be latched onto if we are to truly increase the pie so that we can create a truly sustainable world. Courage, justice, liberty, equality, strength, love, compassion, wisdom, sincerity, humility, service, amongst 100 other possibilities must step out from behind the veils and take their place on the world-stage to reshape our coming years.

Under the crass veil of blind money-making active in every manner of institution, starting from the person and ending with the canvas of society itself, we have lost or are fast losing connection with our inner songs, to become a senseless cog in a wheel hurtling towards its own destruction. The connection has to be reestablished, and bought into a decisive focus. It is only so that the seeming inevitability of destruction will be reversed, and we emerge as co-creators of a world forever recreating itself in images of greater and greater possibility and sustainability.

The drivers behind the creation of product and service have to be recast so that products and business process becomes green. The definition of wealth has itself to be altered to more comprehensively put into focus the full range of human endeavor. The pathways by which economic activity have tread have to be re-laid. The seeds of creation have to be multiplied and diversified so that many ways lead to many beautiful and surprising outcomes.

Our inner songs have to rise to replace the standardized drone that has created the score of our recent paths. It is time to create a new symphony comprised of liberating notes formed in the silence of our own hearts. We have to embrace that Flower that sings to us from the depths of our hearts.

The Desert Flower – Journey to an Ideal

Rare is it when a person's life becomes an ideal. Rarer still when a person's life is true to their name. Yet the life of Waris Dirie meaning Desert Flower, depicts how this became true in her case.

Born into a nomadic Somalian family, she was subject to the traditions that bound such people, and at the age of five suffered the procedure of female genital mutilation. At age 13 she was being forced into marriage with a 61-year old, and it was then that she fled from her home and hazarded the journey across the desert to Mogadishu (Dirie 2011).

What does it take to flower in the desert, to overcome all nature of challenge, and flower out into an ideal that becomes an icon of hope and light?

After all, this situation is true for most organizations, regardless of scale. Whether the organization is a person, family, community, corporation, or country, it is much easier for the organization to maintain the status quo – to continue without change, simply subscribing to the forces that had been in existence even before its own. This phase of maintaining the status quo is like the physical or "seed" state in the 3-phased flower's journey and can easily continue indefinitely.

A first step away from this has to be taken, so that a different set of dynamics can begin to come into being. In Waris Dirie's life this was her act of running away from the familiarity of her home and all her known relationships. An act such as this often requires one to be open to a different voice, something much deeper than that which visible life offers us.

But when that first decisive step is taken, and an organization opens to a different order of being, to the possibility present in the ubiquitous flower journey, then something different begins to manifest. In Waris Dirie's life this something different was finding herself being moved to London, UK. The journey could have ended there, but continual opening to that deeper impulsion so that thought and action is driven by something beyond the comfort and easy familiarity of one's own, allows entry into the vital or second stage of the three-phased flower's journey, the "stalk" stage.

Here there is a growth in different directions, and an increasing interaction with a larger range of forces and circumstances. In Dirie's life this is perhaps captured by her quickly becoming a supermodel. In fact these external forces and circumstances reshape the organization in ways it could never imagine, and if there continues to be that opening to the deeper voice of the ubiquitous flower journey, then the mental or "flower" stage of the journey can be reached.

Then all the stages of the ubiquitous journey are seen for what they really were, a preparation by an Intelligence far vaster than one's own, to create a springing-board for something that transcends the limits of the little person. This is where the idea resident in the seed comes into manifestation, the intent and purpose of the journey becomes clear, and the Ideal begins to develop a life of its own. This is where the little girl born into a life tremendously pitted against her, can turn it around and change established tradition into something far more meaningful.

It is the reaching of such Ideals that make life worth it, and that reshapes possibility along the unimaginable contours, surfaces, and beauty of even unknowable flowers.

Personal Transformation and Power

Our reality does not end with what the eye can see. This is where it begins. There is the whole informing edifice of which what the eye can see is only the final outcome. To focus only on the physical or on the husk of the seed, on that which can be seen, is to focus on the surface of the edifice only, and by definition misses the causal dynamics that marks the real meaning and intent within the seed. To focus on the seed or physical only is to focus on established reality and to miss the reality of all the possibility that is seeking to manifest from within the heart of the edifice. And being that the heart of the edifice is the real center around which the entire edifice and all physical manifestations revolve, to focus only on the physical, as though it were an independent reality with no connection to anything deeper, is to miss the context of life.

To imagine therefore that each of us are entities existing in a physical world to fulfill a part as determined by our common and most likely programmed physical-vital orientations is to consign ourselves to littleness and lack of possibility. We each become then a cog in a wheel, and depending on the randomness or luck or even effort of construction of our physical resources or vital capabilities, will play either a more or less central role in driving or moving a wheel that is headed ultimately toward its own destruction. If there is power in this, it is not power to bring about change, but power only to accelerate debilitation of a poorly perceived and believed world-system.

Meaningful change can come about only when the reality of one's relation with the heart of the system is rightly perceived, and by identity, the dynamics of the heart of the system begin to determine the dynamics in oneself. For this to happen though one's psychology has to go through a sea-change, and the existence of a universal fractal system epitomized by the ubiquitous Flower, of which each of us are potentially significant or insignificant actors depending on if we choose to or not to exercise the journey implicit from the seed to a flower, respectively, must become a reality. In other words a basic re-contextualizing, so that rather than experiencing ourselves as independent and isolated entities existing in the world to fulfill or aggrandize a narrow physical-vital view of ourselves by catering to dominant physical-vital dynamics abroad in each institution of life, we must begin through an essential mental-intuitional orientation to experience ourselves as a flower that draws inspiration from the ubiquitous Flower.

Such a re-contextualizing implies that we become heroes because every manner of limitation as evidenced by the pervasive and incomplete seed-stalk (physical-vital) outlook will then need to be faced, overcome, and successfully replaced by the flower (mental-intuitional) outlook that by definition begins to open us to the heart of progressive life. The re-contextualizing in fact begins to become more real, with each stagnating or opposing fractal that we successfully overcome. In this view we are not just cogs in a wheel but creative centers of a continually and sustainably progressing world-system for which we are each ultimately co-responsible. There can be no more power than this.

The Importance of Managing Stress

Managing personal stress is more important that one can imagine. There are of course the common reasons that existence of stress compromises the functioning of the body and results in its accelerated break-down. But here I focus on a couple of uncommon and equally important reasons.

First, who one is being, through fractal-pressure, invites the reality of one's circumstance and creates the reality of one's world. This theme has been amply explored in Connecting Inner Power with Global Change. If one lives in states of physical, emotional, and mental stress, then those states act as attractors of corresponding physical, emotional / vital, and mental stresses in layers of organization more complex and removed from the organization characterized by the level of the individual, to ripple out to the layer of organization characterized by the global playing-field itself. In my perception, hence, global symptoms such as climate change and the global financial crises, have their roots in states of stress experienced at the level of the person.

Further, living in states of stress keeps one locked into the surface of one's being. One is driven by myopic surface-oriented physical, emotional / vital, and / or mental states of being. At the same time one is locked out of deeper possibilities resident within oneself. Lack of managing personal stress, whether it be states of the physical nature such as inertia or fatigue, or states of the emotional / vital nature such as fear, anger, jealousy, doubt, or depression, or states of the mental nature such as anxiety, mental noise or short-sightedness, perpetuates the trivial and wasteful reality of these states of being.

On the other hand, managing these states of being so that they do not exercise themselves or form the kernel of one's action in the world, means that one is now potentially open to deeper possibilities that are no doubt resident in the depths of one's being. It is only when the common surface

44

dynamics we are habitually used to can seize to be operative, through a process of managing stress, that one can enter into meaningful silence and become more aware of who one is at one's core and who one stands for in the play of the world.

Personality Types in the Flower Chronicles

In the corporate world there has been increasing focus on personality types and as CPP Inc, the publishers of the Myers-Briggs Type Indicator (MBTI) state, as many as 2 million MBTI tests alone, are taken per year (CPP 2013). Such Typing is meant to be a measure of preference in using certain faculties of consciousness, as opposed to a measure of ability. Yet, it is often, as is the case in any general physical-vital anchoring, positioned as determining the very type of an individual, and if so, is a dynamic that can become stagnating as opposed to freeing.

In a study of the System we live in (Malik 2009), the very fact that progress is inevitable, as defined by movement of the fractal for progress, and as tends to happen from the seed or physical-orientation, to the stalk or vital-orientation, to the flower or mental-intuitional orientation is significant. This fractal for progress is epitomized in the journey that a flower makes in becoming itself, and is therefore referred to as the flower chronicles.

For this pattern of progress is found to exist regardless of industry, regardless of region, regardless of field, regardless of race, regardless of person, regardless of circumstance, and in the end the fact that this pattern manifests inspite of tremendous opposition to change, without preference to location, with incredible intelligence seizing on any opportunity for progress, and with an overarching principle of love and caring, signifies fundamental properties of the system we live in –

omnipotence (overcoming all opposition to change), omnipresence (happening all over), omniscience (happening with an incredible practical intelligence leveraging levers, people, circumstances magically), and omnicaring (happening with an overarching care).

In fractal fashion, where a seed-pattern repeats itself on different scale, these fundamental properties of our containing system manifest in more practical terms or types, as power or strength (omnipotence), service and perfection (omnipresence), wisdom and knowledge (omniscience), and harmony and mutuality (omnicaring). These types then also reproduce themselves in fractal fashion, and are the very soul-force of different personality types.

Yet, so long as we, as individuals are caught at the egoistic end of this ubiquitous flower pattern, the seed-stalk or physical-vital end, these types are going to remain hidden to us. It is only when we overcome the dysfunctional and egoistic patterns that define our behaviors that we can progress along the flower journey, and in opening more to the flower or mental-intuitional end, become aware of that deep soul-force that in reality drives us.

Any personality type test or indicator that does not map or suggest these two fundamental dynamics of: 1) moving along the P-V-M-I journey described by the growth of the flower, and 2) reorienting our meaning and inner drive to the four soul-forces, are incomplete and can never provide a progressive framework to align and move us in the direction that all life is inevitably moving in. And such an alignment is arguably of increasing importance in today's world where decades-old operating assumptions are simply falling apart. In fact, in giving too much credence to the test that does not capture these two fundamental movements, the types so derived will, as mentioned, tend to forever lock us into one insignificant frame or another.

The axis of Introversion-Extroversion is perhaps the most illuminating feature of the common MBTI test. It parallels the journey from the seed or physical (outward, sense-based orientation), through the stalk or vital (energy-based orientation), to the flower or mental-intuitional (thought and even deeper, inner-based orientation). The importance of an integration of these modes of operating manifests in the age-old and archetypal journey a Prince makes in becoming a King, or a Princess in becoming a Queen.

While we might say that a Prince starts from an attitude of often-foolish self-assertion (the egoistic, vital anchoring), through the resulting adversity and fall becomes the King, more tempered by freeing thought and even inner sight. The foolish extrovert becomes the wiser extrovert-introvert (a mental-intuitional anchoring). On the other hand, we might say that the Princess generally starts from an attitude of shyness (the egoistic, physical anchoring, or perhaps a form of subdued introversion) and through the resulting adversity and fall, becomes the wiser Queen, more open to the powers of elevated introversion and necessary extroversion.

Both the King and the Queen typify a fundamental balance between introversion and extroversion, and are the result of a personal journey in which many contrary-fractals emanating from one's own self, had to be faced and overcome. The fruit of the journey is the accumulation of a treasure beyond measure - full awareness and assimilation into active being of the soul-force that drove one from behind.

The other abilities referenced in MBTI, Sensing and Intuition (different from the Intuition suggested in the P-V-M-I model), and Feeling and Thinking, when seen from this perspective, are lateral or horizontal capacities only indicating preference in information processing (Sense or Intuit) and decision-making (Feel or Think) in the fundamental journey to balance introversion-extroversion. They are not in fact exhaustive capacities, but something that was obviously in the field of Jung's experience at that time.

This sense of the journey, of change as a result of the journey, and of the journey leading to a goal or true type that was implicit and hidden, must be the true value in any personality test. It is hence, and based on the deeper insight of the Fractal for Progress that the web-based tool, PowersWithin (Aurosoorya 2013a), that seeks to help a person identify the soul-force or deep driver that they are within them, is designed. It is also based on the deeper insight of the fractal for progress and the practical and personal limitations that the deeper soul-force may manifest as, that the web-based tool, EmotionalIntelligenceBuilder (Aurosoorya 2013b), has been designed. EmotionalIntelligenceBuilder provides an index of common fractals and contrary-fractals that may drive one's journey, and that have to be overcome. PowersWithin provides insight into the deeper soul-force that indicates truer and deeper personality. The juxtaposition of the four soul-forces and the P-V-M-I framework provides insight into how the soul-force is likely seeking to develop practically.

Recreating the World Around Us at Every Instant

When one takes a good, hard look at oneself, one will find there many active voices housed within the self. There may be a voice that wants fast promotion in the workplace, a voice that wants to balance work and family life, a voice that is continually frustrated by one's own boss, a voice that is driven by idealism, a voice that is somewhat scared and shy, a boisterous and self-righteous voice, a voice that is enamored of technology, amongst many other voices.

These voices are not unlike different "players" within one's small self, and in this manner of looking it is as though one were a team comprised of many different players or members.

Sometimes these team members are at odds with one other, sometimes one member imposes their will to the dismay of all other members, sometimes the team seems to be getting absolutely no where – lost in a task that can hardly be defined, and sometimes there is forward movement – at the cost of delayed retribution because one of the voices feels that its agenda has been severely compromised, for now.

The dynamics of self when considered from this point of view is not unlike the dynamics of team, as illustrated by the forming-storming-norming-performing model. In fact, these dynamics repeat themselves on different scale, and are therefore fractal in nature.

Note though, that it is NOT that there is this happy, coincidental similarity between the way a team functions, and the possible dynamics in one's small self. Quite the contrary – the dynamics in the small self is the dynamics of the many voices, and this is causative, fractal in nature, and ripples out so that teams are in fact an accentuating mirror held up to throw into relief the conflicting dynamics in oneself.

After all, if one find's frustration in interacting with another team member, it is not that that team member is fundamentally frustrating (they after all, are themselves a conglomeration of many possibilities), but it is that a voice in oneself gets triggered into frustration because that voice has stagnated around a dysfunction that is particular to one's self.

If immediately, when this voice of frustration arises, there is a stronger movement in oneself that coalesces around a voice of compassion or a voice of love, then the whole external dynamic will shift, and the apparent frustration that was beginning to crystallize will get dissolved.

In other words, if the myriad team members in one's self coalesced around the emergent leader of compassion and love, then the forming-storming-norming-performing dynamic would accelerate through its stages and the team (or self) would display attributes of 'performing' [budding flower chroniclers will immediately recognize that this movement through forming-storming-norming-performing is none other than the movement through the all-present seed-stalk-flower or physical-vital-mental fractal for progress, where physical = forming, vital = storming, mental = norming + performing].

When looked at from this point of view, each one of us is a repository of incredible resourcefulness, possibility, and power. A whole environment can be understood if one learns that the environment is a reflection, an image, a projected world, with its origin in the dynamics in one's self. A whole environment can be shifted if one learns to shift what one is feeling and thinking when in that environment. A whole environment can also be recreated if one recreates the dynamics one experiences in one's self.

It seems that the human was after all made in the image of God. We are powerful beyond measure. And knowingly or not, we create and recreate the world around us, at every instant.

The 1,000,000 Lives Paradigm

Imagine that you had 1,000,000 lives yet to live. How then, would you live this one?

For starters, in the 1,000,000 lives that lay ahead, chances are that you would be a citizen of every part of the world – Brazil, China, Japan, South Africa, Israel, Palestine amongst every other space and clime. So one thing that would likely come to mind is why on earth would you want to fight or oppose that which you your self have already been or lived? Many that you will oppose are likely your very own bloodline, ascendants or descendants of your own flesh and blood. So you might as well do all you can to foster peace between your various homes in the world now.

If you had 1,000,000 lives ahead of you, you would likely be part of every ideology and -ism that will ever surface and develop on this earth. You will be Christian, you will be Muslim, you will be Jewish, you will be Hindu, you will be Buddhist, and more. So you might as well do all you can to become tolerant now, and understand the essence that drives these different religions and ways of life. You will be capitalist, you will be communist, you will be anarchist, so you might as well see right now, the truth in each system and try more and more to embrace that so that your own understanding increases. You will be black, will be white, you will be yellow, red, and you will be brown. So you might as well treat all these people as an integral part of one extended family now.

If you had 1,000,000 lives to live then every aspiration that you could ever have now, would likely be fulfilled at some point or another. So you might as well enjoy this time without disappointment and without stress, without anxiety, and without irritation, knowing that this life is a stepping-stone into another. You might as well fully master what you are doing now by focusing on the inner drive, on the essential things that matter.

If you had 1,000,000 lives to live then you will have experienced every limitation possible, whether self-chosen or imposed. You will have lived with disease, you will have lived as a minority, you will have lived in poverty, and you will have lived as an outcast. So you might as well exercise compassion, and treat those as you yourself would like to be treated if in those circumstances.

If you had 1,000,000 lives to live then the earth and all that is in it now, is going to be the base of all that you will experience tomorrow. So you might as well act as though tomorrow mattered. You might as well learn about and respect the different types of life that exist – whether of stone, water, air, plant, or animal. You might as well learn the truth about each respective system and ecosystem and how its health today determines theirs and your continued existence tomorrow.

If you had 1,000,000 lives to live then no more would you have to rush about imagining that all that mattered was your fulfillment in any given short space of time. For all time and all space would then matter, and your decision-making would need to change to account for that. You would conceivably become a being unbound by what you currently see in the mirror, and all lives to come and the circumstances of all those lives to come would define your becoming and reorient your being now.

If you had 1,000,000 lives to live then too, you would likely expand your understanding of life to seek behind the continual becomings to link to that which perhaps stands forever behind. And if you could link to that which stands forever behind in the here and now, then all your heres and nows would forever be changed, for then it would be THAT that guided this, and this would more completely and surely become like that. And what greater felicity and source of love to be with that that is perhaps the source of all this? For then the Flower behind all flowers would be revealed, and seeing that, this flower would offer itself even more completely to bring more of that Flower into THIS.

So if you lived your life now as though you have 1,000,000 lives to live, brotherhood and fraternity, equality, freedom, unity, sustainability, compassion, felicity, love, and the Flower behind all flowers, would even more become a part of today.

"A Man Does What He Can, Until His Destiny Is Revealed"

This quote from The Last Samurai, an inspiring 2003 movie, becomes meaningful when taken from a flower chronicler's perspective (Wikiquote 2013). In the movie itself it refers to a situation when the Samurai Lord, reflecting on a series of conversations with a Captain of the US army focused on Custer and his attacks on the Native Americans, is about to attack a far larger imperial Japanese army. Death of the outnumbered Samurai seems certain, and that is when the Captain says, "A man does what he can, until his destiny is revealed".

The movie was inspiring for a number of reasons. It portrays the bravery and nobility of a wise warrior clan fulfilling its dharma without calculation. It captures the dynamic of sacrifice to awaken a country to its soul. And it ends with a synthesis in which finally the old and new are both respected and become the guiding light for a more meaningful integration.

But these inspiring outcomes are the result of significant shifts that occur in the character of key people. The life of a person, after all, is the conglomeration of many different fractals – that is repeating patterns on different scale. These fractals determine how the person will perceive, behave, and act. These fractals consequently will also draw circumstances consistent with their root-pattern. Hence, the texture and significance of one's life will be determined by the conglomeration of underlying root-patterns.

If man does not do what he can, then forever he will be subject to a class of fractals that will keep him locked into a

53

certain way of being. In such a case the past lives on, often unendingly, and it is only when powerful external patterns intersect with the existing ones, in an act of Grace, that the resulting shock and pain may cause these habitual and stagnated patterns to dislodge, and progress on their respective dynamic journeys.

If man does what he can on the other hand, meaning, if all the myriad journeys that he is composed of are completed, then something else can be revealed. When all the journeys are completed, then stagnation whether at the seed or physical, stalk or vital level is overcome, and the past is transcended. History is undone, and in the moment of NOW so created, something other than habitual physical, vital, and mental patterns can step forward. This is destiny, this is creativity. This is to live.

In the contemporary movie portrayal of Thor, of Norse mythology, the power he possesses is subject to stagnations at the vital level. Hence Thor is impulsive and short-sighted. For him to own his power, for it to become the platform of his destiny, he must fall - and this is so because he is unwilling, and even quite unaware of what he must do to overcome his stagnations. In other words the patterns that animate him must intersect with other powerful patterns so that the stagnation can be undone. When he is stripped of his power, and has fallen, and is willing to die for a greater cause, it is then - when the stagnated patterns have completed their respective journeys – that his destiny is revealed, and he is able to return to his home as a wiser heir-apparent.

Whether with the sword or the hammer or any instrument - internal or external, a man must do what he can to overcome his physical, vital, and mental stagnations. It is only so that Destiny, the living ambassadress from earth's glorious future, will consent to incarnate in him.

Summary

All change begins here and now, with the small and the present, and what we have immediate access over. All change hence begins with the self. The flower journey and its stages reveal much that is going on in the self. It gives an understanding of the psychology that must change for all to change. More often than not dysfunction is a result of stagnation in the journey. And since this journey is the same journey made by all organizations understanding it in the self is understanding it in many different times and spaces.

We have to therefore embrace the flower in ourselves first, regardless of what we may want to do in the world. Waris Dirie's life is an example of what it may mean to embrace one's flower. Not embracing this flower means we may succumb to the stresses or dysfunctions that seek to perpetuate their own being. But embracing the flower changes all this and can open one out to imagined wealth. Imagining we have 1,000,000 lives to live can often impel the flower journey here and now, because the stagnations that often accompany us are more easily overcome.

Our truer personality and what is driving us from behind can come to the surface. The power to change our circumstances, that is nothing other than a reflection of ourselves, comes into focus. And if there is something greater that Life wants from us that too then can more easily happen, as the conversation with the Samurai suggests.

Part 3 – Organizational Design & Development

In this Chapter we will begin by highlighting the importance of increasing job satisfaction. Individual psychology is a powerful force that lies at the base of far more complex organization change. The interplay between the individual change and the organizational change and how these move in lock step, is focused on in the piece on the Dark Knight movie series. The power of this relationship is further explored when we delve into a case study of organizational change at the high security ward of the Hawaii State Hospital. Finally we will consider an underlying equation for organizational creativity that must be considered in developing any organization, and conclude by summarizing a radically different approach to change management.

The Importance of Increasing Job Satisfaction

Increasing job satisfaction can be a tough nut to crack. It requires becoming aware of multiple facets of individual psychology - the way an individual interprets the world, all the attendant interactions that result from that - and being able to monitor and change at least some of these over time.

As a colleague and co-founder of JobSatisfactionGuru.com (JSG), Kailash Joshi, has often emphasized in our on-going journey in arriving at JSG, specialists and clinics to help with all kinds of ailments and pains exist - doctors, dentists, psychiatrists, podiatrists, chiropractors, and so on - but for one of the most common modern-day ailments, job dissatisfaction, there is little recourse for those experiencing this ailment. And yet, numerous studies indicate that 70% of employees experience job dissatisfaction and that this number appears to be growing.

Many models have been created to understand job satisfaction. These include the Dispositional Model, Affect Model, various communication models, Emotion Model, Attitude/Orientation Model, Two-Factor Model, Maslow's Hierarchy of Needs, amongst other models. Each of these addresses some aspect of human psychology and suggests an approach to increasing job satisfaction based on that.

Hence, in the Dispositional Model satisfaction is positioned as being a function of innate individual characteristics, and will remain stable over time, regardless of how the job may tend to change. In the Affect Model the basic premise is that the gap between what one wants and has determines satisfaction. In various communication models job satisfaction is driven by the level and character of communication. The Emotions Model considers how dissonance, suppression, and amplification of emotions influence job satisfaction. In the Attitudes Model inner orientation towards the job will determine satisfaction. In the Two-Factors Model satisfaction is driven by "hygiene" and "motivational" factors. In Maslow's Hierarchy, for instance, "low" physiological and safety needs need to be fulfilled before "high" ones such as self-esteem needs can even be considered.

There is truth in each of these models, and these need to be integrated into a baseline model built on different layers that together determine individual psychology. These layers the seed or physical, the stalk or vital, and the flower or mental, and it will be found that increased levels of job satisfaction is determined by an individual experiencing greater degrees of freedom, which implies that it is the mental layer that leads, even while the vital and physical layers are forever present and actively influencing individual psychology and perception. In other words, a person is further along in one's own flower journey. Scaling the flower model, the Dispositional model is about reinforcing the status quo, and hence is reflective of the seed or physical. The Affect Model, communication models, and the Emotions Model are reflective of asserting one's energy, and hence have to do with the stalk or vital stage. The Attitudes Model has to do with an inner or mental orientation, hence more reflective of the flower stage. The Two-Factors Model and Maslow's Hierarchy in fact integrate each of the three levels.

In fact a 2011 Job Satisfaction Survey by SHRM (SHRM 2011a) drives home the huge possibility of dramatically increasing job satisfaction, if a mental or flower-leading model is leveraged. This is so because primary drivers of job satisfaction such as job security, compensation, benefits, flexibility to balance life and work issues, are part of the physical layer or orientation, and suggest the leverage that will be achieved if an employee shifts their basis of satisfaction to the mental orientation.

Fractal power is increasingly being leveraged in creating any successful initiative. Harvard Business School's Teresa Amabile recently co-authored a book "The Progress Principle" (Amabile 2012), a case in point, that highlights how most effective managers have the ability to build a cadre of employees who have great inner work lives - consistently positive emotions; strong motivation; and favorable perceptions of the organization, their work, and their colleagues. In other words these employees are further in the their personal flower journeys. The worst managers undermine inner work life, often unwittingly. My own experiments at Stanford University Medical Center covered later in this book, suggests the same reality - how shifts in individual perceptions, emotions, and behaviors will enhance team dynamics and team.

The ubiquitousness of the flower journey suggests that innovation potential and positive events will occur in those demographies where job satisfaction is genuinely higher. That is why higher job satisfaction must be achieved at the individual level. Gallup polls and Advisory Board employee engagement surveys are well and good. But these are biased toward the organization and do not provide an accurate picture of job satisfaction in that they are based on a snapshot in time. Further they do not provide the immediate means by which an employee can increase their job satisfaction. What is needed is a solution that aims at altering the patterns at the base of the fractal – hence a solution targeted toward the individual: a place where employees can get down-to-earth and wholesome advice on how truly to assess and increase their own job satisfaction.

If every worker all over the world were truly satisfied, this would imply that their individual psychology has gone through a significant shift. I believe that the more profound this shift, the lower will be the likelihood of ills such as Climate Change and the Global Financial Crises occurring. In my book, Redesigning the Stock Market (Malik 2011), I explore the fractal link between micro-level psychology and macro-level effects of this nature much more deeply.

The Dark Knight and the Flower Chronicles

In the recent Dark Knight trilogy, society in Gotham City is portrayed as decadent, and the extinction of Gotham City positioned as the solution by the League of Shadows, to maintain a balance between forces of light and darkness. At its very base such a solution is counter to the Flower Chronicles in which all organizations have an in-built urge to transcend their littleness. It is only when that is at all costs not possible, that extinction naturally becomes a possible outcome.

And certainly the costs were stacked high by the machinations of the League of Shadows, and in the 'Dark Knight', the second movie in the trilogy, The Joker. In 'Batman Begins' the League of Shadows is intent on destroying Gotham City and this outcome is reversed through the heroics of Batman. Like the mythical Atlas, he shoulders Gotham City's burden - in this case of decadence, and continually reverses the intended outcome. In the 'Dark Knight' another force, of extreme anarchy, is released through the character of The Joker. So strong is this force of chaos that even the overt hero, the District Attorney, is transformed into evil and emerges as the doomed Two Face.

In terms of the journey implicit in the Flower Chronicles (seed or physical, to stalk or vital, to flower or mental) The Joker is the overt and dark vital force causing a society to move away from its established status quo of decadence. The Joker's ferry experiment like his unintended creation of Two Face reinforces the volatile yet dark-bias inherent in the society of Gotham City. The Dark Knight has no creative power, but exists only to arrest Gotham City's movement into anarchy. Anarchy is avoided by The Dark Knight shouldering the burden of sin, and allowing Two Face to emerge as the hero that he thinks the city needs.

Such a dynamic is clearly an early stage in the Flower Chronicles, whether of Society or the Hero, and is marked by maintaining the Status Quo and erecting a false hero that will satisfy a small sense of greatness that perhaps people are adequately moved by. Atlas remains Atlas, and as Ayn Rand suggests in Atlas Shrugged, Atlas would simply shrug with the added burden of an increasingly decadent society (Rand 1996).

In the finale of the Dark Knight series - 'Dark Knight Rises', the flower journey surges ahead, and the timeless and never-moving Atlas, who thus far seemed to use all his power to arrest the plunge into anarchy, is able to emerge as something different. This ability was accompanied by a subtle yet corresponding transformation in society itself. In response to the seeding of possibility through the figure of the future Robin, and the more important growing collective urge for change, the downward pointing anarchy that had held the Dark Knight as a dark knight, changes and he becomes more of a knight in shining armor.

He becomes an Ideal, something greater than any human, and in that movement embodies more of the intent and intuition at the progressive end of the ubiquitous Flower Chronicles.

This dynamic then is perhaps the secret of any organizational development. The hero or champion shifts the set of possibilities available to an organization by furthering the journey of the flower in herself or himself. The organization embraces this possibility and also surges forward in its own flower journey.

The Brave New World of Organizational Development

In Connecting Inner Power with Global Change I present a fractal framework, built through observation of progress, that unifies different layers of complex organization, from the person, to the team, to the business unit, to the corporation, to the market, and to the containing system. These different layers emerge as expressions of an underlying unified system, which in fact is perceived as being intelligent, loving, all-present, all-powerful, and more.

Further, I identify common dynamics that exist across each of these layers of organization, which I term broadly as physical, vital, and mental dynamics, that in fact completely determine the behavior of each of these layers of organization. I posit that this behavior is the result of how the physical, vital, and mental strands combine together, and that there is in fact one particular pattern, termed the P-V-M Fractal that is progressive and allows the system to arrive at the most sustainable and fruitful outcome possible. This P-V-M Fractal is succinctly summarized by the journey a flower makes in becoming itself, and hence the way of seeing and being of a flower in this journey, or the term Flower Chronicles is fully interchangeable with P-V-M Fractal.

I suggest that there is a tight and causal relationship between the base-patterns existing at the level of the person, and the patterns at each of the subsequent layers of organization, from the team all the way through to the market and system itself. Hence, the key to solving seemingly complex problems, whether they exist at the system, market, or corporate levels, is in fact the seed or physical, stalk or vital, and flower or mental dynamics that exist in root-form at the individual level.

For after all, if everything is essentially One, and as practitioners if what we experience out there actually lives in such fractal- or root-form in our own beings, then the question is how much control can each of us have over our environments, and how should the field of Organizational Development be reconstructed because of this? In Connecting Inner Power with Global Change, it is clear that every single individual is bestowed with great power and therefore great responsibility in changing this World. In such a view there is no such thing as a victim, and the only thing that has to be done is for the individual to awaken to the often deeply-ingrained fractal-programming that drives them, and 'complete' the many stagnated fractals resident in their own being so that each of these progresses along the eventually inevitable PVM or Flower Chronicles arc.

This may seem theoretical, but in fact as one experiments with the completion of stagnated fractals in one's own space, and sees the impact in the world around, it will be found to be quite practical. A documented case in point, structured in a different language and background, but I believe, based on the same underlying principles is that of Dr. Hew Len clinical psychologist who worked at the Hawaii State hospital in the high security ward for the criminally insane from 1983 to 1987, where he cured an entire ward of violent mentally ill patients using the simple ancient Hawaiian healing method of Ho'oponopono (Vital 2008)

In a 9-part youtube interview conducted by Rita Montgomery and Dr Rick Moss (Youtube 2013) Dr Hew Len talks about "data" that is running everyone. In fact he posits that perception itself is the end-product of this data that lives in every one's subconscious. He says that we are not free, but are always driven by this data. There are millions of bits of this data that constantly drive us. Ho'Oponopono is the practice of letting go of this data.

To me this is remarkably like the myriad stagnated fractal patterns that drive us. 'Cleaning this data' or 'erasing the data' is like completing the stagnated fractals that not only animate one's own perception and behavior, but by fractal-contagion much of what is around us. One can only become free when one has let go of the data. Healing another, entails first becoming aware of the data in oneself, when one thinks off or experiences another. Then through a process of surrender to the One Reality, and knowing that each and all are emergences form that one reality, of offering the data in oneself to That and asking That to forgive or complete it. As a result what may change is the data in oneself, which by fractal effect may change the data in another.

To me it is such a practice that constitutes the brave new world of organizational development. In a talk I gave recently in Silicon Valley on leveraging fractal technology to scale change initiatives (Aurosoorya 2013c) I emphasized how organizational development (OD) is going to be the most important profession in the world. I said this precisely because of the focus that OD practitioners have on dynamics at the individual and team levels, and their resultant fractal effects on much larger corporate, market and system outcomes.

But for this to happen the focus of OD practitioners has to shift from out-there to in-here. OD practitioners have to become acutely aware that their own being is a precise field that mirrors many, many dynamics in the corporations they may be working in. It is by shifting the nature of dynamics in oneself, that dynamics can be shifted in the world around oneself. Mahatma Gandhi summarized this well in his statement, "Become the Change that you wish to see in the World".

An Equation for Organizational Creativity

It has been said that the Universe is re-created at every instant (Aurobindo 1986). But even if we cannot wrap our minds around that insight, it is evident that we are continuously creating.

Every instant of our lives is a creative act. We cannot but help that. It is our inherent nature. If from nothing else, this should be evident from the fact that we are at least the result of the interaction of two generously creative entities - the Earth and the Sun.

But the question is – what is it that we are creating? More often than not our acts of creativity reinforce the past that exists. Being so, we do not notice what is being created because the output already exists. This dynamic is captured by the equation: P(centeredness) + V(centeredness) > M(centeredness), where P signifies the physical-orientation, V the vital-orientation, and M the mental-orientation.

What this is telling us is that the sum of our P-centeredness, that is centeredness in what the eye can see and hence the past, and V-centeredness, that is centeredness in self-referencing energy or egoistic movements, is greater that our M-centeredness, that is centeredness in genuine curiosity and progressive questioning. In other words we are subject to stagnated patterns that are generally anchored around the physical or vital orientations.

It is only in completing the stagnated patterns, that something other than what had already structured the past can appear (Malik 2009). When stagnated patterns are completed, then our creativity, which is happening ALL the time becomes more visible, since what is produced is something OTHER than what had existed before. The equation that describes this condition is: P(centeredness) + V(centeredness) < M(centeredness).

Being that every element is creative, and in fact seeks to reinforce its raison d'etre wherever it can, it can be said that creativity is fractal in nature – that is, it tends to repeat itself on different scale. This insight suggests that the set of equations are true for organizations at different scale. Hence the psychology of a person, practically determined by the play of P-centeredness, V-centeredness, and M-centeredness, will also determine the creativity that may or may not exist at a department, unit, corporate, market, system, or global level.

When linearity and simple cause-effect models are the dictionaries by which we ascribe meaning and purpose to our lives, the inaccuracy and resulting action in that view cannot but cause us to encounter formidable obstacles at every step of the way, that then manifest as the many larger-than-life problems we are faced with today. Today's challenges demand nothing less than a sea-change in the definition and dynamics of many common components of our lives. Our notion of self, our notion of world, of leadership, of progress, of money, of business, of society, and of myriad other institutions needs to be turned on its head, not out of any frivolity, but based on more penetrating observations of progress and stagnation that animate many practical aspects of our lives. The contradictions that abound in our life do so because there is a huge disconnect between the common meanings and purposes we ascribe to key components of our life and the meaning and purpose that the truth of our reality demands.

If that is accepted as true, the approach to achieving effective change naturally changes. Usually the approach to bringing about change is restricted to one or the other level. There are frameworks that deal with making personal change. There are frameworks that deal with making organizational change. There are frameworks that deal with making market or system changes. These no doubt have their place and utility in the scheme of things, and will no doubt assist various organizations in completing their respective flower journeys.

The demand placed before us by world circumstances themselves, however, cannot any longer be addressed by such piecemeal and disconnected approaches. The time has come for a radical reconstruction of the notion of drivers, motive forces, causality, and the very map and way of change. This alternative approach to change that integrates the micro with the macro, that gets into deeper subjective drivers and their objective effects, that considers all events, ideas, circumstances, not to mention people, teams, corporations, collectivities, countries – instances of organization – as being constructed and therefore even reconstructed by common building blocks, in effect an approach that connects the micro with the macro, is what is introduced here.

New postulates for change emerge. These include the following:

• There are common building-blocks that animate each level of organization. These can be thought of as the seed or physical, stalk or vital, and flower or mental-intuitional building blocks.

• Organization refers to an idea, a theory, a habit, an event, a circumstance, a person, a team, a corporation, a collectivity, a market, an economy, our world; basically anything whose structure, processes, meaning is defined by the common building-blocks.

• Dynamics of a particular organization are entirely determined by which of these building-blocks are active at that level of organization.

• Like DNA, the stringing together of building-blocks in a particular sequence or with particular dominance, determines the active dynamics of that level of organization.

• There is only one particular sequence of stringing together building-blocks that allows an organization to progress sustainably. This sequence is summarized by the journey that a flower makes in arriving at itself – starting from the seed, through the stalk, to the flower.

• This particular sequence exists in all progressive organizations, regardless of level of complexity.

• When organizations embrace sequences other than that of this progressive journey, they become a part of 'as-usual' as opposed to progressive life.

• All sequences tend to repeat their raison d'etre and way of being not only at their own levels, but by influence, at other levels also.

• When a journey toward flowerhood inevitably encounters contrary forces a rite of passage is created by which deeper identity can emerge.

• The existence of the ubiquitous flower journey leading to progress, regardless of level of organizational complexity and regardless of formidable opposition by forces to the contrary, implies its reality or even an essential and pervasive and four fold reality of power, presence, knowledge, and love.

• An opening to this essential four-fold reality of power, presence, knowledge, and love is perhaps the most effective way for an organization to complete its own flower journey of progress.

• The flower's journey opens a zone of possibility that causes the world-system to progress in the most sustainable way possible. This is because of the resonance created when a journey is in tune with the deep Flower journey behind all things.

• The insights just described sets the stage for a vastly different set of dynamics with which to bring about change in organizations.

Summary

In this chapter we began by considering the importance of increasing job satisfaction. Job dissatisfaction is the result of stagnation in personal dynamics and this can only be sustainably altered through shifting individual psychology. I believe that individual psychology lies at the base of larger organizational dynamics and the lock-step relationship between individual change and societal change is in fact explored anecdotally in the Dark Knight piece. In fact the secret of organizational development is positioned as being this change in individual psychology. The power of shifting external phenomenon through individual shifts is explored in the case of Dr. Lew. The trajectory of the shifting parallels the flower journey and is summarized by the equation of organizational creativity. The power of the flower pattern and its parts in affecting organizational change is brought together in a Radical Reconstruction of Change Management which summarizes what is to be done to bring about complex change.

Chapter 5: Organizational Design

In this chapter we consider some deeper forces necessary to successful organizational design. There are PowersWithin, in the seed of things that have to come to the surface in the flowers so expressed. Utilizing and tapping into these will allow the design of more stable organizations.

The Time For PowersWithin Has Arrived

We live in unprecedented times. The confluence of crises ranging from Climate Change, signifying a fundamental macro-level restructuring of the very physical foundation we have come to rely on, at one end, to the global financial meltdown signifying the breakdown of the very vital foundation replete with various flows our economy and present-day society have come to rely on, leads us squarely into the necessity of a basic mental level reorientation at the other end.

Our conception of ourselves must of necessity alter such that the subjective powers, the powers within, begins to count for more than the objective. It has become a necessity that we restructure all manner of organization so that these PowersWithin may find a more concrete platform to exercise their influence in practical life. It is only in the re-equationing of the fundamental balance between subjectivity and objectivity that whatever is seeking to express itself through the chaos of the time will find its most secure surfacing.

PowersWithin can be thought of as those exceptional drivers that come to the surface where the oft-common journey characterized by the physical-vital or seed-stalk stages comes to an end. Hence these are perhaps those dynamics that were inherent in the seed. Utilizing or tapping into these drivers can provide exceptional stability to organizations because of this.

The time for leveraging PowersWithin has arrived. There are several concrete indications of this:

• The knowledge of the physical world has increased to such an extent that it is trying to break its own bounds. The search for the bases of matter is leading to more and more subtle particles that are themselves increasingly subjective in quality.

• The veil between the outer and inner physical, vital, and mental capacities and powers are breaking, and the outer physical, vital, and mental possibilities are awaiting to get more power from within rather than from the external material level as in the past.

• Manifestation of excessive vital powers and its practices in the material world exerts such a high pressure that it has resulted in the formidable problems such as Climate Change and the global financial meltdown and is leading to the collapse of the very foundation we have based much of our activity on.

• Conventional industry is dying before it is even declared as sick.

• There is an increase in the collapse of all hierarchical and patriarchal structures around the world.

• Any contemporary crises are very deep rather than superficial.

• The consequence of practicing falsehoods is becoming concretely visible.

• Nothing can be hidden any more.

• The strength of women, naturally more subjective beings, is on the rise.

• There is more and more awareness of and focus on the unknown.

• There is a growing urge toward freedom and equality.

Every thought, word, and act, which already is a means for the vaster powers of all-love, all-knowledge, all-presence, all-power, to manifest themselves, must more completely surrender to that which is seeking to manifest. For on closer examination one can perhaps see that it is indeed these powers from within – harmony and mutuality, knowledge and wisdom, service and perfection, power and energy - that stand behind all that we see manifest around us.

Consider a simple example of a chair. For centuries perhaps, people sat on the ground, or on boulders. Then one fine day somebody had a flash of insight, and the concept of sitting on a movable, comfortable chair became real. The concept itself was the result of the power of knowledge. Having had the sure vision of the thing to be done, the force and energy to do it became real. This is the result of the power of energy, a derivative of all-power. Now, of course, was the issue of making the concept real. Elaborate plans were then drawn out, specifying materials to be used, implements to be used, alternative end-designs, and even the process of production. This was the result of the power of harmony and mutuality, a derivative of all-love. Finally the blueprints needed to be executed. The skill and workmanship and overseeing of the project had to be embarked upon. This was the result of the power of service and perfection, a derivative of all-presence.

Or consider the example of the human body. One can again see the action of the archetypes in the very creation of the human body. Thus, the archetype of wisdom and knowledge creates the thinking ability resident in the brain and mind. The archetype of harmony and mutuality creates the lungs and heart, by whose action the individual can remain connected to the rhythm of the vaster breath all around, and keep connected the different parts of the body whose individual rhythms are in tune with the heart within. The archetypes of power and energy create the entire digestive system by whose action food is assimilated and provides power and energy for all that the body needs to do. The archetypes of service and perfection combine micro-elements into atoms, and these into molecules, these into plasma for cell, these into organs, and these into the body itself, which then becomes the sac within which all the other archetypes and their representatives can act.

The Archetypes of the PowersWithin

When the researcher, thus, is seeking after a new insight, it must be done with a one-pointed commitment and concentration so that the very wells of knowledge resident in hidden suns feel compelled to reveal their great secrets. When the manager is seeking to motivate his team he must do so with such conviction and energy that the very powers of the wind and fire feel compelled to manifest in the team. When the organizer is seeking to design and arrange parts of an organization he must do so with such a sense of rhythm and harmony that the beauty of nature becomes apparent in the designed forms. When the engineer is constructing his device he must do so with such a sense of accurate detail and attention that perfection itself arises through his touch.

These four powers must be allowed to express themselves in their purity. Currently, and in accordance with the unrefined vital tendency of the age, all the sub-powers of the four powers have submitted themselves to the dynamics of commercialization, itself an unrefined power of mutuality and harmony. Thus, Art is created and valued for its ability to generate monetary wealth. Sports too have become big business. Knowledge is valued only for its ability in generating monetary gains. And so on. When we say that everything must express itself in its purity we mean that knowledge must be pursued for the sake of knowledge, art to express beauty, sport to perfect the body, enhance organization skills, and develop many other noble qualities, and so on. But it also means that the myriad capacities contained within these four powers will more easily exercise themselves in our functioning.

Thus the development of the archetype of knowledge within oneself will perhaps imply not only the seeking of knowledge in areas related to one's immediate work, but even seeking of knowledge in other areas, of a need to research and create new knowledge, of a temperament that is calm and turned to introspection and even meditation, of a tendency to want to dominate all emergence of passion and vital tendencies by reason, by the urge of wanting to spread knowledge amongst all, and by the seeking after truths too profound to perhaps even be contemplated.

The development of the archetype of mutuality and harmony within oneself will perhaps imply the understanding of rhythms of all kinds, the understanding and even mastery of the great laws of interchange by which organizations are built, of the need of amassing in order to throw out in even larger measure in order to create an even greater return, of even the ability of compelling others to unite through harmony, and of turning insights into practicalities – of making even abstract thoughts and ideas manifest practically.

The development of the archetype of power, leadership and energy within oneself will perhaps imply the development of an unflinching courage, of the ability and need to be a leader in noble causes, the need to protect the down-trodden, the ability to muster and possess great energy for any new endeavors, the ability to see the new and needed, and the ability to convince others of the worthiness of new adventures.

The development of the archetype of service and perfection within oneself will perhaps imply an extraordinary attention to detail, a need to labor at any discipline in order to achieve perfection, a giving of oneself to that which one loves without concern of the self, a sense that nothing is too small to be the object of attention, and a sense of what has already been accomplished and what remains yet to be accomplished.

PowersWithin and the Creation of a Stable Mega-Organization

Once each power is developed and expressed in purity then only will multiple motive forces become the engine of development. When this happens, then truly robust organizations, flowering organizations, can begin to come into being.

Consider the example of Silicon Valley. While it may be primarily a commercial organization, yet we begin to glimpse something of what may become possible when the powers just talked about can begin to interact with one another in free fashion. That is, without the motive of doing everything for the sake of generating money only. In the case of Silicon Valley we see that the climate and beauty of the Bay Area began to attract many talented people into the vicinity. Over time the talent pool became progressively diversified.

Educational institutes, such as Stanford University and University of Berkeley cropped up and became centers of cutting-edge research. The Armed Forces were attracted to the area for the same reason, and came with their huge requirements for research for research's sake, and their huge funds in support of the area. Graduates from the universities started companies that began to in turn support the universities with handsome funds. Talent moved around from company to company like people from department to department. Thus we see that even when individual companies failed, Silicon Valley functioned as a larger organization and was able to retain the talent in the area, was able further, to buffer the shocks to some extent, hence preparing the ground for future waves of innovation.

Pragmatically speaking this dynamic of functioning as a larger mega-organization meant that some level of commercial-immunity began to develop, so that people losing their jobs was not necessarily considered as that stressful an event. There was a freeing, thus, from the purely commercial element. If the various powers of beauty, aesthetics, knowledge, power in the form of money, plus the myriad streams of talent – from engineers, scientists, managers, lawyers etc., did not exist in such close proximity, and further, if the various professionals could not thus support each other through their continued informal meetings, through the urge to create the next wave of innovation, through the urge to pursue progress for the sake of progress, then they would have left for other areas and the phenomenon of Silicon Valley would never have been.

Modern day organizations cannot provide these various buffers and opportunities for interaction that Silicon Valley provides, and hence when hit with adversity, more often than not, simply crumble. This is perhaps due to the fact that it is always only one-dimension that drives them, and when the health of that is threatened or falls, the organization resorts to tactics that will ensure that that dimension looks good at any cost, in the bargain sacrificing the development of the other dimensions, and therefore its longer term health.

The PowersWithin-led organization will be something like a community. Having attained freedom from an exaggerated commercial impetus, people will 'live' their 'jobs' because it is what fulfills them. Such a freedom is what will allow the four primary powers to manifest to greater and greater degree within them and their environment. Seeing thus, their ability to become centers of knowledge and wisdom, or mutuality and harmony, or power and leadership and energy, or perfection and service, or some unique combination of these primary forces, so increase, a sense of satisfaction with life will more easily accompany all that they continue to do. Under the freer flow of these powers their uniqueness will be refined and flourish, and correspondingly, so too will the uniqueness of their respective organizations.

An organization may be political and hence be primarily driven by the power of leadership and courage, or it may be social and hence be primarily driven by the power of service and perfection, or it may be commercial and hence be primarily driven by the power of mutuality and harmony, or it may be research-oriented and academic and hence be primarily driven by the powers of knowledge and wisdom, but always each of the other powers will also be behind it, fulfilling and completing its primary urge. Even the number of PowersWithin "savants" will continue to increase, become guiding lights so that the community will spontaneously begin to move in holistic directions consistent with the urge of people, of the sub-organizations within the community, of the community itself, and of the larger system of which the community or mega-organization is a part.

Even perhaps, something that may be behind the four archetypal powers, something that may be behind the building of all uniqueness – individual and organizational, if something like that exists, that is, may be compelled to come forward, seeing how developed its means of expression and action have become.

Summary

So long as we remain focused at the physical-vital our way of life is going to be determined by the externalities of life. In such a situation the habit of who one is is reinforced. It is only at the flower stage that the balance of dynamics is changed and forces of subjectivity become more important than objectivity. It is in such a condition that the PowersWithin, the deeper archetypes that are part of our containing system, can exercise themselves. It is these deeper powers that require free reign for truly sustainable organizations, regardless of scale, to come into being. Hence the flower must be traversed, and the very forces that stand behind all individuality must become, through organic interaction, the foundation of organization design.

There are several properties that exist by virtue of the ubiquitous flower journey that by definition repeats itself in many different places (Malik 2009). Here we explore some of these that also will allow a different way to converse with our environments. These powers are critical in the consideration of sustainable organizational development and design.

Universality

The flower's journey into itself is characterized by the physical-vital-mental sequence. This journey is ubiquitous and exists in each type of organization regardless of scale and regardless of type. By knowing the intimacies of this journey or sequence, one can develop significant insight into this similar journey at another level. Thus, for example, in fully living the physical-vital-mental journey as it occurs at the personal level, replete with the nature of the phases and the transitions between the phases, one can have insight into the physical-vital-mental journey as it appears at the level of the corporation or the economy, or even in the evolution of a system of science, such as physics. Many distinct fields of experience and knowledge, which simply have no connection with one another in a linear view of the world, now share an intimacy when viewed as a manifestation of the same underlying flower pattern. This property is one of universality. The implication of this property is that knowledge of progress in one field of human endeavor can be transferred to another field, to gain at least a gut-sense for how progress may happen. Another implication is that if one does one thing really well, thereby by definition going through the physical-vital-mental journey in the mastery of that activity or field, one should be able to not only understand, but also have sufficient insight into the nature of progress in many different fields. A corollary of this is that the notion of specialization is overstated.

Influence

Influence is another Flower Chronicles property. Influence is the property by which a shift in the journey at one level of organization tends to cause a corresponding shift at another level of organization. Hence, at the individual level a shift from the vital to mental state of being in a leader may tend to cause a corresponding shift in the functioning of a corporation from the vital to mental state of being. It is to be noted, however, that this will unlikely be a one-to-one mapping. That is, it will require a certain momentum or threshold of influence before an actual shift will be seen at the subsequent level. This said, however, the fact remains that the shift itself even if emanating from one individual has put a new repeating pattern or fractal possibility into place that must have its repercussion in the scheme of things precisely because it represents a new possibility in the play of progress.

Influence can work bi-directionally. Hence, if a segment of the economy shifted from a vital to a mental functioning, corporations that may be lagging would need to make this shift in order not to get marginalized. Note, however, that the shift from one phase in the flower journey to the next at the level of the economy, is usually made by leading companies where the shift from the physical to the vital, or from the vital to the mental outlook, has already taken place in the leaders of those companies. Hence, in effect, the influence from earlier leaders is now reinforcing itself from the top-down. This kind of magnification cannot but exist in a world characterized by a ubiquitous flower journey.

Another property is that of recursion. That is, one should be able to apply the flower journey to any sub-phase within the flower journey. For instance, in applying the flower journey to the mental or digital phase of the global economy fractal we find that the digital economy itself goes through the physical, vital, and mental phases in building its possibilities. Applying recursion upward, we also conclude that the current global economy is in a vital phase, and that the agricultural, industrial, and digital phases, were all sub-phases of this overarching vital phase, that is only now hitting the boundary that could possibly lead it into a mental phase, were we to fulfill the conditions of a successful transition.

Similarly, applying both downward and upward recursion to the evolution fractal we can explore activity at the atomic and molecular levels through the physical-vital-mental sequence, resulting in the culmination or starting point of matter, the downward recursion, if you will, and subsequently using granular and distinct material building blocks, in an upward recursion to explore the journey through the physical-vital-mental sequence, to arrive at the physical foundation of evolution.

In this manner we see how the recursive property of the physical-vital-mental fractal can be used to piece together likely development of entities. In a similar vein, at the level of the individual and the corporation, we can apply the physical-vital-mental sequence to shed light on what physical, vital, and mental could mean within these levels of creation.

Completion

Another property is that of completion. This implies that for progress to happen, the physical-vital-mental sequence must be completed. But it also implies that the flower journey in progress wants to complete its journey. At the personal level, for instance, if one experiences anger, a vital state, then introduction of a mental state, bringing in reason into the situation, will diffuse a potentially destructive cycle. At the level of corporation, if the leaders are consumed by greed, a vital state, then unless a higher reason for being, or thinking about the longer-term, both examples of mental states, becomes alive, the corporation could experience an Enron-like demise. In the case of a country, such as the USSR, a fixed notion of how things should be run, a physical state, resulted in its demise, perhaps because the country was not able to rise to the next level in the fractal. Hence, for progress to occur, the fractal must be completed.

Intersection

Intersection is a property that holds when two flower journeys are made to intersect with one another. There is the possibility that both journeys can move to the next level through this intersection. Consider the unfortunate destruction of the World Trade Center (WTC). The WTC can perhaps be thought of as the symbol of the global economy flower journey. It was destroyed by religious fundamentalists, representative of the flower journey that religion is going through.

Supposedly, vitalistic, that is egoistic and self-aggrandizing dynamics, characteristic of the present phase of the global economy flower journey led to oil-related aggression in the Middle East. This spurred a radical response from fundamentalists that led to the destruction of the WTC.

Two vitally-centered journeys, both characterized by possible arrestation, were made to collide, and in the shock, perhaps both stand a chance to progress to the next level. On one side, the destruction of the WTC leads to a deeper realization and consequent questioning of some of the methods of modern business, and perhaps forms an important stimulus to the acceleration of the global economy journey. On the other side, peaceful members of religion the world over are simultaneously led to a questioning of what religion could be made to stand for, thereby also leading to deeper question of what it should stand for – also an important stimulus to the acceleration of religion's flower journey.

When viewed from this lens, or through examination of this property, a different and hopefully more revealing light might be shed on many conflicts the world over. The conflict should be recognized for what it is – the intersection or collision of two arrested journeys that through the collision are being given a chance to progress to the next levels in their respective journeys. Boundary conditions are always difficult, especially when the resistance to cross over to the next phase is strong.

Facilitation

Facilitation is a property that can be applied to a situation that appears to be stuck. Essentially this implies applying a form of the physical-vital-mental journey to the point or situation of stagnation. The physical-vital-mental pattern can be thought of as a pattern of moving from status quo, the physical, to chaos, the vital, to questioning or reforming, the mental.

Applying the step of 'status quo' allows one to more fully grasp the current situation – what are the facts and the visible signs characterizing the situation. Applying the step of 'chaos' facilitates movement away from the state of stagnation. The direction in which the move takes place is relatively insignificant – the point is that the movement needs to take place. This sets into motion a new energy of a different nature than that of stagnation. The final step is that of 'questioning', by which a new light is shed on the situation that caused the stagnation, and possible new directions in which the energy that has been introduced through chaos, can now begin to mature towards.

Flow

Flow is somewhat related to facilitation, and is a property by which a range of energies, of themselves, enter into a situation. The starting point is that of concentration on the activity at hand. If such a concentrated engagement occurs, then the physical-vital-mental journey manifests of itself.

The beginning of the activity, whether it is reading a book, playing tennis, conversing with someone, amongst many other possibilities, may often be characterized by a state of relative resistance or inertia. This is akin to the physical level. If the activity is pursued with concentration, then a 'flow' begins to arise, which makes the activity easier to do. This is perhaps parallel to the vital level. Continued engagement in a concentrated manner will likely result in that same activity becoming effortless, and even perhaps in various insights related to it beginning to arise. This is akin to the mental level.

This unrolling of energies is inevitable if indeed we exist in a world where progress, and progress as characterized by the physical-vital-mental sequence, is an essential underlying trait.

Up-Scaling

Up-scaling refers to shifting the context or orientation from a 'lower' or previous stage in the sequence to a higher or next stage in the sequence. Shifting from a physical to a mental orientation, for example, necessitates thinking and operating in a wholly different way. From a basic outward or objective orientation the field of relevance shifts more toward an inward or subjective orientation. Degrees of freedom associated with a situation also correspondingly changes, as does the essential psychology of the actor or instrument exercising the shift. Up-scaling is a powerful approach to consider new and different possibilities in any situation.

World-Wiseliness

World-wiseliness is a property related to the mastery of several different physical-vital-mental journeys at different levels or different arenas of life. The idea here is that the more physical-vital-mental journeys one masters, the more world-wisely one becomes.

One experiences a broader range of similar phases garbed in different expressions or languages, and gains more insight into boundary conditions, and the requirements in pushing from one phase into another. A more complete sense of the mosaic underlying progress emerges, and one can more easily perhaps extend one's experience into previously unconsidered areas.

The property of world-wiseliness is perhaps very relevant in today's world where many different ways of being are being melded together through force of convergence. World-wiseliness may also shed insight into knowing which converging journeys may prevail, because they are inherently more aligned with the imperative of progress.

Mirroring

Mirroring refers to the fact that regardless of where we look, what we see is a reflection of our inner state. This cannot but be true in a world characterized by a pattern repeating itself on different scale. Seed-patterns that live in us, through force of fractal pressure, find expression and manifestation at each level of creation.

Climate Change, social depravities, severe resource shortages, are outer expressions or mirror our inner states. Nothing in the world lies, and all events are signs of changes we must make at the level of the seed-patterns, in our essential internal outlooks and way of being, if we wish to truly change the world we have created.

Affirmation

Affirmation is a property that reinforces the very notion of progress. This property asserts that any successful outcome in the world must have described the essential flower journey characterized by the physical-vital-mental stages. A simple proof – man is the master of his environment, and not the donkey or rubber-plant, precisely because in man the fractal journey has reached a higher level of completion.

Integration

Integration is a property with many applications in this Flower Chronicles world. In its application to leadership for example, it implies that while leaders may exist at each phase in the flower journey – the physical, the vital, the mental – there must be an overriding leader who is a summary of the journey. That is, he must possess mastery over all levels, while being led by the very sense underlying the meaning of the Flower Chronicles.

It is only such a leader who can successfully integrate and coordinate all that is going on in an organization, and yet ensure a constant freshness in direction and approach. A leader, hence, who draws inspiration solely from the vital or financial level, for example, will not be appropriate in times of major change. On the other hand, a leader who just has an intuitive sense of the underlying progress, without having mastery over the material or physical, the financial or vital, and the conceptual or mental realms, may be relatively ineffectual in getting things done.

Uniqueness

Uniqueness emerges as fractal journeys are completed and may to some extent be defined by the particular shades, circumstances, or capacities experienced and developed along the way. Uniqueness uses the journey to emerge from the trials and tribulations of it. Crossing between or through phases often necessitates encounters with contrary-forces that cause something essential that is experiencing the journey to begin to express something more of itself. Finally there must be a shaking off of the physical, vital, and mental garbs used on the way for something to emerge from within that then may use the experienced physical, vital, and mental capacities to more fully express itself.

Summary

The emergence of a flower journey in many different quarters of life suggests that our conception of life as linear needs to be changed. Things are not simply determined by what is visible only. We live in a complex system with intent, and operating in this system can be further optimized through leveraging Flower Chronicles Calculus. Organization design and development need to leverage such properties, as becomes apparent in this calculus.

On Dec 27, 2012 I visited Machu Pichu for the first time. It is spectacular from the point of view of location and environment, the actual construction and architecture itself, and the depth of response that it can invoke in a visitor.

My experience was extraordinary, as though the Incan Spirit were guiding me through a visceral vision of the Chakana also known as the Inca Cross - a depiction of the world tree with its embedded triple worlds of the snake, the puma, and the condor, and its vaster implications in understanding Machu Picchu itself.

The Physical or Snake Level

We arrived at Machu Picchu shortly after 6am, hoping to experience the first rays of the Sun as they streamed across the complex. Instead it was raining and foggy, and we could barely see a few feet in any direction.

The hired guide's narration was summarized by one concept - Agriculture. According to him many of the constructions at Machu Picchu - the temples, the windows, the extraordinary sun-dials, the huge, flat rocks, the rooms, all existed to either propitiate Pachamama (Mother Earth), to house the workers and nobles, or to maintain precise knowledge with respect to seasons and cycles of various crops, which in turn would ensure that the Incan people were productively busy and happy, and could therefore be more easily ruled.

Budding Flower Chroniclers may recognize that this initial experience parallels seeing and being at the physical level.

First, the weather itself did not allow a macro-experience of the Machu Picchu complex. Instead it was decidedly micro with attention only on what was directly in one's narrow field of vision. The guide's interpretation was itself also driven only by what the eye could see - that is, it was entirely anchored in the physical level. There was no room in this view for any higher reality or possibility that may exist behind the surface.

This experience felt much more like that when life first emerges. There is consciousness but it is narrow and bounded. Strong and hardly rational forces that wish to maintain the status quo exist. There is much fear about the unknown and when something is seen its nature is already "known" by attribution and past feeling. This is true of the visible and the invisible. This then becomes the law and it cannot change. Hence even if the surface is penetrated there is no access to knowledge or power that may change things. What is, determines what will be. There is only narrowly bounded reaction in this world. This is also the sense of the "underworld" or what the Incas call the Uka Pacha, whose totemic representative is the snake.

At about 9am we exited the place because of the continuing downpour of rain. I knew though that I had to get back inside.

The Vital or Puma Level

At about 11am it seemed that the fog was going to lift and so I coaxed one of my sons who was strongly advocating calling it a day and going back down to the town of Aguas Calientes at the base of the Machu Picchu mountain, to reenter Machu Picchu and hike up to the Guard-House from where one could get a view of the entire complex. We reached the Guard-House thirty minutes later. The fog was coming up the mountain in insistent waves, and just for a few minutes we got a clear view of much more of Machu Picchu.

In preparation for the trip I had just finished a rapid read of Inayat Tal's Unveiling Machu Pichu (Tal 2012), an insightful book that contends that the Inca were highly gifted and that there was not a stone at Machu Picchu that did not serve some higher purpose. He offers a key to understanding the complex architecture, relating different regions of Machu Picchu to the character and energy of split white light, going from red to violet, but also including the color before light, blackness, and a color after white.

I resonated with the book, could feel aspects of truth in it, and wanted to at least try to experience Machu Picchu the way Inayat Tal had portrayed it in his book. Because of the weather, and the pressure from my sons I could not quite do this, even though I experienced a definite elation from seeing so much more of it all at the same time, if even for a few minutes. The narrowness of the physical experience and the dull interpretation from earlier that morning that had been weighing me down was broken, and my senses, sight, and imagination began to roam more freely.

This second entry into Machu Picchu, was hence at the vital level. The waves of fog, the insistence of old ideas competing with new, and the play of forces asking for a quick exit versus those that wished to continue to adventure, were characteristic of this level. Energy had been awoken and there was a more adventurous freedom that I was experiencing as a result. Like dynamics on our Earth, the active level in which we live, it is more often the strongest, rather than the most rational force or energy that wins. The law is still that of the jungle, and it is the Puma with its strength and swiftness that reigns here. The sense of the Inca's Kay Pacha, with the puma as its totemic representative, seemed therefore to be very much that of a Vital World.

It was still drizzling though and the fog continued to arrive, and I had promised my sons if this was the case even at noon, I would call it a day, and head back down with them to Aguas Calientes. And so we headed back down. My wife though, decided to stay at the entrance of Machu Picchu, continuing to hope that the fog would lift. We had to catch a train to Ollantaytambo at 6 that evening, so I never expected to come back up a third time to Machu Picchu in the same day.

The Mental or Condor Level

A couple of hours later though, it became sunny, and my wife called the hotel to insist that we come back up to Machu Picchu. And so at about 3pm we reentered Machu Picchu for the third time that day with the strong Sun overhead. Now my experience was going to be something entirely different.

As we walked through the Sacred Square, and to the Temple of the Three Windows, it was as though the huge rocks had come alive and were beginning to converse with me. Standing in front of one of them I felt a response and a dialog of energy involving several energetic centers in my own being. It seemed I was opening from the inside out. A different way of receiving became alive.

As I continued to look at the Half-Chakana facing the Three Windows it was as though a seed was being sown within me. Over the next 2 days insight began to dawn. This became the basis of a new interpretation of Machu Picchu.

The Temple of the Three Windows and The Chakana (The Inca Cross)

I had read previously that once a year the Half-Chakana became a Chakana, when the Sun was low enough in the sky so that its light streaming through the Three Windows created an image of the other half of the Chakana on the ground.

It occurred to me that the always visible portion of the Chakana, represented by stone with its three ascending and three descending levels, was a reminder or symbol of the human effort that had always to be made. This effort is the movement through the physical-vital-mental or shall we say the snake-puma-condor journey, that in fact any organization, regardless of scale, needs to make to continue to progress.

It is easy for an individual or an organization to want to continue at the level of operation that they are most comfortable with. The reality of the physical-vital-mental journey implies at least two things. First, there must be a constant reorientation or seeing and being such that the deeper truths and possibilities that are the fruit of sincere questioning (a dynamic of the mental/condor level) become the anchor points for all practical existence. Second, there must be an integration of all the gifts of each of these levels around such a higher/highest anchor point.

The movement through the three levels on the upper left-side of the Chakana, hence, is the representation of the human-effort to be made in any scale of time - seconds, through minutes, through hours, through days, and so on. Summarizing, this effort is a reorientation from the physical (or snake-view) to the vital (or puma-view) to the mental (or condor-view). To the degree that this reorientation is successful there will be a corresponding descent of the higher orientations into the lower orientations that begins to change the lower orientations. This descent is represented by the upper right-side of the Chakana.

The Temple of the Three Windows gives first therefore, insight into the meaning of the Chakana. For the lower half of the Chakana is visible only on the Winter Solstice (June 21-22 in the Southern Hemisphere) when the Sun's daily maximum elevation appears to be the lowest in the sky, hence giving a sense that it is 'closest' to Earth. Considering the Sun to be a symbol of the Divine or of some higher truth, this implies that the whole Chakana appears only when the Divine or some higher truth "descends" to Earth. Human efforts are hence justified or assume their full meaning when the lower half of the Chakana appears.

The lower half of the Chakana then represents something other then human effort. It has a divine character to it. Further it operates on a relatively macro time-scale when compared with the micro time-scale of the upper half. Intuitively it would make sense then that this occurs once a year only since it likely requires many, many human micro-efforts made continuously across small scales of time to invoke a divine response. The lower left-side of the Chakana then, signifies the descent of the Divine through the three levels of manifestation. The lower right-side of the Chakana represents an ascent by the Divine in which these three levels are themselves lifted as it were to a progressively higher way of being.

This higher way of being then becomes the bases for a new series of human-efforts or the start of a new cycle. In the Incan/Andean context it could be that the Spanish conquest of the Incas, which took place 500 years ago, has only been the cover or means to allow one such descent and ascent through the figure of Jesus Christ. One of Christ's gifts is a different relationship between humans allowing for increased compassion, love, and brotherhood, which once assimilated brings a greater comprehensiveness to the Incan Way.

The center of the Chakana is a circle, and in this interpretation could represent a couple of things. First, it could indicate the cyclical nature of the human-divine dynamic. As mentioned, the dynamic of the upper half of the Chakana has to occur many times before the dynamic of the lower half can meaningfully occur. From a Flower Chronicler's point of view, the ascents and descents of the upper and lower halves of the Chakana are four physical-vital-mental journeys that occur at different time-scales and through the efforts of different primary actors.

Second, the circle could represent infinity. The Earth could be placed in this circle, or the Sun, or Christ, or a New All-Embracing Golden Light, or any other possibility inherent in Infinity. In this case the Chakana becomes a symbol for the constant progression manifesting more and more of the possibilities inherent in Infinity (the Chakana or Inca Cross in the following picture then indicates the constant progression of the archetypes of the Snake, the Puma, and the Condor).

The Chakana and Its Implications for Machu Picchu

In this interpretation then, the Chakana thus completed by the Sun's light and appearing in the Sacred Square is a key or central feature, and becomes the root-pattern of which the entire layout and architecture of Machu Picchu is a fractal or a pattern that repeats itself on larger scale.

There is then a portion of Machu Picchu (the far end toward Wayna Picchu or the 'new mountain') which embodies the Physical or the Snake energies, a portion more towards the center that embodies the Vital or Puma energies, and a portion more towards the peak of Machu Pichu (Machu Pichu means 'old mountain) that embodies the Mental or Condor energies.

Note that the three windows in the Temple of the Three Windows likely relates to a view or more overt opening toward each of these three portions or energies. There are also portions that represent the pre-physical and the postmental energies. The stone-apparatus in each of these portions are not just random stones (as Inayat Tal points out), but technology by which an individual can enter into relationship with each portion to gain insight into their own physical or snake, vital or puma, and mental or condor make-up and energies, and as a result more quickly push themselves through their individual physical-vital-mental/snake-puma-condor fractals, to thereby enable the descent of divinity.

The complex of Machu Picchu actually lies between the peaks of Machu Picchu (old mountain) and Wayna Picchu (new mountain). The condor-energies that are representative of mind and beyond are thought-forms and thought-forces, and from this perspective house or mold archetypes of everything that will appear physically and vitally (in the snake-portion and puma-portion) in time. Hence they are "old" and it makes sense that they appear on the side closer to the peak of Machu Picchu (old mountain).

Further, the key buildings (minus the agricultural sector and the housing complex) in the Machu Picchu complex exist in a shape that is a half-ellipse. Taking the lead from the Half-Chakana, this itself is significant. For just as the Chakana is completed by the play of the Sun's light and shadow, the half-ellipse can become a full-ellipse when the physical structure of Machu Picchu is similarly extended.

This full-ellipse is none other than a vesica piscis, the mystical intersection of two circles, through which it is said manifestation issues forth. Just as in the two halves of the Chakana, the two circles thus created may represent the effort to be made by humanity (the visible structure of Machu Picchu), and the ever-present Divine that supports and leads humanity (the extended, "invisible" structure of Machu Picchu).

Therefore what we may have in Machu Picchu is likely a universal pattern and technology for progressive development in which the Human-Divine connection is central and strengthened. Further this pattern is fractal in that it occurs first on a micro-scale in the figure of the Chakana in the Sacred Square, then on larger scale in the architecture and layout of Machu Picchu itself, and finally in the extension of the macro half-ellipse into the full-ellipse, which may itself be a womb for manifestation.

Magnifying the root-pattern thus represented by the central Chakana, Machu Picchu may perhaps be thought of as a dynamo of a new dynamic accelerating the development of humankind.

Summary

In this case study we see the concrete application of the flower journey applied to the architecture of an archeological site. The architecture is laid out as a flower, with the physical at one end, the vital in the middle, and the mental at the other end. These also represent the key aspects of the mythology of the Incas in the form of the snake, the puma, and the condor. But the whole site is not just a metaphor. The arrangement of stones is technology by which to enter into contact with corresponding parts of oneself, which is also summarized by the flower.

Introducing a new paradigm into an organization is itself a journey. The key, as with any journey, is how to organically move it along the three stages so that there is a culmination in some kind of flower possibility. For the flower always has its hidden treasures, and sooner or later the seeds contained within it will sprout, and start a thousand new journeys.

The following journey highlights some developments with fractals and the Flower Chronicles that took place over the course of 3 years at Stanford University Medical Center. Starting from the very first event that was very much like the seed, through various experimentations as in the stalk phase, and culminating in a flower, that also marked the end of an adventurous cycle.

Formation Of The Seed

A former client, Todd Prigge, became the new Director for Organizational Development at Stanford University Medical Center (SUMC) some years ago. About 4 years ago he invited me to become part of his team. I found his invitation compelling, primarily because he offered me an opportunity to experiment with the organizational development models and software I was in process of developing.

Soon after I joined his team my book Connecting Inner Power with Global Change was released. Todd was more than supportive and as things worked out we began a regular study circle with his team to discuss the book. Shortly after that I was invited to host a radio show on the same book (iTunes 2013), and Todd and another member of his team

99

Laura Gottlieb, became permanent members of the 13-week panel on the radio show.

This allowed us to explore the fractal and flower concepts in the book in some detail, and subsequently Todd and I developed a field guide related to the same book that is soon to be published.

This was the formation of the seed, and was to lead to a number of related events ranging from the offering of Flower Chronicles courses, working with leadership teams to improve team and departmental performance, and incorporating some team mirroring software I had developed, over the next 3 years.

Aurosoorya's Fractal-Based Stress Management Program Debutes at Stanford University Medical Center

In April 2010 Aurosoorya's Fractal-Based Stress Management program debuted at Stanford University Medical Center's Center of Education & Professional Development. This was an important milestone in organizational development, and marked the use of software-based tools to begin to manage fractals that emanate from the individual level. Such management allows individuals to more easily complete their individual flower journeys by more quickly moving through the seed (physical) and stalk (vital) levels

The program was focused on allowing individuals to become aware of their own stress patterns, along the physical, vital, and mental dimensions. In particular, two web-based tools were used – StressManager (Aurosoorya 2013d) and EmotionalIntelligenceBuilder (Aurosoorya 2013b). These tools can be used by individuals, team and business units, allowing a deeper analyses into seed-patterns that are at the heart of dysfunctional team and corporate dynamics.

In this very first event at Stanford University Medical Center, participants were interested in understanding the order underlying chaos. Decision-making can oftentimes seem chaotic, and so can the various dynamics at a team or business unit level. Yet, the chaos is just a veil, and behind it the inevitable journey through the physical, the vital, and the mental is taking place. In the fractal-based model the macro is a reflection of the micro, and pressing problems, whether of a failure to fulfill project-based ROI, or of lack of department productivity, can be addressed by changing seed-patterns at the individual level.

The participants were interested in the core question of the course - "What is the fractal imprint that shapes your reality?", and what was intriguing was the appetite of the participants to know more about fractals and the system-behind-the-system, even though they had not necessarily been introduced to these concepts before. To me this reinforced that we are surely at some significant bridge-point in the scheme of things.

Aurosoorya Course on Accelerating Team Development Took Place at Stanford University Medical Center on October 12, 2010

Aurosoorya's full-day course on accelerating team development took place on Oct 12, 2010.

This marked the second course at Stanford University Medical Center's Center of Education & Professional Development within 6 months. Like the first course on stress management this too represented an important milestone in organizational development, and will further push the use of interactive web-based software tools to manage fractals that emanate from the individual and team level.

The course focused on accelerating a team's journey through the Forming-Storming-Norming-Performing levels to drive a team to a higher level of optimal performance in a shorter time frame, thereby increasing ROI and productivity, while lowering organizational costs.

Participants broke into teams and were given different real-life like scenarios. Each of the teams was at a different level of maturity and had to play the part of being either in the Forming, Storming, Norming, or Performing stages. Through entering observations and comments in real-time to describe how simulated team interactions went, overall team patterns were computed in real-time, and gave each of the teams and participants insight of what it meant to be at that level.

This course along with the previous one, were both focused on introducing the concept of fractals and their power in the workplace. The possibility had been introduced and the 'field' was being prepared for something more dynamic.

Aurosoorya's Web-Based Software Powers Team Development at Stanford Hospital & Clinics' Leadership Academy

In a move that set another new standard for the field of organizational development, Stanford Hospitals and Clinics (SHC) began using Aurosoorya's web-based team-development software to accelerate team development through its 6-month long 2010-11 Leadership Academy program. The new standard is set by using an easy-to-use, real-time tool that makes computation of fractal patterns transparent and that illustrates the true and often unstated dynamics occurring at the level of teams. Insight into fractal patterns are important because it is the "small" behaviors,

102

attitudes, perceptions at the individual or team level that correlate with and in fact determine larger outcomes at the team, unit, and corporate level. The Leadership Academy is an annual program in which close to 50 leaders from across the institute participate to develop and put into practice key leadership skills that SHC has identified as critical to its future. Leaders are placed into teams that work together on strategic projects.

Aurosoorya's team-development software was used to help these teams move through the forming-storming-norming-performing stages of team development at an accelerated pace. Oftentimes project teams get stuck at the forming or storming stages. In reality very few teams make it through to the norming and performing stages. Through tracking issues and accompanying states of being which are usually anonymously entered into a web-based issue and state tracker, the software draws attention to fractal patterns that causes the team to stagnate around a particular state of dysfunction. Identification of fractal patterns unequivocally identifies the stage of development that a team is at, and sets the bases for the team to begin to work away from such patterns to more desirable ones.

If there is a prevalent pattern of states such as 'synthesizing', 'reasoning', 'calmness', 'patience', and 'enthusiasm', punctuated by only instances of states such 'haste', and 'fear' for example, this would seem to indicate that a team is operating at the norming stage.

The software allowed teams to become more aware of the patterns holding them up, allowed them to begin to surface and address issues in a safe way, provided insights into the particular circumstances that typically cause such patterns of dysfunction, suggested numerous ways in which to begin to move to better patterns of functioning, and allowed tracking and shifting of fractal patterns in real-time.

The Mirror Effect: Experiments in Accelerating Team
Development

There is an incredible value in holding up a mirror to
teams. Planning and tracking plans – whether tasks
completed, milestones met, outcomes realized - is part of this,
but only captures a fraction of the image. As important, if not
more so, is the capturing of softer, feelings-based team
dynamics.

What makes team members excited, or complacent, or
fearful, or angry? What is the intensity of a feeling? What
team dynamics may have caused it? Did a feeling persist
beyond the boundary of a team meeting, to perhaps keep the
team-member up at night? After all it is the nature of
persistent feelings that at the end of the day will make or
break a team.

In a six-month experiment, Stanford Hospital and
Clinics' Leadership Academy equipped a group of 50 hospital
leaders with a tool developed by Aurosoorya, which sought
primarily to capture the softer feelings-based team dynamics.
The tool in effect held up a mirror to the team and helped
them to address team dynamics that are more easily avoided.

The nature of the feelings that each team member,
anonymously or openly, depending on how transparent a
team chooses to be, was asked to capture in the web-based
tool included those such as complacency, fatigue, flexibility,
depression, inferiority, jealousy, humility, determination,
gratitude, anxiety, mental noise, amongst many others.

Tracking such information sheds light on the culture of
a team in process of being created. Focusing on feelings is
critical because failure to do so erodes team environment and
accelerates destructive dynamics. Successfully managing
potentially destructive feelings, on the other hand, allows the

team to scale the team maturity curve faster. Hence, changing the nature of interaction between team members allows the team to shift through the forming-storming-norming-performing stages of team development at an accelerated pace to thereby increase team productivity.

While all this is well and good the critical question is whether it makes any real difference at the end of the day. The following experiment suggests that this was the case.

The approximately 50 leaders at the 2010-2011 Cohort of Stanford Hospital and Clinics' Leadership Academy were divided into 7 project teams, worked on a strategic hospital-based initiative, and were asked to track team dynamics on a regular basis. In fact, they were given a choice of whether to track team dynamics or not to. While individuals in those teams who chose to use the tool reported increased sensitivity to feelings-based team dynamics, the question is did the use of the tool actually increase productivity at the team level? Results from a simulated subarctic survival exercise that each of the 7 teams went through, indicated this to be the case. In this simulation, involving a plane crash, each team member is individually asked to rank 15 items necessary for their survival. The team then collectively ranks the same items. If the team score is better than the best individual score, then synergy is deemed to have occurred. If the team score is worse that the best individual score, then synergy is deemed not to have occurred.

The experiment revealed a couple of strong correlations. First, those teams whose use of the team dynamics tool was low exhibited lower synergy. Second, those teams whose use of the team dynamics tool is at the ideal level even for a period of time, registered a higher degree of synergy as measured by the survival exercise. This is likely because the nature of interaction between the team members was positively impacted by becoming aware of, or calling out, and acting on negative dynamics. It is also likely that the very act of becoming aware of and calling out positive dynamics tended to reinforce them. Mirroring, therefore, allowed teams to make adjustments and accelerate their development in real-time.

Working With Nursing Leadership Teams At Lucile Packard Children's Hospital

Following the work at SHC I shared some of the approaches experimented with there with Pam Wells, the Chief Nursing Officer, at Lucile Packard Children's Hospital (LPCH). She cascaded this through her organization and shortly after that I was contacted by a couple of her Directors who ran various nursing departments.

They were interested in having an intensive team development program for their leadership teams. Each of these multi-month engagements started with a dedicated one-day immersion. In this immersion I first introduced the overall fractal team development program to the team. The team also learned to use the web-based software and began to get their feet wet by running through fictitious real-life like simulations that leadership teams often face.

This lasted a couple of hours after which I asked them if they would like to address a real-life situation that their department was currently facing. The teams typically elected to do so. Each member of the team had the web-based software up on a dedicated computer. In addition there was a real-time tracking computer that was projecting out the cumulative patterns on a screen for all to see, though this turned on only at the end of the data inputting exercise.

The team elected to input data anonymously and the base question they addressed was how effective the leadership team was in addressing the current challenge under consideration. The Director of the team was also present and was also simultaneously inputting data from her perspective. The data being entered was very personal and was focused on what states of being each member had experienced personally or observed in other members around them in the course of the challenge. These could range from courage, determination, and joy, to fear, irritation, and anger, amongst a slew of other states.

At the end of the one-hour exercise the team focused on the cumulative patterns that were projected on the screen in front and began to discuss the 'fractal imprint' of the team – its representative but unvoiced signature that was determining the culture and results that the leadership team and the larger department, through fractal pressure, was experiencing.

There is a direct correlation between the flower model and the maturity of the team. The seed stage can be thought of as the forming stage, where team members generally prefer to remain relatively inert, not at all acting like a true team. The stalk stage can be thought of as the storming stage and this is where a lot of energy, usually negative, surfaces in passive-aggressiveness or even often, uncontrolled outbursts. Research indicates that most teams never make it past this stage. The flower stage is parallel to the norming and performing stages where the team is truly beginning to come together and not only setting up but also more effectively executing a new contract on how it will operate as a cohesive team.

The patterns that are projected on the screen indicate decisively what stage of development the team is really at. This then allows the team to decide what it needs to do to effectively move forward to the next stage of team maturity, if that is what it chooses to do.

Toward the end of the day the team can elect to disclose their identity while entering data, and it is only the very brave team who is already quite mature in its operation that will elect to do this. In fact, I would not recommend this for most teams when they first hold up such a team dynamics mirror to themselves.

Following the one-day immersion each of the team members of the leadership team agreed to continue to use the software to track various leadership concerns and at the end of the first month a report was generated that the team could then further course-correct on. In addition the team could always see the cumulative results of the whole team at any time on an on-going basis in the web-based software itself. Some teams use this to course-correct in real-time.

These engagements lasted about three months and also involved some individual coaching that I administered to some of the members of the leadership teams.

While the end result was that the teams began to operate at a higher level of maturity I can also say that this was not an easy process. The mirror reflects exactly what is going on, whether one wants to see it or not. Depending on one's perspective and maturity as a leader this can be a good or a bad thing.

Experiencing The Flower Chronicles Through Relational Presence: An Experiment At Stanford Center of Education and Professional Development

On December 6, 2012 we held an intimate and deep workshop at Stanford Cenetr of Education and Professional Development. This workshop was focused on experiencing the wisdom inherent in a flower's journey into fullness. This journey is referred to as the Flower Chronicles.

The Flower Chronicles is a way of seeing and being that builds awareness of the dynamic reality of progress inherent in the blueprint of Life. This blueprint is present regardless of the scale of an organization and the level of organizational complexity. This blueprint summarizes a remarkable story of sustainability that exists all around us. This story is embedded in the skies and on earth, and can be seen in the way a flower arrives at maturity. This journey repeats itself on different scale, and provides a simple blueprint for organizational learning and development. The flower is a perfect representation of this fractal blueprint.

Hence, whether an organization is a human-being, a team, a corporation, a market, or a larger encompassing system, active real-time dynamics and the change in dynamics over time follows a universal pattern that is simply captured by the way a flower comes into being, or the way a flower would chronicle the world around it in its journey to its fullness.

This journey traverses three stages – the seed-state (or physical), the stalk-state (or vital), the flower state (or mental) – and implies changes in orientation that allow the flower or organization to realize greater degrees of freedom.

To create the visceral feel for what this journey is, throughout the workshop each participant was asked to share thoughts operating from the space created through relational presence. In this mode, one must relate to others in the moment, and being almost as two sides of a blade of grass, as my collaborator and creator of the notion of Relational Presence, Lee Glickstein describes (Glickstein 1999), create thought that is fresh, because the obstacles of the seed/physical and the stalk/vital have a higher likelihood of being overcome in such a state.

In other words, to create afresh, the participant has to successfully traverse the flower journey: habitual thoughts and ways of looking at things (the status quo of the seed or physical orientation) have to be overcome, uncomfortable feelings and reactions that often arise in relation to others (the movements of emotion centered around the small self typical of the stalk of vital orientation) have to be overcome, and if this happens, then there may be freshness – new thoughts, new feelings – that are a result of operating with a new orientation in the moment.

Experiencing this journey can be an initiation into a greater way of seeing and being, because this journey is ubiquitous. It is the journey that all sustainable, successful organizations make. It is the journey made by the emotionally intelligent individual, by the truly productive team, by the innovative corporation, by the triple bottom-line driven market, by the self-correcting and sustainable financial market, by Life as it has been etched into the sands of time, and by the never-ending dance of the Earth with the Sun, since it first came into being over 4 Billion years ago.

Since this journey is ubiquitous and fractal - that is, it repeats itself on different scale regardless of circumstance - the alert participant could very well begin to see and even be as the flower in all situations they may be faced with, and may even see the flower dynamics in all things that they do see. That would be the result of a true initiation. To see and be as a flower is to awaken to the fantastic design that forever holds life in its extraordinary embrace.

The questions are: How many participants truly got initiated? Was 4 hours enough for this to happen? What flowers may arise from the seeds sown in this experiment? And on a broader scale, is the enthusiasm and understanding that we saw in the classroom sustainable? Was what we experienced at Stanford Center of Education and Professional Development indicative that a broader population may be ready to receive this paradigm?

Many questions that only Time can answer.

This workshop was the culmination in a three-year journey at Stanford University Medical Center. It marks the flower end of the journey and we will have to see what may emerge as a result of this journey.

Encounters with a Writer for Forbes

Over the course of my experiments at SUMC I interacted with a Forbes reporter on several occasions. It all started when she found some of my work on fractals highlighted on the Business for Social Responsibility (BSR) website. This work connected fractals to the fields of Corporate Social Responsibility and Sustainability (Malik 2007), and was one of the joint endeavors between BSR and Aurosoorya, the organization I floated to conduct a range of experiments.

When she contacted me through e-mail, Nicole Skibola did not identify herself as a writer for Forbes. She wanted to meet to learn more about my work. I was happy to do so, and only after we met and discussed fractals and the flower model for a few hours did she disclose that she was going to write a piece for Forbes (Skibola 2011).

Here is what she wrote:

'When we discuss corporate social responsibility, it is almost exclusively contextualized in terms of the actions and decision-making at the corporate, organizational level. However, at the heart of every corporate practice that touches upon an environmental or social issue, there are individuals weighing the costs and benefits of taking social responsibility factors into consideration.

Long-time organizational change consultant Pravir Malik has recently begun working on mindfulness in the workplace as a tool for individual, team, organizational, and ultimately, societal change. Through his research

111

organization, Aurosoorya, Pravir introduced a fractal-based system of mindfulness into the Stanford University Medical Center's Leadership Academy training four months ago. His hypothesis suggested that by addressing dysfunction at the micro level (i.e., personal discontent, frustration, anger), that larger patterns at higher levels would be affected in a positive manner. He envisions these growing scales of collective consciousness as fractal in nature, all part of a larger, inseparable system.

Pravir equipped medical team members with a software tool to track their feelings throughout the day, with a focus on emotions felt right before, during, and after team meetings. By consciously identifying emotions, both positive and negative, team members became increasingly conscious of the "levers" that caused their happiness or unhappiness. Coupled with the support to deal with personal and team challenges, the exercise enabled team members to resolve particular states of dysfunction.

The seven teams went through a Subarctic Survival Exercise. Team members first prioritized a list of 15 items required for survival, following a simulated plane crash in the subarctic region:

"Each team then had a discussion and prioritized the same list of items as a team. If team scores were better than any one individual's score, their team dynamics are judged to be synergistic. On the contrary, if any one individual's score remains better than the overall team score, their synergy is judged not to have occurred."

Pravir found there was a fairly tight correlation between those teams that performed best and their use of the web-based team dynamics tool, and those teams that performed worst and their lack of use of the tool. The exercise suggests that by purposefully recognizing and recording relational dynamics, teams were able to create positive dynamics, enabling them to perform better as teams in stressful circumstances.

So what does this all tell us about corporate social responsibility? By creating greater consciousness at the individual level, Pravir believes that humans will become more mindful of how their actions impact others, and ultimately, the world around them:

"Fractals in organizations involves self-similar patterns across different scale. Scale can be thought of as the different layers that comprise an organization, including the individual, the team, the corporation itself, the markets in which the corporation operates, the environment and the societies in which the corporation is involved. Examining self-similar patterns in these layers inevitably thrusts us into the heart of CSR, which focuses on the practical interaction between these layers."

Changing thought at the individual level uncovers new possibilities. By integrating more holistic environmental, social, and governance considerations into the strategy and operations of business, new opportunities emerge, to reduce externalities that cost society and business. With better organizational design and increased emphasis on personal and team mindfulness, businesses can become more dynamic and adaptable.

Pravir envisions these dynamics providing insight into the future of CSR. It's time to think about how corporate attention can shift from current compliance-based practices to a fundamental corporate repurposing based on truly addressing human, social and environmental needs. Pravir explains,

"It is perhaps of little surprise that fractal dynamics was intuitively grasped by such effective individuals as Gandhi and Einstein many decades ago. Gandhi is known to have stated, "Become the change that you wish to see in the world."

This statement is imbued with fractal reality: by changing the base-pattern [at the individual level] the subsequent levels of an organization, and its entire interaction and approach to the market, environment and society, are also fundamentally changed."'

Summary

In retrospect the flower journey that was traversed through the three years at Stanford University Medical Center was itself through the physical or seed-state of an overarching flower-journey. While to expect anything more is optimistic, it is perhaps not realistic given the large array of established dynamics in an existing organization. In other words, while three phases of the ubiquitous journey were traversed, they happened within the confines of an overarching seed-phase.

At the end of the day the best that may have been achieved is that the seed itself began to germinate, and with continued influx of energy, may yield to a more energetic growth on a larger scale within the organization. When I last talked with Nicole earlier this year she was disappointed to hear that my experiments at Stanford had not by now become a lot bigger and more impactful. As I reflect on this one of the conclusions I reach is that the lack of a greater outcome is certainly also related to the dynamics in my self. If I were able to shift things more in real-time within myself, so that encountered negativity or obstacles were more quickly worked through, no doubt the outcome could have been greater. In other words I should have been able to apply more of my own flower model medicine to myself. Hopefully this is something I will get better at over time.

What the experiment in its totality does point to, including the iteration between shifts in myself when dampening dynamics are encountered from the outside, is a likely step-by-step approach by which truer change happens. The change agent always holds the key to larger change, provided they are willing to see this. This I would say is true not just at Stanford University Medical Center but at all manner of organizations, of which Stanford University Medical Center is only one type.

Part 4 – Industry Development

This chapter starts with a poignant look at the BP oil spill that really tells us that we are witnessing the death of an old-way of being. The Industry journey appears to be transitioning to the possibility of being more flower-driven. We look at the Food, Beverage & Agricultural industry and see how it is really at the physical-vital level, and needs to move to the mental-level, especially when highly organized retail players are on the verge of making the large developing markets potentially part of the global machinery. There is the possibility that this could be a good thing, but only if policy is set to allow Retail as an industry to operate from the flower possibility.

We also look at Antibiotics and Pharmaceuticals and their current operating paradigms, which are primarily at the vital level, and propose ways in which these powerful industries could also make the needed shift to operate more from the mental-level.

The Internet has grown rapidly in recent years, and we take a look at Facebook and Google, and more mainstream ERP players, in particular SuccessFactors, now acquired by SAP. These industries can truly become facilitators of positive change, if they complete their own flower journeys. For completeness we look too at the Energy industry in general.

Finally we consider the future of consulting, and conclude with a suggested evolution to the standard of business and economic accounting by it transitioning to a solar-like reality.

Deeper Symbolism of the BP Oil Spill

As I consider the confluence of some recent global business events (Eurozone crises, continued Japanese deflation, rippling stock market depression, BP oil-spill), the conclusion that we are witnessing the death of an old-way of being cannot but be reinforced.

Flower Chronicles analyses at various levels reveals that we are at a significant transition between the physical-vital and a more mental way of being. The physical-vital is all about appropriating energy flows to reinforce a myopic perception of self and build it to be even larger, bigger, and become even more aggressive so that it can more effectively do more of the ineffective same. This is the operative mentality that has thus far driven our corporations, markets, and economies.

The short-sighted growth of these constructs has interestingly been driven by a carbon-based energy source, which chemically speaking, is nothing but crushed and pressurized remains of eons-old physical and vital beings (less evolved and even supposedly gigantic plants and animals). So from a symbolical perspective, we have the remains of eons-old physical-vital beings fuelling an essential consciousness that is physical-vital in its manner. That we are approaching or by some estimates are in a reality of peak-oil is in this analysis significant since it suggests that peak-oil too is a sign that an essentially old-way of being is reaching its end.

Transition always tends to bring an old way of being vehemently to the surface, if for no other reason than to try to fight an emerging new way of being to prolong its reign. In this perspective the BP oil spill may symbolically be viewed as bringing that old physical-vital energy source and consciousness that flowed unseen in subterranean passages or pipes, vehemently to the surface. This old way now openly spreads its poison and a valiant battle, which does not include

118

throwing golf balls and tires at it (Morris 2010), which by the way is what BP did to try an control the out-spewing of oil, must take place between the old and the new until the new spreads its wings and makes us soar to new heights.

In this light the Eurozone crises, continued Japanese deflation, stock market depression and crises must be seen as a deep need to want to disengage from a maddening physical-vital way of being. The irony is that our analysts, commentators, regulators, and other economic and public stakeholders continue to see these events in the old physical-vital way of being, and continue to want to resuscitate this dying and outdated way so that it may live again.

It cannot be resuscitated though. Way has to be given for a new, more mental way of being in which possibility can more abundantly come to the surface. De-monopolization of power in all its forms is the inevitable future before us. Realization of this will help all involved to more effectively transition through and manage what is seeking to taking birth.

A Time to Remake the Food, Beverage, and Agricultural Industry

Food is essentially a source of energy for people around the world. Its nutritional value is directly proportional to its freshness and the conditions within which it is grown. In ideal circumstances food, to promote freshness, should be grown locally. In reality it has today become a major global enterprise. And once it has entered the realm of global business that means that it is now subject to a different set of criteria to make it financially viable. Instead of operating from the flower-level, the industry, like any global business is operated from the physical-vital level. The creation of food has to become a business and be operated as a business, and in that translation the essential condition for its effectiveness is cast aside. Instead of being a labor of love, with consideration for season and local ecosystem and the health of people, in its creation, it is driven by global competition and economies of scale.

Therefore, when serious drought hits Russia, a primary provider of world-wide wheat, and the prices of many commodities such as corn, soybean, rapeseed, barley, jump in the bargain (Gorst 2010) threatening the established supply of these basics, and causing panic and the threat of significant starvation, it is time to pause and ask what really has the global food, beverage, and agricultural industry done for the good of humankind?

Being run as a global business means that at every phase of the supply chain compromise has to be made and costs have to be assumed by the locality or region within which that supply chain phase exists. Starting from growth of the essential raw materials, we see increasing instances of ecosystems, complex forests, marshlands, amongst other natural habitats that have been built up over millennium and are embedded into the very fabric of life often in ways that we do not completely understand, being wiped aside in favor of regimented and for that locality unnatural growth of crops. This has huge costs to the soil and natural life in the locality, the environment, the surrounding community, the economy, and future generations. Destruction of ecosystems destroys ecosystem-services provided to humanity, such as water and air filtration, carbon sequestration – essential to counteract climate change, flood control, enrichment of soil, destruction of species – with their effects such as creation of food, pollination, provision of medicinal compounds, amongst others. None of these tremendous costs are ever considered as costs. They are taken for granted and externalized to the other entities unfortunate enough to be the context for that phase of the supply chain.

Further down the supply chain where there may be a processing plant, a whole new level of costs that are usually not considered come into being. The first order of costs is usually environmental. Hence, if water for the plant is needed, or even if water is a key ingredient in the food or beverage, then tube-wells may be sunk and the underlying water-table seriously affected. This has huge effects on the lives of communities in the vicinity. If the plant has bi-products then these are often spewed into the atmosphere, sunk into the earth, or offloaded into a water supply or flowing body of water in the area. This too has serious effects on surrounding communities, and is often not considered in the statement of cost. The agricultural sector is the highest user of water. Hence it becomes very important for it to be used most efficiently and responsibly.

In the processing itself often additives and preservatives and other questionable chemicals are employed that create a food filled with subtle poisons. Our current approach of assuming otherwise until proven beyond a shadow of a doubt is biased toward the big corporation that we have to remember is motivated primarily by maximizing its profit, often at any cost.

Further, is the whole issue of Genetically Modified Foods (GMO). Nature and its output have been created over millennium. There is an inherent wisdom in the array of compounds that constitute any single herb or plant, and there is a long-built up equilibrium in which each herb or plant exists in harmony with everything else around it. To modify the genetic structure of such a construct, without considering or comprehending the huge number of interrelationships that are being changed as a result of that, is to load up the dice in random ways and hope for the best when they are thrown.

One simply cannot maintain long-established equilibriums in such a manner. As Einstein has said, "God does not play dice with the universe." Further, we really have no clue as to how the GMO is going to interact with human bodies, and what the effects on the cells is going to be. This is an irresponsible approach to production, and potentially creates a whole slew of problems in its wake.

At several points in a supply chain large workforces are often employed. Often times in order to minimize total cost of production migrant workers are employed and human rights issues compromised. Women and children are also often exploited. Employees are overworked, not subjected to decent working conditions, and have fewer rights than the normal citizens of a country.

The point of view that an agricultural company or a global food company is doing humanity a service by providing food or beverages globally is flawed. It counteracts the very need for growth and creation of food to become a community-strengthening activity. Contact with, nurturing, and respecting the land is essential in the scheme of things. When I was Managing Director at BSR, a leading non-profit sustainability consulting firm, one of our clients who shall go unnamed retorted when we approached them to assist with their CSR situation, "We provide grains to people all over the world: if that is not CSR then what is!!".

A community or a country that loses touch with its land has lost its sovereignty. Sooner or later it becomes entirely dependent on external flows and then easily can succumb to one of many external or global threats. Today's global agricultural and food industries promote loss of contact by individuals, communities, and countries with local lands. This is a huge cost that is never considered in the simplified, short-term mathematics of asset and liability that animates business today.

Every piece of land is essentially creative. The very fact that all life emerges from this matrix is proof enough. Sometimes the secret of its creativity needs to be teased out, and in working to make this happen communities can be built and strengthened. Creative land lies at the basis of strong local cultures and economies. A vast range of products and services that are today artificially created through remote processing can be localized. Livelihoods can be enhanced through mastering the creation and exchange of these products and services. In today's push to create profit, often at any cost, today's global agricultural, food and beverage industries continually negate all this possibility.

Walmart's Entry Into India. A Time For Tests And New Measures

Walmart has tied up with Bharti to create wholesale stores in India. Beyond marking a new phase in the Indian Retail environment, application of Flower Chronicles analysis indicates why this also marks a crucial phase in the Indian and Global developmental cycles.

Walmart's success to date has been driven by consumer desire for an increasing array of diverse product offered at low prices. Walmart leverages its tightly managed global supply chain to offer just such a mix. But what are the hidden costs of this equation? Insight into this is gained by dwelling further on the nature of the driver behind Walmart's success.

1. This driver is consumer desire, an aggressive stalk- or vital-level dynamic. Such a dynamic seeks for satisfaction of its want immediately without considering the factors that have allowed the product to be supplied in such a manner. The cost, hence, tends toward a marginalization of all longer-term, more sustainable solutions.

2. As this dynamic is reinforced, there is a ripple effect and a similar short-term vital-level dynamic becomes alive at the local, national, and global levels. Affected flower journeys at these levels include the consumer journey, the business journey, the supply-chain journey, the culture journey, and the society journey, to mention some key ones. In other words, the progressive realities possible to each of these entities is stalled at the vital-level, resulting in a slew of additional costs. Cycles of conspicuous consumerism, of business-as-usual, of questionable supply-chains, of stalled culture, and of misplaced society respectively, are reinforced. To illustrate some of these:

a) Vital-level consumer desire reinforces and strengthens vital-level global supply-chains. Such vital-level supply-chains often operate at suboptimal levels increasing the social and environmental costs to humanity in their wake. These costs remain un-factored in the final price of the product and are borne by the locality that has come into contact with the ever-expanding supply-chain. Ironically, as the companies managing such supply chains show increasing profits, they are rewarded by investors, and the very dynamic that it would make most sense to move away from is given additional impetus to continue with its questionable effects.

b) As local communities become part of these supply chains, their dependence on continuing to be a part of the supply-chain increases, and a balanced investment in their own communities often decreases. As a result local and hence regional development at multiple-levels is compromised, and then all must become part of the global business machinery in order to survive. There are, hence, huge costs at the community and regional levels.

c) The culture and the society flower journeys are also hence compromised, and instead of growing to express their own uniqueness and possibilities, outcomes of journeying to the mental or flower-phase in their own trajectories, they continually circle at a standardized level because the basis of creativity has been marginalized by assimilation into a strong global machinery.

3. By the nature of the unrefined vital consciousness the costs to humanity of remaining at that level increase much faster than if corresponding shifts were made to the mental-levels of the respective flower journeys. Mental-level dynamics are by their very nature more inclusive of a wider set of issues and hence more balanced in resulting action. Consideration of such balance has a longer-term positive effect that lowers hidden costs to humanity. By failing to shift to this level there are rapidly escalating opportunity costs.

These same costs that propagate out across the world, are also easily experienced locally at the site of the incoming Walmart.

On the flip-side the incoming of a highly organized force such as Walmart, albeit of a stagnated vital level, that has in fact succeeded in spreading its often welcome vital-way of being in many parts of the world, can as per the reality of intersecting journeys, cause a corresponding counter 'organization' at the point of its presence so that all potential flower journeys have the chance to alter by progressing along their respective trajectories. It is to be hoped that this is the case, and that such a reality may be proactively stimulated through thoughtful policy administered at the local level.

If so, then rather than Walmart displacing local producers and suppliers there is the possibility of local producers and suppliers becoming part of a hybrid Walmart-local 'ecosystem'. Such a development pushes the vital-boundaries of the Business journey to operate in another way that becomes more cognizant of the long-term benefits of strengthening localities for the sake of localities rather than for the sake of business alone or for Walmart alone. This

125

development also pushes possible stagnation in the local Community journey so that there is the acceptance of a new energy in the rearrangement of local activity.

Further, this and other such expanded 'ecosystems' can now feed into the global supply chain, to alter the very nature of the global supply chain itself. Rather than the usual vital-level heuristic of minimizing one-sided or manager-viewed cost - in this case Walmart's as in managing the supply chain, a new mental-level heuristic of maximizing unique and local development could become the arbitrating factor in management of global supply chains, thereby pushing the Supply Chain journey to the next level in its own flower trajectory. Companies that develop localities along their global supply chains, based on respective uniqueness should be the one's rewarded, because in reality such development strengthens the long-term wealth of the world.

As Walmart enters India, there is a chance to cause several potentially stagnated journeys to progress. This can be facilitated by substituting old ways of being and old measures of success by new measures that cause new behavior in the long-term.

As a measure of such real positive development the following should be tracked over the next couple of years:

1. Shift from vital to mental-level consumer behavior manifest in a shift from impulse and desire-based to more thoughtful buying.
2. Increase in price of products as real social and environmental costs are factored into cost of products.
3. Increase in local community, cultural, social capital with comprehensive development of local 'ecosystems'.
4. Change in nature of supply chains so that they morph into robust development chains through acceptance and assimilation of local business / cultural / spiritual ways of

being.

5. Change in reward to companies that cause true development along supply chains rather than compromise supply chains.

6. Change in the nature of development so that expectations of continued short-term financial growth is replaced by expectations of balanced long-term holistic growth.

In many respects what happens in India in the Retail sector over the next few years is crucial to the overall development of the world. This is so for a number of reasons:

1. Retail in India is predominantly unorganized. Greater degree of organization that will accompany the incoming of the likes of Walmart will make it a far more serious, globally integrated industry with much more substantial effects on society and the environment.

2. Such organized retail will integrate a huge middle class, by some estimates twice the size of the USA, into the global market.

3. An unchecked retail sector at the head of what could currently be considered cancerous global supply chains, and driven by continued and unrefined vital-level consumer demand is a recipe for global disaster. On the environmental side GHG emissions will increase by a huge factor, global temperatures will continue to rise, and the rest could be history. On the social side more of the same will reinforce a self-destructive paradigm of business-as-usual, and the rest could be history.

On the other hand, a more well-thought out Indian retail environment, where the emphasis is to consciously shift the intersecting Consumer, Supply Chain, Business, Culture, and Society journeys to the mental- or flower-level in their respective journeys, will usher in a whole different and far-more balanced era in global development.

Weakness at any scale can be traced to a fundamental inability to move out of a condition of complacency. This is true of a faltering global economy, of a failing market, of an outdated culture, of a team that is stuck at a level of dysfunction, of an individual who insists on meeting others with hostility and irritation, or at the micro-level, of the inability to address the rise in drug-resistant infections.

When the UK Chief Medical Officer sounds that the antibiotic 'apocalypse' is nigh (Gallagher 2013), and that one can die from a routine infection because we have run out of antibiotics, it is perhaps time to look for a solution that moves away from the obvious inadequacy of current accepted trends of research, and strike a new path of thought.

One such path is offered by the Flower Chronicles model. In this approach there is a fundamental pattern of progress that is true regardless of scale. Hence, it is true regardless of the type of organization. An organization may be the human body, a complex market, a multi-geography business unit, the World Wide Web, or an academic theory, amongst others, for instance.

In this approach an organization is subject to a certain orientation, such as the seed or physical, the stalk or vital, the flower or mental, which will determine entirely the characteristics, dynamics, and possibility of the organization. The 'physical' refers to experiencing reality primarily through what the eyes can see, the 'vital' through the medium of often self-assertive energy, and the 'mental' through the vehicle of thought, curiosity, questioning, or idea. In its journey a flower summarizes this universal pattern of progress that is characterized by the movement from a physical-orientation (the seed) to a vital-orientation (the stalk) to a mental-orientation (the flower). Such movement is a necessity if an organization is to sustain itself.

An organization that is arrested at any one level will of necessity experience problems, which are the means by which it is forced to move to another orientation. Weakness hence, arises when a system or organization has become complacent and is stuck at a certain level, when in reality it should constantly be progressing.

The "antibiotic apocalypse that is nigh" is the desperate call from a system that is transfixed only by what the eye can see. Infection is not the problem. In reality the problem is the weakness of the system or body, and infection exists to remind it that it has to move away from its current beliefs and moorings that continue to enforce such weakness.

Research that continues to separate the agent of disease or infection from the rest of the system is representative of the physical level because it sees everything as separated and different, and falsely attributes power to something that in reality has none. Introducing poison, whether antibiotics or some other such 'medicine', into the body can only increase the weakness of the body. Obviously then, infection will appear as drug-resistant, because the poison has only functioned to further weaken any natural defense.

Shifting orientation to a vital or more energy-oriented paradigm, one begins to see that strength and weakness are a function of the play of energies and in a reality where infection seems to have the upper-hand, points to the necessity of changing the energetic relationship to strengthen the real fulcrum of control, the body, rather than attribute false power to something that is only a response.

Shifting orientation even further to the realm of thought or idea, the real focus of research needs to be on the inherent power of healing that we know exists in every human-body and have viscerally experienced at some stage or another in our lives. Indeed that must become the focus of all future health approaches and research efforts.

If this journey of progress is pursued, not only will the "antibiotic apocalypse that is nigh" prove to be incorrect, but even the incredible threat of burgeoning medical expense of an ageing population felt now in the USA and also in other parts of the world, be more directly addressed. The Health and Human Services Department expectation that the health share of GDP will continue its historical upward trend, reaching 19.5% of GDP by 2017, for instance (HealthAffairs, 2008) will be reversed, and the budget will be forever balanced allowing future Presidents to truly embark on a path of building strength from within.

The Need to Rethink the Pharmaceuticals Industry

At its core the pharmaceutical industry exists to develop and produce drugs that can assist the healing and regeneration of the body. If we exist in a world with splendor at its base, and if we are all constructs of that incredible possibility that seeks continually to express and enhance itself, there are a few things that are very possible. First of all, the healing power is likely not something that has to be imported into the body, but probably exists resident in the body itself. If we can grow and self-repair through childhood and adolescent years, then it stands to reason that that same ability should continue to exist in adult and later years. If it does not, then perhaps that is the case because certain abilities are being switched off or negated through lifestyle. If this is the case, then the purpose of drugs should be to help this natural healing ability to come alive once again.

Today's common thought on disease though, is that it is caused by external agents such as microbes, pathogens, bacteria, and virus, that invade and compromise the functioning of the body. In this paradigm health is a function of keeping disease away, or if it invades the body, not so much of invigorating the natural healing ability of the body, as killing the invading agents. If this were true though, that is, if it were the strains that create disease, then disease should be rampant because the fact is that some microbes, pathogens, virus, bacteria exist in every intake of breath. All air is like a cocktail mixture with the good and the bad mixed in it. This cannot but be the case since we live in a greenhouse in which all types of agents are free to mix and roam the greenhouse with impunity. The fact that we are for the most part not filled with disease means that it cannot be the external agents that are the sole cause of disease. There has to be something else in our way of being that gives its consent to the potentiality of disease.

Many of today's drugs though, are created to kill these various strains that supposedly create disease in their wake. If disease is not created by these external agents, and if these drugs are now freely moving through our entire bodily system once we ingest or inject them, then the question is what are they really doing within us? If the determining factor behind the expression of disease in ourselves is our power of assent, however subtle this may be, and if our cells and fantastic bodily systems themselves have the power to heal, then what we are injecting or swallowing cannot but have a detrimental affect on our systems since they are based on a false or ignorant set of premises.

But today's emphasis on profit-making has a great masking effect, and the truth of healing is veiled, by evoking fear in its place. Pharmaceutical companies, arrested at the vital- or stalk-level, resort to advertising campaigns that strike fear in people, and through fear, people now take a whole slew of 'medicines' to combat or keep away disease. One of the most questionable practices is that of vaccination. In truth vaccinations are the very diseased potion injected into us so that we may create antibodies if the real disease enters into us. But why take in darkness to fight darkness. Darkness must be met with light, and true light is generated when the cells are allowed to release the healing powers inherent within them.

While vaccinations stand at one extreme of the portfolio of products offered by pharmaceutical companies, at the other end of the portfolio are compounds that are made from plant extracts. But the truth that compounds are something from a thriving, living life-form, is veiled in tremendously complex names that makes it impossible to realize that what the compound consists of is something that could be grown in one's back yard. Regardless, the complication though is that the active-ingredient from the plant in the compound is not harmonized with the plethora of other plant-ingredients that it naturally exists with, but isolated, magnified, so that it in effect it is now out of proportion from how nature intended it to exist, and because of that will likely have a more caustic effect than necessary on the body.

Pharmaceutical companies claim that they are involved in drug-discovery. But everything of use that they have come up with exists in a more balanced form in nature. So what exactly have they been discovering? Further, much of the biotech industry replicates drug-formation processes in nature and then patents the process. If the process already exists in nature then what right does a company have to now patent the process as its own? If the real power of healing is something within each individual being, then the real value of drugs would be in allowing this automatic or profound ability to take effect without in anyway compromising any portion or system of the body. Instead drug use usually has many side-effects, and mixing drugs can be lethal. So under the aegis of profit-making the pharmaceutical company, has pushed something that should be local and in the immediate and accessible province of every individual into a falsely unattainable realm. It has mystified natural processes of healing and in effect claimed to be the sole intermediary of nature's magnificent processes. It has at best inadvertently covered up man's natural ability to heal himself and in that regard continues to do a great disservice to humanity. In the meanwhile it continues to grow rich on plundered money.

Putting Our Faustian Energy Deal to Rest

Energy is existent in every micro-measurement of life. It is present in the atoms that exist all around us. It is present in the light that makes everything visible. It is fair to say that it is present in every fiber of existence. Energy is in fact abundant. It is only the paucity of our own perception that has made energy scarce and burdened humankind with the exorbitant costs that our mishandling of energy continues to create.

Our primary source of energy is today oil. When energy is available locally at every point of the earth, why we have to lay pipelines that move a deadly substance across the earth, really meant to remain in the bowels of the earth, is one of those astounding questions posterity will be forced to ask. Why did we continue to extract a poison to fuel every manner of system is the big question? Why did we play with an eons-old equilibrium in the earth's fluids? And even if we did do so, and extracted these fluids to be used on the surface, what right did a single company or even a group of companies have to claim something that belongs to the earth and to all humanity as its own, and charge extraordinary prices for the use of it?

The simple answer, of course, is that in doing just this, in externalizing all these costs, and in being subsidized by current and future generations, communities, environment and nature, the few have been able to maximize profit to get rich at the expense of the many. And that in itself is a lure too seductive to turn aside from. And naturally, once it is being done, then economies of scale might as well be the arbiter of future decision-making, and make the whole enterprise bigger, faster, and far uglier than before. All this is an indication of this Industry having stalled at the stalk-level in the flower journey as well.

Modern times have seen huge wars being fought for access to oil. Countries have been invaded in the name or the lure of oil, and millions of innocent people have suffered from the disastrous social disorder that resulted from such wars. Dislocated and disenfranchised youth who once had a chance at a normal life have had their lives marginalized and become targets for terrorist groups. Terrorist groups, acting as parasites, have sought to destroy their decaying hosts. The cycles of destruction are huge as local cultures, society, and centuries old ways of being are tossed aside in the pursuit of a deadly poison that ultimately destroys its very users.

Oil causes havoc at every step of the supply chain. At the point of extraction, as just stated the natural equilibrium of the earth is altered as now deeply embedded fluids are extracted from its very being. Imagine a similar procedure being done on the human body, where deeply embedded fluid was continually extracted. It will surely result in serious instability. Then during transportation of the oil through pipes and in storage facilities there is continual seepage, and the fluid that once existed in a natural equilibrium deep in the earth is now randomly distributed in a completely different environment than what is natural for it. The chemistry of the different environment has been altered and species introduced to a substance that is completely foreign to them. In the absence of precise knowledge and balancing action there cannot but be an adverse effect in which the natural equilibrium of the environment is altered.

Further downstream there will be processing and refining plants. This means that water will be extracted and waste-product spewed out where it once belonged, and in the air and general environment around it. Storage facilities for processed oil will inevitably leak the oil into the water and air supply. Carcinogens and a deadly host of toxic substances are now distributed into communities of all kinds. Health of people deteriorates in different ways. People's very cells are now infiltrated with the unnatural and deadly substance, which compromises the workings of all the bodily systems. Ecosystems get affected, and we are faced with the very basis of modern civilization being threatened at its foundation. But further, the oil is now also widely distributed through vehicles. It now spreads across civilization, and when burnt introduces further toxicity into life. The possibility of Energy is replaced by a dark and poisonous binding chain that has wound itself into all aspects of life, breathing its poisonous fumes as it draws us into the lures of lethargy and self-annihilation. Dangerous, fire-breathing dragons that scorch all life around them have inadvertently been unleashed.

As though all this is not sign enough that we have embarked down an incorrect avenue, we have continued to build our systems and cities such that they are fueled by this source. This is a contradiction in terms, and pushes away the wealth and wholeness that must be a natural part of our lives. Sunlight has energy and is available for the asking. We do not have to extract and pull anything out of its natural place and way of being. So powerful is sunlight that all life moves naturally toward it and yearns for it. Life does not shrivel, coil up, and get poisoned as a result of contact with it. How out of touch with reality are we when we refuse to see the signs that are so detrimental to us?

Facebook: David or Goliath?

Analyzing what could be next for Facebook is to a large extent going to depend on the context of analysis. If one were to go by the recently released Facebook movie The Social Network the context comes across as a run-of-the-mill story of the past rather than a defining driver of the future. It is not the possibility of global shift, of Facebook's being a key stimulus in accelerating the much needed and in fact inevitable shift from the current 'vital' milieu to a more meaningful 'mental' milieu that comes across in the movie, but rather the success of a venture that has been intricately woven with the all too known small human themes that represent a humanity of the past, rather than a humanity of the future.

It is lengthy litigations, intellectual property struggles, power struggles, and frustrated or un-flourishing love that are key scenes and themes, all the etchings and motives of a vital world, that are propped up as the drivers of the Facebook phenomenon. In my mind this is a gross misinterpretation and misrepresentation of the promise of Facebook. And the gravity of this misinterpretation is clear from a few summary signs, such as the unanimous 'A' rating by Yahoo Movies critics, 'A-' rating by over 800 users a few days after the movie screened, and the movie's topping the box office on opening weekend (The Hollywood Reporter 2010).

But then again, if it is a vital world we live in, then it is the vital dynamics so well portrayed in the movie that the majority is going to find attractive. And yet, Mark Zuckerburg on his Facebook profile states "I'm trying to make the world a more open place by helping people connect and share" (Zuckerburg 2010). This aspiration is clearly representative of a key movement that must occur for the vital to shift to the mental, or for the stalk to become the flower, at the macro or global level.

At a micro level the dysfunction or common characteristics of the vital are represented by movements such as fear, greed, selfish desire, that in a fractal scheme of things (where a fractal is a pattern that repeats itself on different scale) manifests on a larger scale in such things as lengthy litigations, power struggles, frustrated love, that are the very stuff of the movie about Facebook. On a still larger scale this pattern manifests in the macro-level dysfunction we see playing itself at the global level today – unsustainable business practices, large corporate Goliath-like monopolies seeking only to exercise their self-perceived right to appropriate all resources for their own use and profit, with all human beings being relegated to the status of 'asset' or 'liability', amongst others – the all too common stories most large entities almost unconsciously play out because that is the implicit nature of monopoly alive today.

It is amidst this backdrop, this context, where unnatural monopolies intent on prolonging their devastating grip on humanity - the macro-level vital milieu - that phenomenon such as Facebook become immensely important. For not only does Facebook potentially "make the world a more open place by helping people connect and share" but more importantly it allows collectivities and communities that can challenge the status quo to more easily come into being. It is such communities that can challenge Monopoly, that allow

137

David to overcome Goliath. The movement from the vital to the mental also needs the emergence of identity – of individual identity: this is critical, and Facebook allows an audience to gather around instances and expression of identity, thereby strengthening that identity.

In its own trajectory Facebook must embrace the possibilities that allow the shift from the vital to the mental. It must move away from the gravitation of its Facematch beginnings and the trappings of the themes that have made "The Social Network" apparently so popular, to its David overcoming Goliath promise. This will only be securely done by basing all analyses and context on the underlying Flower Chronicles journey, which alone ensures safe passage from the stalk or vital to the flower or mental possibility.

"Here is the Future": My Interaction with Lars Dalgaard, CEO of SuccessFactors

I was a speaker representing Stanford University Medical Center (SUMC) at the SuccessFactors 2010 Conference. While I presented SUMC's recent developments in the performance management area, I want to focus on an interaction I had with Lars Dalgaard, CEO of SuccessFactors.

Lars launched the conference and passionately spoke about SuccessFactors' growth and product plans. It is interesting to see an organization grow as rapidly as his in the course of only 10 years. In 2010 SuccessFactors had about 8,000,000 users world-wide. No doubt such rapid growth is itself a sign of effectively promising to move the needle on established practices from the status quo (seed/physical) and the irrationally assertive (stalk/vital) to the more rational or mental possibilities in the HR field, which is sorely in need of progressive thinking on many different fronts.

After his address I walked to the stage and introduced myself to Lars. I had a copy of my book "Connecting Inner Power with Global Change", and presented this to him saying, "Here is the future." He replied saying "I can see the conviction in your eyes. I will read it."

Perhaps Lars quickly grasped or will grasp why I approached him. But nonetheless, I will elaborate:

1. SuccessFactors continues to create some powerful tools that are now focused on Business Execution through mobilizing human resources. Goal management, performance management, compensation management, succession planning, work-based collaboration, are key elements of this approach.

2. Effective use of these tools will definitely help an organization more effectively execute on business goals.

3. This does not though, necessarily equate to continued business success. If a business is headed in the wrong direction to begin with then all that the application of SuccessFactors Business Execution tools will do, is expedite the failure of the business. This will be the case because now a set of goals, measurements, and actions will be organized much more effectively around the misdirection to accelerate failure rather than success.

4. The choice of such business direction is in fact the critical issue, precisely because in today's uncertain times many base assumptions that global business has grown up with are being severely challenged.

5. In my opinion, these challenges are in fact the result/reaction of a purposeful, conscious, fractal-based world-system, that is insisting that economy, business, person cut to the chase and realize that big issues out there have their origin in small patterns in here at the level of the person.

6. Paradoxically the choice of business direction is more than anything else a function of the consciousness a decision-maker lives in, the result of small patterns of perception, awareness, assumptions, that define that consciousness.

7. Human-resource focused software has to get to this level of granularity of helping people and organizations more effectively manage the base-patterns that create much of the dysfunction we continue to see at every level of organizational complexity.

8. Further, there is a direction to the development of the world-system, and hence economies, markets, and industries that is revealed by the flower-journey synonymous with progress at each of these levels.

9. In my opinion the real winners in the ERP/HR software space are not necessarily the SuccessFactors, SAPs, Oracles, PeopleSofts of the world, but those software organizations that are able to bring the pattern-based reality of organizational and market dynamics with their underlying links to human-based seed-patterns into focus. It is these patterns that need to be altered for true progress, regardless of level, to take place.

Google Vs. China

Who are we? Are we cogs in a machine whose very movements and thoughts are to be programmed and controlled by a State? Can what benefits the larger business playing-field be taken as law in determining how the individual should conduct herself or himself in life? Is that the meaning of this fantastic world-journey that we are all on together?

Let us assume that on one hand there is a flower journey that China is currently on. Hence, it is self-impelled to traverse the physical, vital, and mental phases of its journey.

In its current state, the world is primarily viewed from a command-and-control perspective. Citizens are assets to be mobilized by central state machinery for the benefit of the State, which both the central machinery and the citizens exist for, solely. Obviously, freedom of expression is curtailed. And obviously there is nothing wrong with invasion of privacy, so long as what the State believes to be true is not compromised. This is a deeply physical-view of things in which all is subdued and held in tight control like a seed, and in this view any dynamic that disturbs this equation is to be shunned. Hence it is perhaps fair to say that China in its journey is currently at the physical-level. Now, there has of course been a lot of progress on the business-front, but we can make the case that this vital-type progress has served the essentially physical orientation.

This orientation is also out-of-synch with what we are proposing to be the fundamental urge of the integrated world-system. The urge is an implicit movement, embedded in the DNA of life, to successfully traverse the journey from the physical to the vital to the mental, and is succinctly summarized in the flower's journey. This means that such views as has created the operative reality in China does need to, in one way or another, be transcended.

Enter the possibility that the Internet has bought forward and the recent interactions between Google and China. These events challenge the physical-phase world-view held by China, and if successful, would cause the China flower-journey to progress to the vital-phase. Remember, that in the physical phase, humans are assets to be mobilized by machinery – they are cogs in a wheel. In the vital phase, there is experimentation and freedom to express. This is a critical phase; for only in completing it can the truer identity resident in each human breast even begin to come to the surface.

Hence, from the larger perspective of closing the gap or aligning the implicit urge resident in the integrated world-system with China's flower-journey, intervention and boldness by companies such as Google is perhaps warranted, and arguably gives them the moral right to lift internet-based censorship. For China to recognize this would be a big step forward.

Introducing another aspect into this analysis, the question, then, is what side of the struggle should one land on? Is it surprising that companies such as Microsoft and Hewlett-Packard, who have supposedly built themselves by and stood for human freedom should now refuse to comment on censorship (Waters 2010) and instead placate the issue by stressing the importance of China as a market? In one way of looking at it, it should be surprising. In another, not at all – because both Microsoft and Hewlett-Packard, and many, many other companies the world over are part of a Business flower-journey which is itself only at the vital level, where each often seeks for irrational growth, likely regardless of true cost to humanity.

So now we have a play of the China flower-journey, The Business flower-journey, that are both stagnated, and the boldness of a company like Google that is perhaps an instrument leveraged to help fulfill the implicit urge for progress in nature.

The questions are, can China win in a struggle that fundamentally is opposed to the urge implicit in the movement of a world-system? If it is to maintain its current view of things, then at what cost? How much human possibility will be suppressed? How much human blood will be shed? Will it have to collapse and splinter as a country, so that some of it has a chance to fulfill this fundamental urge of nature? On the other hand, can businesses, such as Microsoft, Hewlett-Packard, amongst many other businesses, continue to operate with such bottom-line business orientation only, in a world that is an integrated, intelligent, purposeful world that implicitly seeks for true, harmonious, sustainable growth? If they do so, then at what cost?

Both these stagnated journeys will find themselves continuing on their ultimately irresistible journeys. The protagonists of these journeys can do so consciously and pay a lower price for doing that now, or they will be forced to do so unconsciously, in which case they will pay a much higher price than they ever imagined. This is inevitable in a world that seeks for its own progress.

In another way of looking at it, we are saying that there is an overriding world-journey that will progress at any cost. When it is opposed in its movement, by stagnated journeys like those of China or Business, then instruments are leveraged to intersect with the stagnated entities to cause their progress. Progress can be accelerated by such opposition; but ultimately, sustainable shift comes about by shifting the base-pattern at the root of the fractal. The root is none other than the person – and the embodied attitudes, perceptions, behaviors that animate a person.

The Future of Consulting

Like oxygen, money should be thought of as an impersonal force flowing to facilitate activity. Oxygen is available to all without charge, and the more one maintains the health of their body, the more oxygen can freely flow through it to create a reinforcing loop of health. If one engages in activities that diminish the health of the body, whether through ingestion of toxins of various kinds, or through lack of sleep or exercise, the pathways in the body get obstructed and gradually the ability to draw oxygen diminishes. This is like a reinforcing loop that accelerates the deterioration of the body. That same amount of oxygen that was being drawn by one person now flows elsewhere. In this manner Nature optimizes the maintenance of her constructs so that those constructs that are in harmony with a progressive and sustainable way of being continue in this state.

Similarly, if there is positive organizational activity, money should automatically flow to that organization to sustain it. In the case of the oxygen flow there is a natural set of checks and balances that alters the flow of oxygen; hence, when an organization, be it a human, animal, or plant, has ceased from sustainable existence, the oxygen flow is reduced. In the case of more complex human-made organizations, be they corporations, not-for-profits, or societies, the automaticity is obfuscated because of the interference of a common orientation particular to human beings – the physical-vital orientation (physical component - viewing tomorrow's world as the same as yesterday's world; vital component - viewing the world as a field of exploitation).

The physical-vital orientation is like a node that draws activity to it. Only, it cannot be sustained because it tends to be inherently out of sync with the larger system. It conducts activity for its own sake rather than for the good of the system, and for a larger balance to be restored, the orientation of organizations has to move toward a mental-intuitional orientation (mental component - viewing the world as a play of ideas; intuitional component – syncing activities with a purposeful, contextual world-system). In such an orientation the right relationship between self and the larger system more easily comes into focus, and the dynamics so initiated are more naturally aligned with the purpose and sustainability of the larger system. Even the flower-based, fractal nature of life may then be more clearly perceived and the ripple effects of a feeling, thought, or act on larger and larger organizations more easily comprehended.

Yet, the larger and containing system has its own purpose, logic, and way of being, and ultimately all physical-vital orientations are forced to complete journeys to yield to the mental-intuitional orientation, failing which the stagnated organizations face extinction. When today we are faced with challenges as fundamental as climate change, which threaten to alter our very material bases, this is nothing other than a defense mechanism set in motion by the containing system to ensure its own sustainability. Either the stagnated organizations change their mode of being, that is, make the transition from a physical-vital orientation to a mental-intuitional orientation, or they face extinction.

Organizations with physical-vital orientations exist with their small self as reference, and seek to fulfill their existence in small ways that they think will enrich their existence. Hence, they may act to fulfill desire, or short-sighted ambition, or to conquer other organizations. In the final analysis, though, such orientation is self-defeating since it blocks or veils possible symbiosis with the larger, contextual system. In the mental-intuitional orientation the need for symbiosis becomes clearer at the outset, and the possibility and purpose inherent in the contextual system finds easier expression through the strivings of the constructs anchored in such mental-intuitional orientation. The flow of money, resource, idea, capability becomes a relatively seamless exchange between the seemingly isolated organization – be it a person or a corporation, and as in the interchange of oxygen, all proceeds in an optimized way so long as such mental-intuitional orientation is the cornerstone of its operation. In other words, the cost of money is reduced.

Over the last few centuries most organizations have existed in the physical-vital state to aggrandize their conception of themselves – that is, their isolated self. Business principles that epitomize competition and victory over other corporations have been promoted. All resources, including human resources, are viewed as assets or liabilities. This approach has left a long and seemingly unending trail of debris and destruction behind it. The time for such orientation is now ending. What is most needed now is a transition from the essentially physical-vital to the essentially mental-intuitional way of being. This is true for all organizations regardless of scale. Hence, it is true of an idea, of a person, a team, a department, a corporation, a market, a society. After all, each of these organizations draws its way of being from the essential combination of physical, vital, mental, and intuitional building blocks that then define its existence. Further, the combination of building blocks that define a society's way of being can only be changed when there is a parallel seed-change at the level of the person. Hence, there is a fractal reality that animates organization. For a pattern once in existence at the base level tends to reinforce itself on larger and larger scale.

Most organizations have reinforced yesterday's patterns in today's operations. They have learned how to reinforce their essential physical-vital orientation even by appropriating mental elements to do so. The mental capacities and capabilities are in service of a physical-vital outlook so that at the far-end it seems that even possibilities like sustainability and CSR, that are generally themes one associates with the larger system and hence naturally to be more mental-intuitional in nature, are not really that possibility, but appendages that make the essential physical-vital reality look more compelling. The point is that the essential reality remains the same, and therefore its impact on society, through fractal pressure is also of almost the same nature as a physical-vital construct without this mental appendage. Nothing really changes then, and confrontational walls like climate change that challenge and destroy, have to be erected by the conscious, purposeful world-system.

What organizations need most, whether they realize it or not, is this transition from the essentially physical-vital to the essentially mental-intuitional, starting at the root – the level of the person. It is only so that global recessions, climate change, and other massive debilitating dynamics will seize to be, because it is only then that the conscious and purposeful world system will be assured of its own comprehensive sustainability in which more and more organizational constructs are expressing both uniqueness and diversity by seizing on game-changing mental and intuitional dynamics that push these possibilities to the surface.

The Flower Chronicles is about seeing the deeper relationship between individual organizations and the contextual world-system that we are all a part of. It is about becoming aware of the fractal links that bind one layer of organization with the next, from the micro to the macro. It is about becoming aware of the fundamental building blocks that determine the active dynamics of a layer of organization – the physical, the vital, and the mental building blocks. It is about rearranging these fundamental building blocks so that the mental-intuitional leads and the physical-vital follows, thereby forever and sustainably altering the dynamics of society and environment. This is the future that organizational operation has to move toward. Obviously, this is also the future that consulting has to move toward.

Yet today there are consulting companies that continue to assist corporations in maintaining and winning the short-sighted self-defeating physical-vital game. The Big Four – Pricewaterhouse Coopers, Deloitte Touche Tohmatsu, Ernst & Young, and Cap Gemini fall into this category. So do other consulting companies such as McKinsey, BCG, A.T. Kearney,

Booz, and Bain, even though they charge a higher price for it. It is imperative that the world-views of these consulting companies changes radically so that they can become agents in bringing about Flower Chronicles type consulting that can alone truly help longer-term and sustainable existence of any scale of organization. Even the younger and more sustainably-oriented consulting companies, of the likes of Business for Social responsibility, SustainAbility, and BluSkye, while tending to appropriate more of the mental-intuitional elements still seem to continue to reinforce the essential physical-vital reality of corporations. Hence, the fractal-based analytics and foundation being created by organizations such as Aurosoorya becomes very important because it is focused on assisting organizations make the transition from an essentially physical-vital to an essentially mental-intuitional way of being. An approach of this nature will alone create lasting and secure sustainability because it addresses the issues of unsustainability at its absolute core.

A New Bases And Standard Of Financial And Economic Activity

The support stone of the old stable arch of financial operation was removed in 1971, when the gold standard was exited. According to the World Gold Council only 20-cubic meters of Gold have been mined through human history. This is the consummate symbol of the physical or seed phase of financial evolution. Physical implying that the world and its laws are fixed, determined by what the eye can see. Under the Bretton Woods system the gold price was fixed in dollars at $35 per ounce, and other currencies' exchange rates were fixed to the dollar. Hence, gold anchored all currencies. This meant that the money supply was limited. This also meant that it was hard for inflation to rise and that bubbles of all kinds would largely be avoided.

As John Authers, in his insightful book The Fearful Rise of Markets (Authers, 2010) points out, by removing the gold standard the rules of world trade changed overnight. The price of gold rose, which meant that governments and traders who had been accumulating surpluses of dollars, found that their dollars purchased substantially less gold. This caused currencies to float (as opposed to being anchored to the dollar) and exchange rates to diverge. But most significantly, oil exporters, represented by OPEC now received far less gold for oil. This caused OPEC to raise the price of oil. This further triggered inflation in the US and a weakening of the dollar, which led to a further increase in oil prices. The US, hence, and the rest of the world, thus found itself tied to a new global standard – the oil standard. Irrational monopolies of all kinds, to hold on to limited interpretations of power were reinforced and the world economic activity continued feverishly and unsustainably into the vital phase.

Oil is a flowing source of energy – and is representative of the vital phase. And this is what the shift from gold to oil signifies. However, it is not openly and easily available energy, such as exists in the sun, but the result of dead and crushed plants and animals existing now as fluid in the depths of the earth. The energetic possibility contained in this crushed material is in the first place obtained from solar energy. Hence oil is a derivative energy obtained from the past, made up from essentially physical-vital beings that once existed on the surface of the earth. Given this, its utility has to be finite, and this is borne out by the phenomena of peak oil, which suggests that once the extraction of oil has peaked, there is less of it available in the earth. Estimates suggest that we have already passed that point in time. In other words, oil as a medium of energy, and even as a symbol of financial

149

operation, has only a finite life. But during that life, symbolically speaking, being of the essence of the physical-vital, we can expect its era to be characteristically physical-vital. That is, an increasing energy driven by myopia, rather than order, driven by selfishness rather than selflessness, driven by destruction, rather than creation.

This trend also has an implication for what kind of standard will be created next. Following the notion of the ubiquitous flower journey, with base orientation shifting from the physical to the vital to the mental, it is clear that an attempt to create a 'mental' standard needs to be next - for progress to happen, that is. The physical standard was handed down to us through centuries of habit. The vital standard was driven by a perception of exploiting limitation - the oil standard emerged, not through holistic thought, but through limited vital-bound thought. With the reality of peak oil the next standard could very well be some other limited resource like water. But that would mean entering another round of perhaps even heightened global irrationality. The standard must therefore become something that should shift us away from the control and rigidity of the physical, embodied in the gold standard, and the recklessness and irrational monopolies of the vital, embodied in the oil standard, to the encouragement of bottom-up and globally distributed innovation, perhaps embodied in a solar-like energy standard.

Solar-like energy is by definition globally distributed and available forever. Money flow and creation of wealth needs to be tied to the ability to harness this type of energy, which in effect is infinite, which means that progress and development can in effect become infinite. Solar energy, for instance, in its passive action already fosters many ecosystem services, and therefore foundation of commerce whether we realize. If it or something like it, solar-like energy, could also more consciously, thoughtfully, and actively be harnessed, way beyond everything that is currently being done today by all the futurists around the world, then a new standard of wealth, that is non-monopolistic and available to all through acts of creativity, would come into being. This creativity, measured in how such solar-like energy is being harnessed, stored, used, and leveraged, could be the basis of new money creation, and in effect become a new standard for ordering global commerce.

When we ask the question - "Who controls the gold that money will buy?" it is clear that because of its relative scarcity there will always be only a few in power. When the gold standard existed it was clear that USA was the sole power in the world. When we ask the question - "Who controls the oil that money will buy?" today's reality of cartels, government-corporate-military oligopolies, corporate monopolies with all their attendant ugliness becomes real. When we ask the question - "Who controls the solar-like energy that money will buy?" the possibility of the shift from monopolistic to democratic systems of power becomes real.

That solar-like energy will be used as the standard to anchor all commerce is inevitable. The sooner we realize this and take steps to reorient our systems of business and economy around this, the sooner will truer sustainability come into being.

Summary

In this chapter we began with a symbolic analysis of the end of the oil industry, which really signifies a movement away from the physical-vital or seed-stalk reality to something different. This 'different' is of course the possibility of the flower reality in the ubiquitous flower journey. Consistent with the symbolism of the BP oil spill, the examination of widespread industries such as food & agriculture, retail, pharmaceuticals, and energy suggests that for their own sustainability they absolutely need to move from the current stagnation around the seed-stalk reality to embrace the possibilities inherent in the flower. Not to do so will spell demise for these indsutries.

But is the presence of the other industries, such as social media and ERP/HR software that facilitates such movement even in the 'traditional' industries. For this facilitation to become effective though, these more software based industries have to embrace their flower possibility as well. Facebook has to move away from its Facematch beginnings and the allure of The Social Network in order to become something different for other organizations. And, the effect of these software-based possibilities can also impact countries, as suggested in the case of Google versus China.

But even for the possibility to become sustainable, leaders and dynamics within each company will need to be shown the way out of their current habits and assumptions, and that really becomes the true raison d'etre of an industry like Consulting. Finally, the very basis of business and economic accounting has to change so that a solar-like standard replaces the current oil standard.

Part 5 – Financial Rebirth

In this chapter we will look at some common responses to crises, lay out a flower model against which to assess global market crises, and look more deeply at several market crises against this model, to thereby see a different kind of sense of what has happened over the last 4 decades.

The Flash Crash Of May 6, 2010: How Out Of Touch With Reality Are We?

What the Flash Crash of May 6, 2010 really affirmed was how out of touch we are with the reality we have created. In a few minutes the hard-work of hundreds of thousands of people toiling day-after-day to earn an honest living was by some estimates negated because of automated sell orders. In a few minutes the ideals that many hold, high ideals of democracy, equality, fraternity where all citizens are treated equally and have a say in how life should develop came crashing to the ground as the surge of sell-orders, not motivated by a balanced perspective seeking the greater good, but motivated by that same physical-vital consciousness seeking its own selfish gain, played itself out yet once again.

In a few minutes the absurdity of what we continue to create smashed into our fragile order with its massive face of chaos. In a few minutes we reinforced the tremendous price we are willing to pay for a continued physical-vital way of being. Our Karma boomerangs at us with tidal wave like disaster, and like the increasingly powerful storm-systems of

Climate Change confront us with the poor choices of our own doings.

Instead of facing the question of the absurdity of our global financial system, where we have effectively given up control to an absolute casino-mentality, we seem to be more concerned with creating circuit breakers to avoid future flash crashes (Mackenzie, 2010). This is no doubt of some practical importance, but unfortunately pushes back the dealing with the real issue confronting the very survival of the ideals we believe to be true and self-evident - democracy, liberty, equality - and that of ensuring a reasoned and sustainable progress of our global civilization.

For in reality, the continually increasing sophistication of technology further increases the power of monopolized flows of money, that are not monopolized by reason, but by an unfortunate and uncaring short-sighted mentality of speculation. The risks are now too large, and the price we will pay for not taking action to reverse the global monopolization of money-power that we have inadvertently allowed to arise out of continuing to live in a physical-vital consciousness, will be the continued economic and even cultural and ideological weakening of larger and larger regions of the world - Greece, Spain, Ireland, Iceland, Japan, USA, the EU - as is already evident.

The signs are clear and action to reverse the inadvertent monopolization of the very power - money power - that has come to drive our progress needs to be taken now.

The Common Response to Crises

Every time an economy threatens to fail, it results in upheaval in the global economy, and the same inadequate responses from the financial and political communities.

155

I believe that the underlying cause is continued adherence to a simple linear view of things, when in fact the world we live in is, in my view, an integrated, purposeful, conscious, flower-based world-system. Within this system, there is a special class of journeys – the physical-vital-mental or the seed-stalk-flower journey that I am proposing is the key to aligning with the underlying system to therefore allow the System to work its magic in our lives.

From time-to-time there are more system-based theories of this nature that find their way into the mainstream press. I remember pausing when in the Financial Times I read an opinion on the Greek Crises coming to USA (Ferguson, 2010). The author Niall Ferguson, also author of Ascent of Money (Ferguson, 2009), referred to the 'fractal geometry of debt' in suggesting that the Greek crisis, Iceland crisis, Ireland crisis were all similar, just on different scale. This is the first time I have seen an analysis of this nature in the Financial Times – and to me it illustrates how the mainstream is beginning to move away from linear to even fractal-based systems thinking. I will also quickly mention that what the author, Niall Ferguson, was pointing out, is in fact an illustration of a contrary-journey - a journey that is led by the physical or vital component, rather than the flower or mental component. If we were to replace this contrary-journey with the seed-stalk-flower or physical-vital-mental journey, in effect the financial crises will begin to be more effectively solved.

Why such tremendous power has been given to one dimension of life only, the unrefined economic aim when life is quite evidently multi-dimensional, is the underlying question. This dogma of economic growth often at any cost, and the demand that all in an economy exist as assets to further the one-dimensional goals of the economy is quite frankly an outmoded way of being quite simply rooted in a physical-vital or seed-stalk orientation.

Its time is fast drawing to a close, and if we listen carefully enough in the silence behind the actions we see that this physical-vital orientation is seeking for completion of its journey, to tend toward the flower orientation. Hints of what this may look like flash into the inner mind: the meaning of wealth expanded; money de-monopolized so that numerous communities, rather than Central Banks, have power over their respective destinies; Creative activity democratized – themes I will continue to return to in these chapters.

Every time an economy falls the same rote actions are followed – austerity measures proclaimed, watchful eyes cast on debt repayments, stress levels amongst the common people escalated, potential fire walls set up, and vultures on the side-lines waiting to swoop in for the kill. It is interesting to note that in a staff paper from the IMF (Giles, 2010) where thinking on financial crises has been fixed for 30 years, it is being proposed that Central Bankers expand their portfolio of tools, beyond interest rate adjustment. This is a huge change – clearly moving from the Physical to the Vital. But it cannot or will not be enough.

It is time to examine the system behind the system, and enter into the deeper logic that is beginning to surface.

Making Sense of Market Crises

Established wisdom suggests that one crisis is the same as the next. Hence each of the following crises tends to be addressed in similar ways.

1.   The 1973-1974 Bear Market
2.   The 1987 Synchronized Global Crash
3.   The 1990s Japanese Asset Bubble and the South East Asian Crises
4.   The 2000 Dot-Com Crisis
5.   The 2004 Housing Crisis

6.   The 2010 Greek Debt Crisis

However, I propose a contextual framework against which each of these crises has to be assessed. This framework is based on a universal pattern of sustainable progress that is very commonly visible and is in fact summarized in the journey that a seed makes in becoming a flower.

I start from the 1973 - 74 crises because that was a result of a major shift in global economic reality when the Gold Standard was abandoned. For a good 3 decades the global economy had functioned in a relatively predictable, stable way, always maintaining the status quo because all currencies were pegged to the US$. This state of affairs was more like the inert seed of a plant, the physical state where the world is what the eye can see. Little inflation exists, the money supply is fixed, and what happens is the result of stable recycling of possibilities. This state can be thought of as the starting point in the seed-to-flower trajectory.

When the Gold Standard was abandoned though, currencies de-anchored from the US$ and began to float, and there was a lot more volatility that was introduced into the global situation. What had been known and what we had relied on for decades was abandoned, and no nation could anymore be assured of the wealth in its possession. Hence another standard was sought and the transition from the seed to the stalk stage, or the physical to the vital stage was securely put into place.

The oil embargo of 1973 precipitated the emergence of the Oil Standard, giving OPEC far more power on the global economic stage. Prices all over the world began to escalate and dynamics of inflation reentered the global economic situation with force. This resulted in the 1973-74 bear market in US and elsewhere and accelerated the destructive vital or stalk dynamics that has had relatively free reign over the last 4 decades.

By 1987 there was the first global economic synchronized crash. All major stock markets around the world lost significant value at the same time. From a rational perspective this makes no sense. Different regions around the world and different markets should be subject to different market conditions and a more local cyclicality in investment rhythm. For markets and regions around the world to divert from this, implies that dynamics have become irrational. Such irrationality is a sure sign that the vital level has become far more active since is now aggressive self-seeking that drives things.

Subsequent crises of the 1990s, such as the Japanese Asset Crises, the Asian Crises, and the Russian financial crises quickly came into being as money unleashed from rationality and reason sought a home where it could make quick returns regardless of larger issues of sustainability.

Rationality, reason, purpose, sustainability are the dynamics that are more prevalent when the flower or mental stage are reached. That must be the aim of any policy-maker and regulator. The good news is that impelled by the flower in circumstance, the first decade of the 2000s has seen this urge coming more to the forefront.

Hence in 2000 the dot-com crisis was of a very different nature. This signified the possibility of the mental or flower stage where a whole new infrastructure allowing power to shift from monopoly to democracy more practically came into being.

The US Housing Crises of 2004 and on, powerfully brought to the surface some of the perversities in a Finance led solely by the vital-level. This is the shadow that emerges to remind us of where never to go again. The 2007 – 2009 Bear Market was more of a tug-of-war between the past and the future, with the past, represented by the dynamics inherent in industries such as Pharmaceutics, Oil & Gas, Retail, Food &

Agriculture vying for further attention and investment to continue their self-serving patterns of the past, against the new dynamics represented by the Internet that we all know has begun to arise at the same time.

The Greek Debt Crises and the European Union Sovereign Debt Crises and the Occupy movement bring into relief the whole question of wealth. What is it? Is it the one-dimensional metric that has driven the whole one-sided vital development of the last 4 decades to its current state of obvious instability, or is it something else that is multi-dimensional and factors in culture, spirit, human possibility, as symbolized in the flower.

When viewed in this manner, we can more clearly see what must be done to usher in a period of global financial and business sustainability.

Some Lessons from The Asian Financial Crises

The Asian Financial Crises of 1997 – 98 was by many estimates caused because of the massive inflows of speculative money that needed a new home for quick returns. In part this was due to the higher interest rates offered by countries such as Thailand, Malaysia, and Indonesia that were at the epicenter of the crisis. Further, given that the Japanese Asset Bubble had just burst, there was a huge amount of money that had previously been invested there that needed a new home. All this money rushed about, driven by the lure of vital-value, of making that quick buck, regardless of true creation or destruction of value.

Naturally with large inflows of capital, asset prices began to rise. Corporations and individuals alike experienced a rise in their vital-level wealth – whether wealth was really increasing can only be judged by anchoring on the mental-level, where it is truer development that is the focus. This

160

perception that all were richer because some asset – whether real estate or stocks – at the center of the bubble continued to rise in escalated vital-level value, caused heightened irrationality and risk-taking on the part of all constituents, including banks that began issuing loans based on the perceived vital-level wealth.

When it was realized however that underlying development had not really taken place and that many individuals and corporations were naturally beginning to default on loan payments, then there was a massive retraction of capital, and the Asian Financial Crisis came into being. Foreign investors flooded the exchange market with respective country currencies and as a result the value of these currencies began to depreciate. This put even more burden on individual country international loan payments and heightened the default rates on loans thereby causing more bankruptcies and even more pulling out of foreign-originated investments. To try and prop up the currency rate respective governments increased interest rates, which made further loan origination in the country even more difficult. Thus there was a senseless and destructive cycle put into place that naturally exceeded the boundaries of the vital-level notion of wealth to destroy truer mental-level wealth in the bargain.

What this teaches us is that it is necessary to maintain focus on true underlying development. To use mass-scale vital-level euphoria manifesting in a vastly increased demand relative to supply is in fact a highly misleading measure of value. We need metrics that peel these illusionary layers away to focus on what actually is being done with the money, how it is actually being used, and further how that development is in fact development of a true, sustainable, mental-level order. Anything else is going to cause massive turmoil and destroy the hard work and livelihoods of many innocent people.

Some Lessons from the Dot-Com Bubble and Other Financial Innovation

The Dot-Com crisis of 2000 brings into view another set of lessons. The massive inflow of money in fact was highly beneficial in this environment, because the Dot-Com phenomena was fundamentally about moving away from many of the irrationalities of vital-level monopoly toward the possibilities of a more diverse individual-level creativity. Plays such as Amazon, eBay, Yahoo, Google, and more recently Facebook and Twitter upset the balance of vital-level dynamics to bring another set of possibilities to bear. They clearly push the underlying flower journey toward the transition from the stalk to the flower.

Of course there was a lot of wasted money and vital-level euphoria that caused a boom and a bust. But the net-net has been huge. Innovation of this kind, that is grounded in how activity, work, process of socialization are fundamentally altered, and in real, greater freedom for the individual and different scales of collectivity, is of a real kind. People, communities, posterity – all benefit as a result of such risk and such flows of wealth. This must be contrasted to what has been termed as innovation in the financial field though. Innovation in the financial field is not based on real tangible development.

The recent US-based housing crisis is a perfect example. Sub-prime type mortgages were securitized. Traditionally mortgages were a one-to-one transaction. That is, a bank gave a loan to an individual to buy a house after significant due diligence, and the buyer of the loan then made principal and interest payments to the bank until the loan had been paid off. The bank owned the reward and the risk. With mortgage-backed securities however, an Investment Bank created a Special Purpose Vehicle (SPV) to pool mortgages together that it then sold to generate additional revenues. Thus, the originating lender of debt was first rewarded for issuing the mortgage. There was no risk they took on and therefore the level of due diligence and risk monitoring was completely removed. That mortgage was then pooled with many other such mortgages and marketed as a robust investment opportunity.

After all according to portfolio theory, which anyway is more applicable at the mental as opposed to the vital level and therefore quite inapplicable in current times, pooling assets will minimize overall risk and therefore in theory there is no more need to conduct due diligence – just keep adding in assets of different types, even if they are different types of mortgages, and all will be well. Securities were created and these securities were sold to investors around the world. Obviously the value of money gets inflated as a result. The buyers of the securities now in effect get paid a monthly payment by the would-be homeowner. The buyers of the securities can further sell financially-manufactured products based on that same tangible asset, and the value of money is further inflated.

At the end of the day if creation of money is not backed by an equal creation of tangible value then the world suffers in the bargain. But all recent financial innovation has been of this kind. A whole breed of mushroom-type activity is set up, and all the while everyone thinks everyone is getting richer. Financial returns of these mushroom companies increases. This draws more funds, and more of the same irrational type cycles are initiated. A mega-bubble is created that ties everyone to illusory assets. When this one bursts then real trouble results.

The 2008 global financial crisis was the result of over-dependence on toxic assets of this nature. They were toxic because they were not based on any real tangible value. There

163

is one level of toxicity when adequate due diligence has not been performed. This of course was the case. There is another level of toxicity when the very same tangible product, the house, is used to inflate the flow of money in the economy. Creation of securitized mortgage and other products assured that. There is a third level of toxicity when highly leveraged funds such as hedge funds now focus their resources on the securitized products thereby in effect severing all links with reality. For now the game is focused on the illusory bubble and the asset at the center of this, the toxic securitized products, becomes collateral and a starting point for a whole array of additional financial innovation. The fourth level of toxicity is that such assets are viewed as assets rather than liabilities, in the first place. This points to the toxicity of the financial system itself which allows such meaningless valuations to drive, what is at the end of the day, highly destructive activity negatively affecting the lives of millions of people.

Clearly when these two types of bubbles are contrasted, the Dot-Com bubble and the bubbles that followed it, discrimination as to where to invest has to come to bear. If all we focus on is the claims of organizations that they are generating huge profit, because they happen to be at the center of a financial innovation type bubble, at the end of the day that is like spreading a cancer through society because destructive wealth-diminishing type activity has overtaken productive activity. Claims by companies, and fluctuations of stock prices can hardly be taken at face value. A deeper penetration, a deeper, more meaningful array of metrics that indicate the truer ground-level value needs to be front and center, and become the arbiter of whether or not to invest in a particular stock. This will require corporations to become truly more accountable to society.

The Greek Debt Crisis of 2010 brings up some very fundamental questions. The issue of national sovereignty, and therefore centuries-old wealth as established by deep cultural and even spiritual values made evident in the uniqueness of a nation, versus adherence to stability measures at the regional collectivity level of the European Union come face to face in such a crisis. Further, is the notion of wealth itself. Is wealth the one-dimensional trait as captured by modern-day currency, or is wealth multi-dimensional, transcending today's notion of it? Answers to these questions need to determine the limits and rules with respect to investment and speculation.

Is all of life tradable? Or should limits be placed on what can be speculated on and what cannot. If an institution opens itself to seeking for loans, how far should the consequences of default go? As in the deal made by Shylock the money-lender in Shakespeare's Merchant of Venice, what does a pound of flesh mean? Is it okay to reduce the soul or spirit of a country to nothing? Are austerity measures sending many into a state of poverty and compromising deeper spirit, the blood in Shylock's pound of flesh, and therefore off limits in trading or speculative relationships? What is the responsibility of a country to its people?

The US Government's handling of the financial crisis that has hit USA over the last 2 years illustrates this issue well. The Government has set new standards of intervention that that are also being progressively adopted by other Central Banks around the world. Its primary goal has been the facilitation of the flow of money in the economy to counter any possibility of deflation. Hence, not only has the Federal Reserve been a lender-of-last-resort to established commercial banks, thereby extending them an unprovisional line of credit to minimize the possibility of bank-runs, but it has also become the lender-of-last-resort to non-depository financial enterprises. Even those financial enterprises that were at the center of causing the crises in the first place were in effect 'forgiven'. Given the goal to assure flow of money and business transaction, and given the extent to which the financial world is in a sense a monopoly, a domino-effect that may hit innocent business could not be allowed to occur. The Federal Reserve in effect bought all the toxic assets on the balance sheets of US-based financial institutions. Because the US is a leader in the world by contemporary standards, the US dollar still commands respect and has proven to be a currency of investment amidst the global uncertainty spawned by the global crisis. This is so even though it lay at the center and was the starting point of the global crisis. Through these actions the US has preserved its infrastructure and asset base, and at a deeper level its current culture, that very well could have become the target of internationally-led takeovers.

When we think about the Greek debt crises, the question is, does Greece too not have a right to preserve its infrastructure and asset base and deeper culture? Because commercial enterprise is prized in today's world, and the institution of business is generally placed on a pedestal, we recognize and acknowledge the power held by USA. But every country has its strength and uniqueness, even though it may not be commercial. Why shouldn't then, their cultures be held intact and upheld? Greek people, as have the people of Mexico, S. America, S.E. Asia, Russia, and more recently Europe – wherever recent financial crises has struck – have been subjected to austerity measures and many have been permanently displaced as a result of bankruptcies. Arguably the social and environmental capital of these countries has been permanently diminished in the bargain. Does this mean that a country has to be commercially dominant to guarantee its place in the world? Because of its inherent commercial strength the USA was able to preserve its way of being pretty much untouched, for now.

If countries such as Greece have from the outset established a different social contract with their people and have followed deficit spending as a result, it too should be able to wipe the sleight clean and 'forgive' its accumulated 'errors', whether through innovative monetary or fiscal policy, as has USA, or simply as an application of what is to me an inherent principle of existence, whether for a person or for a country. And it should be able to do this on the promise of its unique wealth it brings to the world – not commercial wealth that in any case is incredibly one-dimensional – but on the bases of increasing the multi-dimensional wealth and therefore longer-term sustainability of the world.

If a country is to use fiscal policy to solve its ills, then the choice of where it invests money is critical. Road projects are well and good. But there are many environmental and social issues that need to be urgently addressed, whether of building up environmental capital through the replenishing of ecosystem services, or of building social capital through the creation of robust communities, for example. If Government is going to pull money out of thin air, such acts should be quickly grounded to create real benefit and a source of future wealth, at the very least, for the country. Deficit spending that is going to yield substantial positive returns even if they are 5, 10, or 20 years in the future should hardly be penalized. In the vaster scheme of things such social and environmental investments increase the wealth of the world. For is not every single resource we utilize in every single enterprise of any kind a part of the earth, and even of the possibility of the flower behind things? To therefore reinvest in it, as opposed to groundless financially-based securitization, Ponzi, and other financial-innovation type schemes is money well spent.

Greece as part of the EU is unable to freely exercise monetary policy. This is part of the deal of becoming a part of the EU. Slapping on austerity measures in exchange for better borrowing rates from EU originated loans, means in effect that even Greece's freedom to exercise fiscal policy is being curtailed. As a country, when one compares a Government's range of responses to crises between USA and Greece, for example then, it is clear then that Greece is fast losing control over its country and its people. It is being subsumed into a global financial protocol and machinery that recognizes bottom-line financial return only, and under this trajectory Greece will not be Greece for much longer, but just another clone in a senseless monopoly seeking for a headless and irrational world-dominion. If this is not a tragedy then what is? Clearly this has to be stopped in its tracks.

Niall Ferguson (Ferguson 2010) reflected that it is poignant that the financial crises of the West has started in Greece, the birthplace of Western Civilization, and is spreading from there, just as Western Civilization spread from there. Let us hope that this crises is viewed for more than a spreading financial crises, to get to what it really is – a failure to perceive and align with the deeper and truer meaning of wealth.

What the "Occupy" Movement Represents

On Sept 17, 2011, the Occupy movement started with an estimated 1000 people gathering to Occupy Wall Street. By October 15, 2011, this movement spread to 951 cities in 82 countries to form a single global protest. This single global protest is a unique phenomenon and represents the visceral urge to move the global business machinery to a more sustainable way of operating so that all layers of society and environment are figured in and balanced in the reconfigured 'business' equation that must result.

Government and Central Bank action the world over, following the financial crises of 2008 – 2010, has obviously been focused on the short-term. But let us look at the nature of their short-term interventions. They have done much to allow the flow of money to continue as per vital-level growth models. Therefore they have sucked up junk assets, lowered interest rates, and forgiven parasitic corporations. This intervention is perhaps warranted, because in the absence of this, the world as we know it, would have changed too rapidly and social unrest risen meteorically. Rebellion, a la the French Revolution would have become the norm and Bastille Days the common nature of day. This may still happen if a longer-term mental or flower-level outlook is not quickly worked out. That is why the seed of response has to change.

The Occupy Wall Street movement reflected this inability to truly move things to the mental level.

The fundamental problem has been that value has been equated with vital-level as opposed to mental-level value. This is a form of Nazism. It is a bastardization of all that is sacred, in which standards of excellence are equated to contours on the surface or on the face of things, as opposed to the uniqueness inherent in development and culture and civilization. When value of assets sync up, so that investment in India and investment in Brazil are not related anymore to the unique need in India and the unique need in Brazil, but simply to an investors overall level of fear or greed, then we know that this bastardization has become the way of life. It is imperative that this be reversed in its tracks. The financial system as a whole has to be overhauled for this to happen.

Our current global crisis is unique. It has never happened before in recorded history. This is evident from some simple observations. First, the very playing field of all business is uniquely challenged by the phenomenon of Climate Change – it is not negative local effects from local action any more, but negative global effects from local action now – a dangerous situation. Ecosystems get destroyed as temperatures rise, and the very resource base of any modern-day business is permanently crippled. The perception that it is an exploitable resource base is flawed at its root, and it is the fundamental perception that has to change to right this. This base-pattern, decidedly vital in nature, creates many contrary or stagnated journeys in its wake. Climate Change is the ultimate macro wake-up call pointing to the absolute urgency of shifting the base-pattern at its very root.

If we are at the boundary between the vital and mental way of being, then that has to become the context of truly addressing the current crises. This is not a one-time crises. We have been living in this overarching vital-level arc since at least the birth of the Amsterdam Stock Exchange, if not even before that. Crises have occurred because of the bubbles that keep bursting. And this will continue until we make the needed shift into the mental or flower-way of operating. All crises have been opportunities to shift away from dysfunction. Instead as a result of the crises we have quickly always tried to put things back to the way they were. The Crash of 1929, preceding the Great Depression, has been likened as being similar to today's global crisis. Some important measures were taken then to reverse the bastardization of value. But little was done to democratize markets to really move to the creativity, uniqueness, sustainability more inherent at the flower level.

This is at the crux. We need to democratize markets so that truer local and sustainable innovation is unleashed. Instead we began a much longer arc that integrated more and more of the world into the unstable equation of bubbled business and markets. The integration, and synchronization, and bastardization has reached the limit of its playing-field. We are at the inevitable end of a dysfunctional way of being. In some respects, if we assume that we live in a purposeful world, then we can see that such an integration may have its purpose in that it ensures that there can be no havens that will not finally want to change.

I think this is borne out by the developments of October 15, where 951 cities in 82 countries have joined in a single global protest.

Summary

Market crises can be better understood and addressed if we understand the context within which they occur. In this chapter context has been positioned as related to development along the ubiquitous flower model. Knowing at what stage of the growth from seed to flower a crisis is synonymous with, allows a far more intelligent response to the crisis. The nature, for example of the Dot-Com crisis, is fundamentally different from the nature of the US Housing Crisis. The former, for example, is a definite push into the future. The latter is a dampening pull from the past. The former helps us cross the threshold into the realm of the flower. The latter is a gravitation back to some level driven by the seed and stalk. At stake is the whole question of progressive civilization versus prolonged stagnation, and hence being able to recognize the difference between crises is critical.

While in the last chapter we looked at specific market examples of crisis, and their inner meaning, in this chapter we look at some of what has created the global financial problems of today, and suggest solutions to these. Both the analyses of the problems and the suggested solutions derive from the underlying flower model applied to the field of global business and finance.

Modern Day Finance: The Paradoxical Destruction of Value

In examining global funding over the last couple of decades one can see the massive increase in share trading volume. From a level of US$ 55T in 2000, volume has increased to US$ 120T in 2006 (World Federation of Exchanges, 2010). Such a massive increase can easily result in breakdown if the system that is the recipient of such flows is not ready for it. In this instance it has resulted in the global financial crises. The situation is much like massive flows of water being forced into pipes and reservoirs that are not quite ready for that flow. The pipes and reservoirs were made for another reason: to facilitate a predictable, efficient market-type rise in funding. The rise in funding has been anything but gradual. Stoked by the vital-dynamic of making it rich in the short-term, often at any cost, the source of funding from would-be millionaires has increased dramatically.

But this rise has not occurred in a vacuum. The expectation and the possibility of such an outcome, of making it rich the quick-way, has been built over decades. John Authers, in his insightful book, The Fearful Rise of Markets, has traced the milestones that have made such a reality possible (Authers, 2010). Starting from 1954, in the US Stock Market recovery from the Great Crash, post-Depression regulation forced commercial banks to be covered by deposit insurance. Commercial banks were barred from investment banking. Fixed exchange rates were linked to gold under Bretton Woods. There was a clear division in the financial playing field with banks dominating finance and investment dominated by individuals using their own money. As Authers reinforces, mainstream investors had no access to investing in commodities, foreign exchange, credit default risk, or emerging markets. However all these conditions that in effect held irrational speculation at bay changed over the last 50 years, to create the conditions for unrelated markets to overheat and move as a synchronized bubble.

Another way to look at this is to equate each bubble, and the global synchronized bubble, as similar to atomic bombs. At its basis the atomic bomb breaks the bonds at the atomic level to destroy the fabric of matter-based development. When atoms are split then atom cannot combine with atom to form molecule. Molecule cannot combine with molecule, and therefore the entire basis of creation is toppled. In this way of seeing, the atomic bomb helps us to understand the effect of modern-day finance. For just in the case of the action of an atomic bomb, where complex matter is reduced to coarser and simpler denominations of it, in modern-day finance all value and development is reduced to a simple denominator in which value and development effectively lose their meaning.

When completely unrelated markets that have a different meaning for existing begin to synchronize their movements, it means that the meaning, the value, the raison d'etre, has been stripped away, and something baser, of lesser value has become the means for moving those markets. In effect those markets have been standardized or atomized. And the very fact that today the movement of even what should be fundamentally different markets – such as emerging markets on the one hand and developed markets on the other – for example, move in synchronized manner means that money is not being used to develop the market in accordance with the opportunities and challenges there, as it should be, but is being used to develop something entirely different – the myopic and selfish need of an even distant speculator.

This has to be the case since speculators do not care how they are making money. They just care that they do. Since money is the end-result it is immaterial whether that money comes from the construction or destruction of culture and civilization. It is immaterial if they are supporting the funding of the social destruction of an innocent people so long as a multinational now has access to raw-materials it may need and therefore is able to maximize its profit and the speculator's in the bargain, or if they are supporting the destruction of complex ecosystems such as rain-forests, wetlands, marshes that provide numerous and irreplaceable ecosystem-services, so long as they pocket money in the end.

In the atomic bomb analogy this is like reducing beautiful scenery, intricate richness, and profound architecture to a coarser and valueless denominator of itself by breaking the bonds that hold matter together, and then imagining that we have gotten richer in this deal because now we have the stream of particles or other such denominators from which all is created, in our possession. If this were true, then there would be value in destroying everything with atomic bombs. This is clearly not true. The basis of modern-day finance is therefore perverse and it is necessary to alter it immediately. Let me reemphasize – it is perverse because the very reason that money exists – to engender beautiful creation, is being reversed, and the beautiful creation that should be the end has now become the means to amass the intermediary – money – whose meaning is, in the final analysis, lost when it does not support meaningful creation.

US Recovery and a Touch of Genius

Many times when I read daily financial news it causes me to wonder. I focus on an analysis of a piece that is very typical. This piece, The US Recovery (FT.com Lex, 2010), from June 11, 2010, points to the continued concern that even after prolonged stimulus in US, with interest rates being near zero for 18 months, and the government pouring $787B of stimulus funds in the economy, that there has been a dip in retail sales and building materials in May (US Census Bureau News, 2010). This, by the way, is a repeating pattern we see playing itself out faithfully every opportunity.

The real concern is that there should be concern over slowdown. As Albert Einsten said, "Any intelligent fool can make things bigger and more complex... It takes a touch of genius - and a lot of courage to move in the opposite direction." In essence the intelligent fool is the investor or institution living in the physical-vital orientation, and seeking always irrational growth, often at any cost. It is the intelligent fool who targets money in hotspots thereby causing the phenomena of bubbles.

These seductive attractors seem to promise it all, but inevitably cause much more instability in their wake. Japan crashed in the 90s. The money that the intelligent fool had been pumping in there then had to find other homes. It went into S. Asia and in the late 90s caused a formidable bubble and crash there. Around 2005 that same drive went into securitized housing mortgages, caused a bubble and then a crash there. In 2008 it went into an assorted number of financial products and has caused the global financial crises we are witnessing today.

It is time for the "touch of genius", as Einstein calls it, and time for the surfacing of "a lot of courage to move in the opposite direction". It is time to awaken into the flower or mental orientation, so that bold and innovate growth based on entirely new patterns of development come into being. So what if retail sales go down? So what if housing starts go down? That is good. That means that there is a pause in the irrationality that continues to accompany us into the present.

What we need now is a decisive separation from the old way of thinking about business and the economy. We need a complete de-monopolization in industry, in the established ways of issuing and handling money, and in our prevalent "intelligent fool" syndrome. It is only then that we will begin to witness a sustainable recovery in the US and the rest of the world.

Understanding the DNA of Markets

A secret knowledge will continue to remain a secret so long as one does not look in the right place for the answer. And so long as one does not look in the right place for an answer the behavior and potential behavior of markets, the very DNA of Markets, will remain a mystery.

Financial prophets, gurus, analysts have come up with potential models that explain markets some times. At one end of the spectrum is the Efficient Market Hypothesis (EMH), which itself comes in different shades. But the bottom-line is that prices on traded assets reflect information about that asset. Hence, financial markets are informationally efficient. On the other end of the spectrum are models that define financial markets as stochastic. Mandelbrot has been a big proponent of this model. Then there are models that define price behavior as a function of human emotion, and hence predictable within boundaries. Elliott and Prechter (Prechter

2009) have built models based on this supposition. Thus, we have models that define financial markets correctly, within their prescribed limits, but fall apart when those limits are transcended.

The great secret to understanding market behavior, however, is in understanding the ubiquitous flower journey and the stages a flower goes through in arriving at itself. These stages – the seed or physical, the stalk or vital, and the flower or mental - are like strands of DNA, whose different combinations will in effect create different behavioral paradigms for markets.   Each of the three market-models just referred to are a function of how these basic strands combine together. With the purer vital or stalk mixture, a Mandelbrot-type Stochastic model results. With a combination of physical and vital the Elliott/Prechter model comes into being. When the mental strand tends to lead then EMH comes into being. Continued misapplication of these models during real-time decision-making will exacerbate dysfunction and result in crises - of the type we continue to experience globally now.

Will the Stock Market Crash Again?

Many believe that stock market performance is cyclic and that rise and fall, driven by human emotion such as greed and fear, are predictable. Some have even performed fairly detailed analyses to highlight the fractal nature of stock market performance (Prechter, 2009; Mandelbrot, 2004). Rise and fall themselves follow a self-similar pattern that is true regardless of time-period. Hence rise or fall over a one-year period will display a similar pattern to rise or fall during a one-week period, for instance.

In my estimation however, there is a deeper pattern underlying studied stock market performance that can radically change the predictable behavior of stock markets.

177

Greed and fear are indices of a 'vital' or 'emotional' way of being. In this way of being true rationality or intelligence has been subdued, and naturally fear and greed stand as prime arbiters of speculator, investor, and shareholder action. Hence, greed tends to feed greed and fear tends to feed fear and under this influence trends once started tend to continue in the direction they were initially headed in.

All this can change however, that is the primacy of raw emotions dictating action, if there were a serious shift in speculator, investor, and shareholder perception and way of being so that truer rationality, that is unbiased intelligence, began to dictate action in favor of raw emotion. If this were to happen, the predictable cycles and fractals of the last few centuries would fall apart and stock market performance would follow another and deeper fractal pattern – that of movement from a 'physical' or 'seed' to a 'vital' or 'stalk' to a 'mental' or 'flower' orientation.

Hence, so long as active consciousness does not shift from a primarily 'vital' to a primarily 'mental' way of being, we can be sure that Elliott and Mandelbrot type fractals will repeat themselves and the stock market will crash again. If, however, there is a shift in active consciousness from the primarily 'vital' to the primarily 'mental', then all bets are off, and a stock market crash is unlikely. The bigger question is whether current global crises will act to push consciousness toward the 'mental', or whether further crises will be required for this desirable outcome to occur.

The Misapplication of Financial Tools

Analyses suggest that markets are in the vital phase. The vital phase is characterized by the principle guideline "reality as determined by assertiveness and the myriad play of energies". The emphasis is on the assertion of energy.

178

Organizations in the vital phase are absorbed in dynamic activity. In this dynamism there is interaction of energies. Some energies overpower others. Some express themselves in harmony with others. All seek to grow in whatever way they can. It is hence, assertiveness and energy that dominates. This hence, is Darwin's interpretation of evolution, and the basis of much of today's interpretation of competitiveness.

The energy of each seeks to assert itself, often at any cost. All seek to gather more energy by any means and to establish its rule over other forms. There is experimentation in this phase, but it is not driven by order and thought. It is driven by the primal impulse to assert oneself and grow at any cost. Greed is the law. Fear ensures that greed can continue to live, if not today, then tomorrow. Hence there is a devouring to devour and a conquering to conquer, and it is the strongest and longest-lasting energy that appears to triumph in the end. This is much like the green stalk gone wild – creating a reality that is almost impossible to maneuver through.

There is no rationality in this phase. This is the phase of irrational gains and losses. This is the phase of irrational bubbles followed by irrational bursts. This is the phase of stock market rise and fall. This is the phase in which recessions are caused overnight, where governments lose control of their economies, where brainwashed people are sent to their death to secure resources that never belonged to them in the first place, where innocent people suffer starvation because of irrational speculation, where accelerated destruction of everything we value and accelerated destruction of the body of the earth are the norm.

As already mentioned, the transition to the vital phase was solidified in the early 1970's with the shift from the gold to the oil standard. Creation of market funds, index funds, and mortgage-backed bonds, which further freed up the flow of money, and the easy availability of credit formed bricks

179

and arches around this foundation stone. But at a deeper level, at the level of the root of the repeating pattern the driver of all this loosening and shifting was greed itself, and the expectation that the quick-buck could be made by trading on the stock market. It was the force of greed-driven speculation that unleashed all the consequent changes. And this force has come to be, in large measure, because of the existing mental-level theories and tools applied in markets that were really vital in nature. This has led from one wrong choice to the next.

At the vital-level what we really need is a set of tools that show clearly how greed is the prime driver of trading. No trader cares for the value proposition behind what is being traded. Reality is that all they care about is appropriating or at the very least skimming margin on a deal. Theories and tools must deal with this reality: greed-fear interaction, herd mentality, fractal effects, monopolization effects, and stochastic variance. This is what needs to be in the portfolio of decision-makers. This is in stark contrast to what is actually driving decision-making: variations of efficient market hypotheses, portfolio theory, index modeling, algorithmic trading. These latter tools belong to the mental-phase of market functioning, and we are simply not there yet.

Reversing the Black-Hole Phenomenon: Beyond Financial Crises

As suggested in this book, it is the interaction of three basic ways of being that determines the practical outcome of many affairs in life. The global financial playing-field is no exception. These three ways of being are the seed or physical, the stalk or vital, the flower or mental. In essence the physical embodies the impulse to maintain the status-quo, the vital to move or compete energetically to aggrandize itself, the mental to organize around purpose and ideas. For progress to happen it is the mental state or way that must lead relative to the others. Where the mental does not lead, there dysfunction increases, and sooner or later crises arises. Crisis is a system response to alter the disequilibrium between physical, vital, and mental, so that it is the mental or flower that may be made to take the lead.

When we think of the global financial crisis, it is in effect the disequilibrium that had to arise to set right the relationship between the physical, the vital, and the mental. For even though the tools and theories used in global trading, such as Efficient Market Hypothesis (EMH), Portfolio Theory, and Index Modeling, are modeled around idea and the notion that the market is a self-regulating organism instantaneously reflecting dynamics of players in its space, and automatically adjusting to maintain such an ideal reality - therefore the mental ideal, in reality it is not the mental, but the vital that leads. That is, it is not holism of information, but self-seeking gain that is the driver of things. In other words, the mental-type tools are in fact irrelevant, and another set of tools needs to be used to manage finance and investment at this stage.

But being that it is the vital that leads, the use of such mental-type tools creates incredible distortions that in effect become beneficial to the vital way of being. That is, there is a perverse incentive to continue with the use of such tools and frameworks, and to espouse the mental-level self-regulating ideal, even though we are not at the level where these tools are relevant. The very notion of value at the vital level is not value as described at the mental level. To briefly illustrate, vital-value has an effect of "monopolizing" funds and flows of financial resources – this is so because the real value represented by an asset, its mental-value, is drowned out by a standardizing flow of vital-value represented by such common denominations as 'cash'.

This is parallel to taking a 3-D object and portraying it in 2-D. The true value of all assets suffers this fate, and as a result of this easy 'equality' there is one large, monopolized flow of investment that comes to exist. Such flow ultimately causes serious destruction, and the work of years and centuries is potentially reversed in a few hours. It is because of such a standardized flow that prices of commodities correlate with the DJSI and corporate needs in Brazil correlate with those in Germany. That is, vastly inefficient pricing that destroys true value has come into effect.

The current global financial situation is described by the vital leading, while pretending to be the mental, and relying on the physical impulse of denial by imagining that all is truly the perfect self-regulating market. To alter the situation, to reverse the black-hole phenomenon so that sun-like creative light really does emerge, the EMH type mental-level modeling has to become a reality. This can only become so if the right tools to manage us out of the current vital way comes into being, for a start. Such tools should focus on the reality of the greed-fear cycle and the resultant repeating patterns that create exorbitant costs to humanity. Such tools should also bring into focus the obscuration of value, or the 'reflexivity' causing feature, as George Soros calls it, of herd mentality. Such tools should also focus on the effects of monopolization of flow and fund, and on the vital-reality of stochastic variance as opposed to the more mental-reality of Gaussian distribution. Such tools should also focus on the identification and encouragement of decoupling of asset or market. If such a set of tools were in the portfolio of all fund managers, Central Banks, investment banks, then the destruction of long-term value would become more apparent, and we would gradually climb out of the black hole that currently has us so surely in its grasp.

Here is the paradox. Just before the global financial crisis of 2008 by most reports this would never have been apparent. The news was good and the picture perceived was of global health and well-being. In fact some even suggested that finance had entered a creative new era of "irrational exuberance" and recessions and break-downs were a thing of the past. So when things were about to get really bad, we continued to call them really good.

Today, there is a much higher degree of caution, and as perusal of any newspaper will reveal, we are much more aware of the symptoms that lie before us. This is good news. And yet we treat it as though it is bad.

So why is it good news.

First, our current debt-based financial models are totally unsustainable. Granting of loans is tied to a high cost of accessing debt in terms of on-going interest payments that implies that there always has to be a high rate of economic growth. There is no other way to service the debt, whether at the individual, corporate, or market levels. To sustain such a money supply created through creation of interest-bearing loans, much more than the value of the money has continually therefore to be produced. This means that irrational competition for the same set of limited resources is now in effect, which quite simply is in itself an unsustainable initial condition. The slow down is therefore good.

Second, we are in a reality of global overshoot. That is, the resources that the earth is able to supply, is far less than the demand on these resources. By some estimates our demand on the earth's resources is already 2-3 times what the earth can sustainably supply. A continued focus on higher and higher economic growth rates, as though that were the meaning and truth of existence, is therefore completely irrational. The fact that markets and corporations are pulling back on growth, albeit not necessarily voluntarily, is therefore good.

Third, through the last couple of decades there has been extensive and comprehensive coupling of intra- and inter-asset classes. In other words, the deeper meaning of investment has taken a back seat to a much more crass motive for investment where money is thrown at something just for irrational return on investment. For example, the behavior of investing in commodities should be independent of behavior of investing in corporate stocks. The behavior of investing in an advanced economy should be independent of the behavior of investing in an emerging economy. And behavior should be driven by the needs of the target asset class and its own natural cycles of production and containment. Yet all this deeper meaning has been tossed aside and irrational investments that overlook natural meaning and purpose is now the norm. At a deeper level this means that progress inherent in civilization, the result of centuries, is now being rapidly reversed. Reversal of such coupling, inevitable during a slow-down, is therefore good news.

Fourth, there is worry about the Japanization of the West. This should not be a worry but a sigh of relief. A pause in irrational behavior is a good thing. The slowdown of irrational granting of debt, and of irrational growth rates is what the world needs in much larger measure. The only worry is in this, that two decades later, Japan has still not looked deeply enough into itself to leverage its unique springs of culture and creativity. Perhaps a 'Japanization of the West' will help usher in a collective in-look rather than the current norm of irrational outlook.

Of course, the question is what is it that we are going to do with the opportunity before us. If we are driven by current economic and financial thought, we will do all in our power to get back to irrational growth. But all this will do is create a more wide-spread foundation of toxic assets, exasperate the reality of and the incredibly high cost of global overshoot, accelerate the loss of meaning of investment and therefore of civilization, lose the opportunity to grasp the deeper meaning of culture, creativity, and wealth, and set us up for more and more unmanageable recessions.

We need a new definition of wealth and a new set of success measures. We need an overhauling of the global financial and economic system. This really, is what recession after recession is trying to tell us. Let us hope we do not have to wait until the next recession to begin to make the change that is needed now.

Why Consolidation of Bourses is Myopic

Consolidation of bourses such as between Deutsche Borse and NYSE Euronext in 2011 (Demos 2011) is going to lead to more bubbles and more destruction of real value. Simply speaking, this is because patterns will tend to repeat themselves on different scale – that is they will display fractal behavior.

The consolidation of bourses means that there is even further concentration of money power. Vicissitudes in this variable will have a magnified effect on the companies, industries, regions of the world that stocks represent. When money flows into a larger bourse, and is focused on a particular sector, the real effect is that it will more easily create a bubble in that sector. When money flows away from a larger bourse, then correspondingly the created bubble will burst. Traders close to the initiating flows will tend to make money regardless of direction of flow. So such a scenario will usually be welcome by them. In contrast the region, sector, and industry affected by these smaller patterns will see the tide of

185

fortunes ebb and flow, and focused on this, instead of underlying value means that true value will be destroyed in the bargain.

Let us look at this more closely.

Such concentration and effective disbursement of money power is in effect further removed from the reality of where and how it is actually being used. Money begins in reality not to serve true development, but instead to serve short-sighted investors. Portfolios or mutual funds will contain a larger set of distant companies, and meaningless correlations will be strengthened. Rather than investing in a region or a sector because there is a true need and a real return that will result from that investment, investment in one region or sector will become related to investment in a completely unrelated region or sector, often because they sit in the same portfolio.

Further, stock markets indexes based on price-weighting and market-share weighting will further exaggerate their biases, and act to magnify irrational patterns. A price-weighted index is a stock market index where each constituent makes up a fraction of the index that is proportional to its price. For a stock market index this implies that stocks are included in proportions based on their quoted prices. A stock that has a higher price will therefore have more of a weight in the portfolio. In such a case there is a bias toward rewarding that which is already in demand. It is not necessarily fundamental underlying value that is attracting investment, but herd mentality. Sooner or later, if what is receiving funds is actually destroying underlying value, then a bubble will burst, and even more value will be indiscriminately destroyed. A price-weighted index is more appropriate when we are at the mental or flower-level in the global economic journey, where price more truly does embed all available information. But we are simply not there yet.

A market-weighted index is one whose components are weighted according to the total market value of their outstanding shares - that is, the total number of outstanding shares multiplied by the price of that share. This kind of index will really capture the herd mentality, and if investment decisions are driven off the movement of this index, it will even more forcefully than the price-weighted index, reinforce the direction in which the market is headed. Irrationality will be followed by even more irrationality and bubbles will be created much faster. Market-based indexing will also cause bubbles to burst much faster and value to be even more indiscriminately destroyed than in the case of price-weighted indexing. This device is also based on Efficient Market Hypothesis and is best suited in the mental phase. Applied at the vital-phase, where we currently exist, it is going to create a lot more damage than good.

While a free-market allows consolidations of this kind without adequate consideration of the true cost to society, it is time to wake up, and for governments, policy-makers, and financial regulators to become clear on the long-term costs of short-term irrationalities.

Changing The Way Trades Are Made

Many relatively recent developments, such as Global Reporting Initiative (GRI), Principles of Responsible Investing (PRI), Socially Responsible Investing (SRI), and the Dow Jones Sustainability Index (DJSI) indicate a new set of expectations on corporations. Voices of holism that demanded that business action be integrated more fully with the field of life began as marginal and soft. Many of these voices have arisen from the religiously minded, and those who are more socially aware, that have been advocating another way to invest money. At its core these proponents

187

have seen life as more multi-faceted than the typical breed of business juggernauts. For the former there tends to be a larger wholeness in which aspects of life meet in practicalities. For the business world the opposite has been true – generally speaking. Therefore, all has been viewed as a business asset, and things like spirit and possibility are only meaningful if there is a financial return associated with that. This business-juggernaut perception of life is largely vital-physical. That is, the prime orientation is one of aggressively imposing one's point of view and one's own interest on all of life. Life is only a field for appropriating or commandeering what is needed for the small self in its pursuit of selfish, myopic gain.

Realistically speaking, the issue is, how much will this orientation change in the short-term, and this is the crucial question, since by many estimates the life of humanity can hardly sustain such continued short-sightedness. Climate Change, for instance has to be acted on in a finite time-bound window, before a tipping point that yields disastrous returns is unleashed. The global financial environment has urgently to be reconstructed if humanity is to preserve any wonders of creation and proceed along a path of more enduring sustainability. There is no choice in these matters – failure to address these situations will cause the already forming forces of destruction to grow exponentially so that developed countries will topple, the bases of intermediate and larger organizational activity will get seriously compromised, and people will lose whatever freedom they have become used to, not to mention the much longer-term damage of the base of wealth from the earth being pillaged and unable to return to a pristine state for at least a couple of millennium if not for longer. Of course, in one way of looking at it, perhaps humanity needs challenges and measures of this magnitude in order that the base consciousness at the root of the tremendously destructive Business journey we see playing itself out now, may shift from its decidedly vital to a more mental or flower state of being.

The flower-state here means that a truer force of inquiry, of curiosity, of questioning base assumptions has come alive, and as a result holism, sustainability, a larger bases for life, is beginning to become the guiding principle for even business standards of operation. SRI, PRI, GRI, DJSI are meaningful attempts to make business operation more holistic. But the reality of these is that it is always difficult to make companies and especially investors, in the heat of the moment, abide by these deeper standards. In such moments there is a bastardization of value and only a very surface rendering of events, people, and possibility becomes means for decision-making. That primal instinct that belongs to the vital physical consciousness is unfortunately so alive in the consciousness of humanity that all higher possibilities are often tossed aside, and whether the field be business, religion, or science, what matters most at the end of the day is whether the thwarted instrument is able to fulfill on its small, myopic, meaningless desires.

It is in light of this reality, of this real operating principle, that what is suggested now, has to be put into action. This is important, since even abstracted out one level, to the level of regulation and policy, the same problem exists. In spite of best intention, of well-thought out principles, when push comes to shove, either the actors find loop-holes, or the regulator is unable really to regulate. If human consciousness is such that the investor and businessman, and even the executor of regulation and policy cannot act with foresight as though the whole of life were the field of operation, then the situation has to be forced. The setting of stock price has to be determined as though a whole lot more about the market were known. We have to approach the reality of an Efficient Market, even if it is not the Efficient Market that is real. In other words it is not just simple demand and supply that will determine price of stocks, but a whole lot more that is being pointed to by the movements such as SRI, GRI, PRI, and DJSI (Malik 2011).

We have to embed in the act of buying and selling a broader intelligence that matters. Filters, heuristics, circuit-breakers that emulate the essence and matter of GRI, PRI, SRI, DJSI have to be bought into the very act of trading. It is not enough anymore that they remain as conduits that funnel money into stock markets from the outside. This is especially so in these times when so much is at stake and when the act of trading has become such a way of life. If trading cannot normally consider the fullness of life, then more of the fullness of life has to be forced into the act of trading.

There are a lot of current constraints of the type just discussed that this will overcome – in the short-term. Further, the bases of organization will have more meaning, since what is intended from the top, down, will actually matter. If a government wants to govern, so that managing GHG emissions, or water quality, or working conditions in factories is critically important for the next 3 months, for instance, it does not have to do so by tax cuts, and fiscal spending, or other unpredictable incentives, but embed that need into where it matters most – in the actual and instantaneous setting of stock price.

If an oil rig leaks, then, it is pretty simple. The price of all oil stocks will be suppressed, reduced, until and unless there are measures that are taken and proved that illustrate beyond a doubt that the environment is being cleaned up, that affected ecosystem services are being restored, that social reconstruction is taking place, and that new technology that avoids such mishaps in the future is immediately being invested in. These filters are programmed into the way stocks are sold, and in fact, there is a moratorium on the sale of such stocks unless certain base conditions are immediately fulfilled. As another example, if there is a lot of unsubstantiated financial innovation taking place, so that derivatives and a whole host of other tranche-like products are unleashed by the financial sector, similarly a moratorium is placed on investment in companies engaged in such activities, unless it can be proved that these products are not potentially toxic and undermining of the true value that must be the bases of money-creation. Further the stock price is automatically depressed and gets un-depressed in stages, based on sustainability-driven action that the company undertakes. These sustainability driven actions are definitely in part determined by GRI, PRI, SRI, DJSI. But there is more that needs to be considered.

Redesigning the Stock Market

When I was a management student at Kellogg Graduate School of Management in the 1990s, I would often glaze over during lectures on Finance. The reason was that many times what was being said did not make sense to me. It seemed disconnected from the realities of life and totally non-intuitive.

About a decade later I had a progressive 'awakening' following which I saw the incredible story of possibility and sustainability etched into all of life. This story took the form of a pattern summarized in the journey of becoming a flower. I have delved into this ubiquitous journey in great detail in Connecting Inner Power with Global Change (Malik 2009) and as the global financial crises continued to unfold, decided that I would like to analyze markets and financial theory from this perspective.

And so I wrote Redesigning the Stock Market (Malik 2011). In this book one of the key themes is the inadequacy of current-day financial theory in managing markets. In fact I propose a more comprehensive theory, with aspects already introduced in preceding materials of this book, that will forever remove the disagreement between behavioral finance and mainstream portfolio and efficient market hypotheses theories through leveraging the wisdom in the ever-present story.

Here is what someone from the mainstream financial academic sector had to say about this book (Gupta 2012).

"Redesigning the Stock Market: A Fractal Approach has come at a time when the whole world is thrown into a financial and political turmoil—at a time when people all over the world are doing some soul searching and are looking for their identities and are strongly protesting against the very systems that they not very long ago stood and died for. The timing of the book could not have been more opportune. The structure of the institutions of business and stock markets require a serious relook as to what objectives they were set forth to achieve but in the process what have they become. This book looks into this in a very philosophical and thought-provoking manner.

The book reflects Malik's depth of thinking, profound knowledge about business processes and his ability to take a contrarian view. The philosophy with which it is written is simple. We are what we repeatedly do. That is we are the end result of a pattern. The author has very eruditely extended this phenomenon to explain the present-day functioning of the financial markets and business. He very logically explains that these institutions have become dysfunctional because of the existence of micro patterns. And if the financial markets and business have to become highly functional then we would have to first look at the root cause of the problem, which is nothing else but patterns that have shaped them. Therefore, these patterns need to be changed and then everything would fall in place. This is the basis of analysis that has been used throughout the book."

"Malik has attacked the very basis of creation of money. He has put forth strong arguments to show that the stock markets of today are irrationally funneling money into those areas that are many times highly destructive to the very fabric of life. Therefore, in place of such markets, he suggests a new breed of stock markets that would encourage needed development—social, environmental, artistic, knowledge based and service focused. He favors those stock markets that increase multidimensional as opposed to single-dimensional type of wealth. This he envisages through a stock market which has environmental and social investment filters embedded at its core of functioning. The whole basis of trading at the stock markets would have to change."

"Without going into many technical details, the book succinctly provides a meaningful insight into the major theories of finance and portfolio theory that are normally used in explaining the present-day functioning of the financial markets. Malik questions their applicability and argues that a continued misapplication of these approaches has played a key role in the creation of the global financial crises that we witness today."

"It is important to understand the history and creation of the stock markets if one is to understand why financial crises keep on reoccurring. This book amply looks into that. The crux of the matter is that the very basis of the stock markets has to change; the author looks into it by analyzing the seed, placing it securely at the vital level, and suggests that unless the seed is changed, it is futile to expect that the nature of financial crises is going to change. This is the focal point of the book about creating a new seed with which to change stock market-related activities for the benefit of generations to come."

"This is an intellectually stimulating book. The author has researched the topic very well. I have thoroughly enjoyed reading it and it has been an enriching experience. The book is intelligently written in a straightforward, easy- to-read style. It forces one to think deeply and look at the seriousness of the multitude of issues raised. One is amazed by the simplicity and the freshness of answers put forward to address these, though one would find some of them very amusing and impractical in today's socio-economic scenario. But then, that is the whole purpose of the book. It brings in a different perspective; it is a huge repository of innovative ideas, shows very eruditely what ails the present business and the society at large and provides revolutionary suggestions to get rid of the same.

It is also worth mentioning that no other book has looked into the need for redesigning of stock markets. So, such a book is rare and one should not miss an opportunity to read it when it makes an appearance as it has now. It provides a fresh line of thinking towards how stock markets can be reshaped to minimize future financial crises and ensure business and societal sustainability. The book is highly recommended for those who would like to take part in the process of change as envisioned by Pravir Malik and particularly to those who are interested in the complex worlds of business, finance and stock markets"

Creativity & The Global Financial Crises

The financial crises can be viewed as a result of the insistence by a critical mass of corporate and government decision-makers and individual and group consumers to remain obstinately centered in a way of being driven primarily by fear, greed, and short-sightedness. As a result of this the field of business possibility has been contracted to one of acquisition of short-term monetary wealth often at any cost. This has led to a hi-level of unsubstantiated risk-taking with its resultant creation of pie-in-the-sky asset bubbles increasingly disassociated with any semblance of real development. The inevitability of the bubble bursts has led to the global financial crises.

In such a milieu the notion of true enterprise - of creating for each what he or she lacks simply does not exist. For such creation implies the understanding of deeper drivers behind individual, corporate, and even country development and some insight into respective uniqueness. In the lead up to today's world, creation of financial wealth has been the prime driver behind corporate action. This driver is a sorry caricature on all that can potentially fill its place were uniqueness to become the lens through which the notion of driver was reinterpreted. For then the worlds and possibilities inherent in drivers behind uniqueness, such as courage and adventure, or knowledge and wisdom, or mutuality and harmony, or service and perfection, would come more forcefully into the forefront. This would unleash a far more sustainable creative power.

To be creative in the business world means to create wealth, even financial wealth, through developing such uniqueness. This development of uniqueness - be it at the individual, corporate, societal, or country levels is what is needed today. Business needs to be deconstructed and then reconstructed around the afore-mentioned drivers as seeds, such that the deeper need that allows uniqueness to flourish becomes the center of the reconstruction.

The deconstruction is already in progress as more and more corporations and markets around the world fail. Such failure can be viewed as an inevitable passage spawned by a conscious and purposeful world-system seeking its own fulfillment. The consequent reconstruction can also be viewed

195

as an inevitable passage spawned by a conscious and purposeful world-system seeking its own fulfillment, and will require repeated acts of creativity to succeed. For instead of the reconstruction proceeding along the fruitless lines of yesterday's development it has to proceed along the fruitful lines of bringing into relief the raison d'etre that each unique entity is secretly seeking to express.

This act of creativity necessarily begins with each individual person. For the power in each one's life has to be taken back by rejecting the unconscious or even conscious support for the ways by which the flawed corporations and markets of yesterday were built and continue to exercise their influence, and instead allowing who one is at one's core to come forward and become the mantra for development.

Toss out the insistence on blind money-making and ask instead, to what extent can business and markets truly provide avenues for the courage and urge for adventure in people to come and importantly to remain alive? To what extent can business and markets truly provide for the urge in people to uncover purer knowledge and become recipients of lasting wisdom? To what extent can business and markets truly provide for the need of certain individuals to exercise and create living and growing harmonies that progressively interrelate and connect together disparate elements of life? To what extent can the very spirit of service and uncompromised perfection be made to manifest such that all becomes a fire of sacredness?

The process of seeing these deeper needs, the process of making it okay to be able to develop along such unique lines, and the process to fulfill development started along these lines requires further acts of creativity to even succeed. For the shift from viewing the world as a machine set in motion to increase cumulative GNP or as a field of ROI trees to be pruned in exact precision with requirements of scheduled cash inflows and outflows, has to give way to a view of the world in which business is not only an organically developing way driven by the clearer expression of multiple drivers, but is just one way amongst others, by which the world seeks its own fulfillment and arrives finally at the establishment of a vast and intricate creativity.

It is only in the birth of a creativity of this nature, through which uniqueness and possibility can replace the established and oft-tread way, that any future financial crises can be avoided.

Summary

Albert Einstein has said that any intelligent fool can make things bigger. And what this chapter shows is the root drivers behind things becoming bigger, and its consequent destruction of value. When we think of recession we think it is a bad thing, because it means we are not growing bigger. But that is the extent to which we have been brainwashed, and the question is how can this deep-rooted brainwashing be reversed.

In this chapter we propose such a reversal by understanding the DNA of markets. What is a vital market, or a physical-vital market or a mental market, for instance; and what are the tools to successfully manage the kind of market we are actually in. If we could match the right set of tools to the right circumstances, we could effectively reverse the global, value-sucking black-hole that we have created for ourselves.

Financial rebirth implies that a new light is shed on the very reality we continue to face today, such as recessions, market crashes, continued consolidations that lead to bigger problems. This light is a function of the deeper understanding of markets, tools, and new drivers of creativity that we have introduced in this chapter, and if applied should result in a gradual disappearance of market dysfunction.

Part 6 – Global Political Development

Many very pertinent issues relevant to true and sustainable global development surfaced in the recent 2012 US Presidential Debates. To place these in context we first consider a chapter from earlier US political development in the life of the 33rd President of USA, Harry Truman. We also consider a general philosophical view offered form the summit of a hill or mountain that provides insight into political party development. These considerations lead us into some of the issues and lessons for global leaders that surfaced in the recent 2012 US Presidential Elections.

The offices of the small are dead. Long Live the Office of the Future!

Recently I watched Truman, the movie. In contrast to the prevalent dynamics of our times it was refreshing to see the story of a person who becomes the U.S. President without trying to or without the desire to do so.

And yet, there were incredibly significant decisions that Truman made - the containment of Communism by supporting South Korea against North Korea, the use of atomic weapons to defeat Japan, the rebuilding of Europe using US funds after World War II, the recognition of Israel, the ending of racial discrimination in the armed forces, the instinct to veto an act that monitored the activities and powers of labor unions in a time when Business was strongly incarnating the unrefined vital dynamic – amongst others.

Many of these are historic decisions that have altered the course of the world, and to even debate if these were the right

200

decisions, one has at the very least to not be bound by the dynamics of the small self. In terms of the ubiquitous flower journey this means beginning to move away from the P-V (physical-vital or seed-stalk) orientation toward the M-I (mental-intuitional or flower) orientation. Further this movement toward the flower orientation is seen as necessary and inevitable for any progressive or sustainable organization, regardless of scale.

The P-V orientation is dictated by a sense of small bounded-ness (P or seed) and animated by the need of constantly fulfilling desires to satisfy that smallness (V or stalk). In today's world we see this dynamic alive everywhere.

Truman, because he was arguably less motivated by the P-V orientation, could more easily open to the flower or M-I orientation. To consistently choose the flower orientation over the seed (or P-V) orientation becomes a rite of passage, an initiation, in which one progressively opens to dynamics of a different order. This means Truman conceivably became an instrument for something more progressive than perhaps he or others around him could imagine.

Perhaps his insistence that it was the Office of the President and not Truman who was more important, and his deliberate putting of himself into that state in his interactions with those around him, hints at this orientation that drove him, and to the initiation that had seized him.

In this day and age the issues we are faced with are no less in magnitude than those the world had faced between 1940 and 1950. What manifested then as the struggle between freedom and small bounded-ness, the struggle between race equality and race superiority, the struggle between peace and war, the struggle toward a more holistic orientation of business as opposed to the continuance of business-as-usual, the struggle for the use of money for selfless as opposed to selfish aims, has vastly amplified itself today. It is therefore the requirement of today to invite the flower initiation on a much larger scale. The P-V dynamics so alive in the institution of Business and Finance, and in the running of countries around the world, has to be replaced by the dynamics of M-I, so that it is the flower possibility that leads the bounded, selfish P-V orientation.

But whereas in the 1950s it was the few who led the many, the big difference today, is that the many now have the chance to lead. The Arab Spring, the Occupy Movement, the EU Sovereign Debt Crises manifest in the Greek Rebellion, the Indian Anti-Corruption movement, the uprise in South America, amongst others, hang in balance waiting the incarnation of this greater dynamic.

It is the Office of the Future that must become alive, and that every individual and collectivity must help ground through initiation into M-I. Verily, the Office of the President must replicate and replace itself in fractal fashion by the similar yet different Office of the Future, so that all presidents, all corporations, all organizations, all institutions, all countries will be accountable solely to it.

The offices of the small are dead. Long Live the Office of the Future!

The Way of the Summit: Some Insights for Election and Re-Election

If you were to look down from the summit of a peak, you would perhaps see different paths etched into the ascending terrain. These paths of course all meet at the summit, and in fact merge at that plateau to become one. In their ascent though these paths may have started at different places, travelled through different conditions, and may or may not intersect, depending on what is encountered on their journeys.

The structure and dynamics of these paths sheds insight into Party Politics and Governance of a country, and understanding of these will benefit the Presidential Candidate or Party that can so learn from them.

Imagine the summit as being the goal, the haloed destination of an intense pilgrimage a country may be undertaking to arrive finally at a foundation from which new journeys and possibilities can be envisioned. The starting point and articulated raison d'etre of these paths may be Democratic or Republican, Capitalist or Socialist, or any other set of dichotomies or uniquenesses depending on the country one belongs to.

The field of Flower Chronicles sheds insight into the dynamics of these ascending paths:

• A path that remains unique to itself represents a possibility needing to be worked out on its own. Clearly as far as Governance of a country is concerned, it will be rare for proponents of such a unique path to remain in power indefinitely. This is simply because the foundation at the summit demands that different possibilities be integrated.

• A path that intersects with another may have stagnated before such an intersection takes place. If so, the shock of the intersection can cause both paths to reexamine their stagnation, address it, and move on wiser, through the next phase in their respective journeys.

• A path that intersects with another, and merges with that, so that neither is the same, but now is the synthesis of both paths, represents a coming together and a prelude to the pattern of the plateau at the summit. This is rare, but will likely signify a victory, and the increasing of that party's electorate.

• The Spiral Path that circles slowly upward is the path of Nature. This is the default path that is activated again and again should the independent paths streaming up the peak never want to objectively consider the others it may encounter. Hence, it must exist so that each independent possibility can be given a turn in working itself out. Imagine the time taken for the Spiral Path to cross over the independent path as being one Presidential Term, or perhaps two, if there is more to be gained from that path at that time, in the scheme of things.

Any candidate would therefore, be wise to ask:

• Is the path I am on wide enough to warrant another term? If not, the Spiral Path will ensure that power cedes to the other possibility.

• Is the path I am on ready to learn from the path I am now head-to-head with, and create a synthesis that is greater than either of the independent paths? If so, then power will likely remain here.

• Is the path I am on going to alter because it has truly learned from the intersection with another path? If so, then power will likely remain here.

Since all paths must merge at the top, that is, must create a whole that loses nothing of the best of each possibility, the repeating and ever-present question is, will the pilgrimage the country is on be broad enough to encompass many distinct possibilities?

If not, then Nature may reveal the active Volcano under the summit, and through the consequent outpouring of fresh lava, create materials and the terrain for the re-embarking on new journeys.

In listening to both presidential candidates during the US 2012 Presidential Debates, it seemed that they were riddled with contradictions.

President Obama's general grounded-ness was a far cry from the 2008 Presidential Debates. It seemed that his trademark self-composure, self-confidence, and idealistic view of the world had all but evaporated. There were moments where that other self came forward, but in general, it was another Obama that stood in front of us on both evenings in October.

It was almost as though there were a great struggle in the being of the President. That voice of idealism and authenticity was still there, but it was subdued and overtaken by another voice. What was this other voice? Was this the voice of the reality of Office? The voice perhaps, of the reality of all the politicking and of the endless compromise that an Idealist needs to make to govern?

It seemed that President Obama is living another life, a life not quite in tune with the authenticity of who he is, and this lack of alignment was manifesting in the aloofness and lack of confidence we saw in general on the evenings in October. From a Flower Chronicles point of view it may be that his voice and stance was being driven by a contrary-journey led by the seed-stalk or physical-vital rather than the flower or mental-intuitional possibility.

On the other hand Presidential Candidate and Governor Mitt Romney's voice seemed to carry more confidence, at least on the surface. But his too was riddled with contradiction. It did not carry the stamp of authenticity. It seemed more a Party Voice, trained to give the illusion of an effective Commander-in-Chief, and representative of the Republican Dream.

For instance, he confidently spoke of how China has not been playing by the rules of the world, and that were he to become president, he would on Day One label them as a currency manipulator. He also spoke of how Obamacare has essentially disadvantaged small and medium sized businesses by making the cost to hire employees too high. The problem is that his approach on China is going to do the very same thing – that is, severely disadvantage business. Assume he labels China as currency manipulators, and as a result they are forced to let the Yuan float freely. All that will do is substantially escalate the cost of doing business for every single American enterprise. This is because China has become the world's manufacturing base and is integrated into every supply chain of just about every company in the world. China is the top trading partner of the USA. YTD 18% of total US imports come from China – the highest proportion of any of its import partners. Further, after Canada and Mexico, China is the top export partner of US companies (US Census Bureau 2012).

So the reality is that US business will be hit harder if Romney comes to office, because it will likely take more than 4 years to truly change ground conditions so that US manufacturers are integrated into every supply chain of even US companies.

Romney's real voice, his authentic self came forward in his closing remarks on the evening of October 16, 2012. Particularly what felt very authentic, were his statements: "My -- my passion probably flows from the fact that I believe in God. And I believe we're all children of the same God. I believe we have a responsibility to care for one another. I -- I served as a missionary for my church. I served as a pastor in my congregation for about 10 years. I've sat across the table from people who were out of work and worked with them to try and find new work or to help them through tough times." (CBS News 2012).

So, Romney too, is really living another life. The general lack of authenticity, though veiled by apparent confidence, is probably due to this. Were he to become the President, and were he to reappear for the debates 4 years hence, there are three possible stances he would take.

If he were riddled with contradiction, as we saw Obama so riddled, we may conclude that perhaps here is an Idealist, and the pressure of Office has caused infighting between separate voices in his self, as in the case of President Obama. If he were confident, we may be left to conclude one of two things: First, here is someone who is perhaps a seasoned and habitual liar and has lost his soul in some deal made along the way. Second, and certainly the more difficult of the two, here is someone who really walks his truth and has made a difference in the affairs of the country and the world.

Clearly, what we want is a President who exhibits the last of these possibilities. We know though, that this is the most difficult and will require the President to truly become a creative force, and new root-pattern of a brave and bold repeating-journey set to sweep the world stage.

Whether an Obama or a Romney, let us hope that this - a creative force putting into effect brave and needed root-patterns - is what we always get, not just in USA, but in all the countries of the world.

Foreign Policy for a Peaceful World

Presidential Candidate and Governor Mitt Romney concluded his remarks (Politico 2012) in the Foreign Policy section of the US 2012 Presidential Election debate with the thought that USA is the hope of the earth. What we need though is a global environment in which it is not just USA that is the hope of the earth, but in fact each country is clearly a hope for the earth. This will require a mix of stabilization, conflict reframing and resolution, and a different vision of the value of global diversity.

The following are some thoughts to be considered in achieving this:

1. While there is value in the effort being made now to contain Iran's nuclear ambitions, this has to be put in perspective. When according to Romney Pakistan already has 100 nuclear warheads and is critically close to becoming a failed state, it seems that the real effort has to be to stabilize the situation in Pakistan.

2. The situation with China is more complex than has portrayed by either presidential candidate. China is often aggressive in its interaction with the world on both a business and a military front. Romney already pointed out some instances of business aggressiveness such as piracy, counterfeiting, and currency manipulation. But further,

• China's human rights records and treatment of workers is in question

• It has converted huge tracts of productive land into desert, polluted running and still bodies of water, and continues to massively compromise biodiversity

• It has reinforced the notion that people exist for State, not only in China, but in Africa too thereby relegating humans to the stature of assets

On the military front:

• Pakistan has received help in advancing its nuclear weapon technology from China

• China occupied Tibet for its strategic position, and has reportedly placed missiles aimed at many key cities around the world. It is further reported that there is a massive build up of infrastructure to convert it into a future war zone (Kanwal 2012).

• China has also claimed Taiwan as its own, and continues to make border incursions into Kashmir and Arunachal Pradesh.

To a large extent the conversion of China into the world's manufacturing center has further enabled this aggressiveness. China's becoming the world's manufacturing center has been driven by vital-level desire, in no small measure led by the consumers of USA itself. This is a short-sighted deal in which USA progressively loses control of its future, and funds China to potentially begin a systematic exploitation of the areas around it to begin with, and other areas of the world in time. Already its reach is firmly established in Africa. The solution is not just to reverse this, though that is part of the solution. In addition, the Business journey in general has to be elevated to the mental or flower-level so that short-term solutions simply become a thing of the past. When Obama refers to Nation Building, and especially the need to Build USA, this is what must be done – the basic business-as-usual mentality has to be converted to a business-as-sacred mentality. In itself this will require investment in many supporting institutions, and into the notion of truly democratizing markets.

4. Stabilization in the Indo-Pak-China region will require that USA choose its strategic partners more carefully in the future. The USA needs to build an exceptional alliance with India, already the largest democracy on the planet and an absolutely needed counter-weight in the region. This alliance should span many different areas – business relationships, educational relationships at many different levels, military partnership, and most importantly, increased cultural and spiritual exchange. Two countries at opposite poles of the world, with originally completely diverse view of the world, cannot but learn from each other and greatly benefit each other in the bargain. This of course has already

been going on at some level for decades. But to make this more clear and overt would be a good thing: perhaps more sister-cities, many more exchanges, not driven by the need for personal gain, but by the need for building a genuine cultural relationship, and culminating in a freer program for double citizenship between the two countries. The need for such an approach is further borne out by the current EU Crises. Mere economic union has manifested in the European Sovereign Debt Crises and the possible destabilization of the whole region, and is simply an inadequate foundation on which to build a future.

5. Conflict the world-over has to be recognized as the intersection of stagnated flower-journeys. The conflict exists to get each independent nation-journey to move to the next stage in its journey. Seen from this point of view there is a freeing reason, engineered as it were by a higher power, by which nations involved can truly move to the next stage in their own development. In the next section of this chapter I look at this in more detail as it has manifested in the Indo-Pak-China region. Similar analyses will yield how conflict the world over can be thought of and potentially resolved. Peace talks will be accelerated as a result of such analyses and the resulting mind-set of all involved.

6. We have to go beyond the economic growth-military might formula for world peace that Romney proposes. This is ultimately a no-win scenario and as Obama points out takes us back a few decades to the era of the Cold War. What the world needs most is the recognition of the diversity of each country and the reinterpretation of global interaction based on inherent values that each country embodies. True global stability will only be arrived at if there are no doctrines, including the western Business Doctrine that is being artificially thrust upon many parts of the world. It has to be recognized that each country is unique, and has its own

trajectory of development that needs to be traversed. Here the field of Flower Chronicles can play a key part. Each country and / or region has to traverse its own flower-journey. A case in point is the Arab Spring, which really is a movement of the region away from the decades-old physical or seed phase it has been locked in, primarily through the device of rebellion. The question is how can this region be assisted to move to the vital or stalk, and then on to the mental or flower-level where it will begin to more securely leverage that which makes it unique. To support uniqueness much has to change in the world, including the make up of the UN Security Council.

Flower Chroniclers will recognize that the very approaches summarized in the points above - stabilization, conflict resolution and reframing, and a different vision of the value of global diversity - are none other than the physical or seed, vital or stalk, and mental or flower orientations respectively. The implication of this is that if vision of the value of global diversity (the mental orientation) were to become the anchor around which other approaches were organized, this would yield the most progressive foreign policy, more in tune with sustainable development of the world.

Summary

One of the advantages of a Presidential Election is that it brings to the surface much of what can perhaps be considered as both 'good' and 'bad' that is happening in the world. The 2012 US Presidential Election was no exception. In the Presidential Debates the underlying struggle between authenticity and playing out a role in Office was brought strongly to the forefront.

This of course sheds light on the basic struggle that an Idealist will likely have to experience in trying to keep on top of the current-day realities of governance. But to put this struggle that we witnessed in the debates in context, we first considered the life of a presidential legend, in the terms of Harry Truman the 33rd President of the USA. We further considered the broader wisdom inherent in paths that move upwards toward the summit of a peak. Such considerations allow us to weigh current presidential terms and parties in terms of ideals that it is no doubt more difficult to uphold.

Such an analysis allows us not to get too deeply embedded in the compromising practicalities of global leadership, and allows us to remain more focused on the right thing to be done. Some of the particulars bought up in the presidential debates, and particularly foreign policy, have been viewed from this perspective.

In this chapter we begin to cast a wider net by focusing on a key region of the world, whose development by many estimates will have a major impact on the development of the rest of the world.   Picking up from the foreign policy discussion in the last chapter we focus attention on what can also be considered one of the most precarious regions of the world, the broad intersection of India, China, Pakistan, and Afghanistan.   Deep-seated   barriers   to   true   global development are embodied in this region and a consideration of how these may be resolved is critical. We will also look at how India could play a key role in changing the prevalent business rules by taking the high road as it were.

The United States and Stability in the Indo-China-Afghan-Pakistan Region

How many fundamentalisms does it take to get to the root of an issue? That is the big question the President of USA will have to wrestle with if the US were to gear up and successfully address the decades-long instability in the Indo-China-Afghan-Pakistan region.

It   is   somewhat   perplexing   to   list   out   all   the fundamentalisms   that   may   have   led   to   the   present conundrum. But in doing so, and in understanding both the direction   that   the   underlying   journeys   behind   these fundamentalisms may be tending toward, and the assistance that   fundamentalism   confronting   fundamentalism   will provide in prodding each underlying journey further on its natural path, will likely allow the emergence of the best approach to stabilizing a potentially lethal global situation.

213

Before continuing with this analysis let us remind ourselves of some Flower Chronicles basics and implications:

1. The flower journey is ubiquitous and leads an organization to a state of flowering.
2. The journey manifests in a shift from a primarily physical or seed orientation to a vital or stalk orientation to a mental or flower orientation.
4. This pattern of progress is observed from the smallest of organizations (an idea or a person) to the largest of organizations (evolution on earth itself).
5. The ubiquity of this pattern sheds insight into the functioning of our containing system, which is as a result seen as being purposeful, conscious, and integrated, amongst other things.
6. The insistence or Will that world-phenomenon, regardless of scale, progress as per this pattern sheds insight into the trajectory that event / circumstance / organization will inevitably display.
7. Stagnation in a flower-journey manifests as fundamentalism. All fundamentalisms are given a chance to proceed out of fundamentalism. Some choose not to, and become contrary-journeys that are eventually removed from the integrated world-system.
8. Stagnated journeys or fundamentalism interacting with other fundamentalism is a mechanism by which one or both journeys can progress along their respective paths.
9. Understanding of progressing trajectories and stagnations emanating within a conscious system that seeks ultimately to replicate a pattern of progress in all its constructs surfaces a unique system of analysis (Flower Chronicles analysis) that sheds unusual insight into seemingly isolated events and their evolution.

The fundamentalisms, thus:

1. It has been stated that US-led neo-conservatism has fostered a foreign policy of aggressively promoting democracy even in those areas of the world that may be inherently more suited to other lines of development. Such neo-conservatism is a fundamentalism because it sees the world in simple black-and-white terms, and in so doing misses out on system-wisdom initiative, that from a flower-perspective tends always toward varied and therefore more robust unity through the surfacing of more complex diversity. Such neo-conservatism can be viewed as an ideological block in USA's own flower-journey aimed at realizing a state of Justice, Liberty, and Prosperity. In its current practice it appears that it is the unrefined vital-state in the progressive physical-vital-mental journey that has surfaced, and that the rooting out of such fundamentalism is necessary for USA to truly realize the promise laid out in its own Constitution. In order to progress in this journey - the USA journey necessary for the country's fruition - lack of self-questioning by the citizens of USA opens the doors to intersection by other journeys and even fundamentalisms, the pain of collision of which causes such intersecting journeys to more rapidly continue to the next stage in their own inevitable journeys.

2. Business-as-usual, aggressively promoted by US enterprise, and perhaps related to its neo-conservative bias, sees the world and everything in it as existing solely for business. This too is a fundamentalism because here too purpose and action in the world are perceived in simple black-and-white terms. Here again, possibility of diversity is suppressed, and potential flower-journeys that independent entities around the world may be on, is simply not in the realm of focus. This Business journey, like the USA journey,

has also stagnated at the vital or stalk level. Shock of impact with another stagnated journey (fundamentalism) will lead to deeper self-questioning and therefore action, which will cause the Business journey to begin to transition to the mental level. The fall of the ill-fated World Trade Center can perhaps be seen as the result of the intersection of the Business journey with the Islam journey, to be discussed shortly.

3. Suppression of possibility on a country-scale, reportedly as practiced by Iraq's Saddam Hussein, and other leaders in the area, is also a fundamentalism. This led to the stagnation of myriad flower journeys that groups and sub-cultures within these countries may have been on. The US invasion of Iraq, when viewed from the point of view of intersection, holds the possibility that the involved entities may be led to another and hopefully more progressive stability. With the Arab Spring hopefully a more sustainable dynamic with each country determining its own future has come into being.

4. Pakistan's roots and continued insistence on the two-nation theory, is also a fundamentalism, because in this approach there is room in the country for Islam only and its active promotion through the device of madrasahs. Activity in such madrasahs on Pakistan soil have led to the strengthening of the Al Qaida, and the creation of the Taliban, which in a fateful maneuver, seems intent now on the conquest of the country responsible for its own birth. Madrasahs, Al Qaida, and the Taliban represent the myopically aggressive side of Islam and can be thought of as manifestations of stagnation in the Islam journey.

5. Mahatma Gandhi's appeasement of a few opportunistic Muslim leaders that led to the division of India into India and Pakistan, with its consequent massive and continued effects on regional destabilization can also be seen as a fundamentalism. Such appeasement of an opportunistic

minority without weighing the good of the generally unified majority, which included substantial elements from the separating minority, represented also a stagnation in the possibility of country-development.

6. Much of India's insistence that Gandhi epitomized the possibility of India's spirit of synthesis, and that deeper and historical synthesis epitomized in India's organic approach to unity-in-diversity is largely irrelevant in modern times, is also a fundamentalism. For in such a view Muslim and Hindu become greater than India. In reality India is greater than the sum of its parts, and it is that underlying greatness that lived in the organic approach to unity-in-diversity that it can even be argued, have given Islam and Hinduism their finest hours. This too has led to stagnation in the Country Development journey.

7. The aggression of India's mighty northern neighbor, China, that insists that many of its neighbors belong to it, is also a fundamentalism, that has so far devoured Tibet, threatens to devour Taiwan, and has begun devouring Kashmir and Arunachal Pradesh, parts of India.

If the President of USA were to analyze the Indo-China-Afghan-Pakistan region and USA's potential involvement in the area, he or she will be well-served to take into account the many 'journeys' and their respective intersections which have led now, to the continued focus in this area. The question to be asked is why the conscious, purposeful, integrated, flower-based world-system we live in is causing the discussed array of journeys to converge now in one area of the world? In realizing that each of the seemingly independent movements are in fact flower-journeys seeking release to the next part in their inevitable physical-vital-mental journeys, the President will be led to the resolution of what really needs to be done in this area.

Summarizing the seven fundamentalisms or more rightly, stagnated-journeys above, we have:

1. The USA-journey stuck at the vital-level manifest as neo-conservatism.
2. The Business-journey stuck in the vital-level manifest as a business-as-usual world-view.
3. The Iraq-journey journey stuck at the physical-level manifest as decades of despotism.
4. The Pakistan-journey stuck in the physical-level manifest as the two-nation world-view and resulting in the stagnation at the vital-level of the Islam-journey.
5. The Indian Subcontinent-journey stuck in the physical-level manifest as self-caused destabilization and synonymous with the stagnated Country Development-journey.
6. The India-journey stuck in the physical-level manifest as denial of its own possibilities and the possibility of truly sustainable development.
7. The China-journey stuck in the vital-level manifest as an outdated and aggressive world-view.

One can hypothesize that the stagnated Iraq-journey possibly needed the pressure of the USA-journey, stagnated at the level of neo-conservatism, to dislodge its own stagnation. On the flip-side the USA-journey needed the shock, waste, and deterioration of its standing in the world, that comes from unilateral invasion of another country, to cause its own stagnated flower-journey to progress to the next level.

One can hypothesize that the Business-journey needed the pressure and intersection of the Islam-journey to awaken business protagonists to the vital-level stagnation in the Business-journey. On the flip-side the Islam-journey needed the pressure of continued suicide-attacks in the name of Islam to awaken other, more rational Islamists to the stagnation and therefore a deeper questioning of Islam.

One can hypothesize that US involvement in the Iraq-journey was nothing more than a stepping-stone for the US to begin to focus on the Afghan-Pakistan region, and in doing so, it is further going to confront the Pakistan-journey, the Islam-journey in even more intense form, the Indian Subcontinent journey, the India-journey, the China-journey, the Country Development-journey, and of course its own USA-journey. It is to be hoped that at the end of this interaction it is not stagnation in one form or another that prevails, but a release for each of these independent journeys so that respective journeying and therefore a more holistic overall development results. This will be the President's big test if he or she chooses to address it.

For, at its roots, it was a misconceived emphasis of country-development as exercised first by Gandhi, and then continued by opportunistic others that gave strength to the two-nation theory. The two-nation theory in turn gave strength to a general platform of destabilization that has manifested in an imminent failed state in the form of Pakistan, and also played a key role in the subsequent strengthening of Al Qaida and the Taliban. Such focus on the two-nation theory, instead of on a developmental approach of unity-in-diversity may also have weakened Iran and led to its reported exploitation by USA. For if development of its neighbors had proceeded along the path of unity-in-diversity the whole region would have been far more stable and sustainable than now. The reported exploitation, it can be hypothesized, is nothing more than a combination of the Business-journey and USA-journey asserting its unrefined vital perversity. This approach supposedly legitimized USA's efforts at subsequent globalization and if the original target, Iran, had been stronger from within, perhaps would never have taken place.

Al Qaida and Taliban, perhaps, would also never have come into being. This exploitation, therefore, can also be thought of as an original error.

For true development to take place both these original errors need to be resolved. This is a system-imperative and the intelligent, purposeful, flower-based system we live in will assure this happens regardless of cost. If we were able, as a species, to make the leaps in our own consciousness so that the physical obstinacies and the vital perversities that have manifested in painful stagnations at the larger organizational and system levels could be avoided, the cost of change would be low. The more we persist, though, at the stagnated levels in each of the mentioned journeys - from the USA-journey to the Indian Subcontinent-journey to the China-journey, the more will these and other system-generated fundamentalisms intersect with each other until the pain of the collision forces us to make the required changes.

The fact that the Afghan-Pakistan region is centered around two deep-seated original errors and has brought together so many stagnated-journeys means that the system is preparing for a major struggle. It will be naive to expect that these problems will be resolved quickly, unless there is a change at the root-levels, in the consciousness of the person.

USA's presence in Iraq may be seen as only a preliminary exercise for what could potentially lie ahead. The fact that USA has ostensibly partnered with Pakistan, the leader in the two-nation theory, instead of India, the home of the concept of unity-in-diversity, perhaps also indicates how confused it is in making sense of the dynamics behind the ongoing struggles and suggests the high price it will pay for successful resolution in the whole matter.

Needless aggression, marginalization of diversity in all its forms, blind business-as-usual, are views whose time has ended. The coming together of the various journeys in the

Afghan-Pakistan region conflict is really about the working out of this. Whether the US President is able to see this and act accordingly as a leader of the world, will determine success in this poignant test.

Successful outcomes will result in the following:

1. The Pakistan-journey proceeds to the next level in its flower-journey by abolishing the two-nation theory once and for all.

2. India realizes that the key to unity-in-diversity is not, in this time and circumstance, a passive and self-defacing Gandhian view of the world. On a more philosophical note it can perhaps be stated that Gandhian pacifism needed the shock of aggression that Pakistan has continually provided, and that China threatens to provide, until a more balanced strength can be properly assimilated into the fiber of India. India must stand up for India. This ushers in the energy whereby the truer essence of unity-in-diversity is resurrected. This causes the India-journey to proceed to its next level.

3. The Country Development-journey hence also proceeds to a reality of unity-in-diversity. This means that the seed of unity-in-diversity is planted in the region.

4. India acts as the true leader in the region exercising more authority in making unity-in-diversity a reality for the region. In this way the Indian Subcontinent-journey will also proceed to its next stage in the journey.

5. Talibanism, Al Qaidism, and other related extremisms are wiped out once and for all, through the efforts of USA, India, and perhaps Pakistan, and others who join in the struggle. These extremisms are likely proved to be instances of contrary-journeys whose only purpose is to cause other journeys to progress.

6. The strengthened area will cause China to reevaluate its aggressiveness, a more visible version of the USA-journey

like approach, and contain itself. This leads to possible progression of the China-journey.

7. USA will come to terms with the truer meaning of democracy and business and cause the USA-journey and the Business-journey to proceed to their next levels.

In this manner all the original fundamentalisms are released and progress continues as per the larger system design.

Potentially very high costs will be paid by each of the actors in the situation if the lessons to be learned are not assimilated at the needed pace. Pakistan, as already mentioned, may face permanent extinction if it fails to move away from the two-nation paradigm. India, were it not to recognize the true and organic synthesis centered in unity-in-diversity, will potentially pay by unending struggles with its neighbors including China. China, if it were to continue on its path of senseless aggression may have to confront USA. USA may weaken itself permanently if business continues as usual and if truth of democracy is not heeded.

But all this can be avoided if the President of USA acts with vision of the true dynamics behind the situation. Let us hope that he or she is inspired to do so.

The Statesmanship Required of India

Global change is only going to accelerate in the years ahead. As already discussed this change is to a large extent driven by the fact that our operating models are strapped to the vital or stalk level replete with aggressive short-sightedness, while our conceptual models, and more importantly the deeper need of the human race is moving rapidly toward a more progressive and holistic flowering.

This disconnect is going to cause expedited breakdowns in the years ahead.

The problem that lies ahead for several countries at the crossroads of possibility is what model of development to assume. Should development proceed along the models easily followed by the West, with its often biased emphasis on profit at any cost? Or should development proceed along more holistic lines that aim toward sustainability in the long-term?

I focus on India, because as already discussed in the section on Industry, India is in a unique position given the fact that some of its key industrial segments have resisted becoming a part of the global business playing-field, so far. It is hence at the margin, and given that by some estimates there are potentially as many as 300 to 400 million consumers ready to be integrated into global retail segments, this is significant. It is not only the number that makes it significant, but also the timing. Growth around the world has primarily been driven by cheap resources, cheap labor, or by some country assuming a high cost in terms of absorbing unjust environmental degradation so that the illusion of profit can be maintained elsewhere. In this equation hence, there is forced or willing prostitution. And it is this reality that has to be changed going forward. As the world seeks for its next wave of growth, it is numbers like 300 to 400 million untapped consumers that comes with an inherent leverage – the leverage to alter the way business-as-usual works.

Consider therefore, the retail segment in India. From a reality of largely unorganized vendor activity just a few years ago, plans to add millions of square feet of organized retail outlets are now underway (Wikipedia 2013f). If this were to happen consumer demand will be rapidly increased. This is inevitable in the short-term. But also implied is the need for organized, predictable business models.   Depending on how this proceeds, it can be either good or bad.

On the positive side unwritten and perhaps stifling rules can be re-written by imposing what global players wanting a piece of the pie need to do to develop India as an environment. Hence mandating that 30% of sourcing must take place locally, or that a sizeable minimum investment in back-end infrastructure and logistics has to take place, is a good thing because it tends to change the easily biased nature of business-as-usual (Kazmin 2012).   Or the allowing of thousands of mom-and-pop stores or even part locally-owned franchisee retail outlets (Chilkoti, 2013) to become the anchor or a key part of the retail ecosystem, as opposed to the Western-type Walmart, also changes the biased nature of business-as-usual.

On the negative side a constant source of a diverse array of raw materials will need to be readily available. This implies that farms, fisheries, mines, factories, public and technology infrastructure, water-bodies, energy sources, will need to be in a continual state of high output. If accepted financial, economic, and business wisdom is to prevail, such a development will be looked at as wonderful as India's GNP and growth rate will continue to soar, in turn pushing supposedly positive growth of the global economy.   But as several environmental studies have indicated, the world is in a reality of overshoot (WWF Global 2013). Demand being placed on the earth's resources far exceeds the level of sustainable supply. In other words nature's capacity to create sustainable crops, fish, livestock, clean water, clean air, minerals, is being exceeded. Recent studies have also indicated that if consumption patterns in India and China equal that of the Western world, two or perhaps three Earths will be required to sustain the supply of needed raw materials.

Such development, where increase in demand fuelled is by increasing population and far better organized business activity, will likely lead to a reality of heightened competition for fewer fundamental resources. When fundamental needs are unavailable, pressure for survival can cause regions to act irrationally, seeking quickest and most aggressive solutions. The likelihood of regional instability will therefore increase.

As several studies on availability of energy have indicated, as a global economy we have likely already or are close to peaking in production of oil (Wikipedia 2013g). Some estimates indicate that within 5 years the availability of oil will be drastically reduced. Given that our economy is primarily oil-based, energy infrastructure for cities, transport, and industry will need to be rapidly redesigned and redeployed. Yet today, we do not act as though oil depletion is imminent. The shock from shortage of oil will alter the rules of our game. The way of life we have become used to will be severely challenged, and the likelihood that this will result in heightened regional instability will again be increased.

If Ethanol and bio-diesel is opted for as the viable option, there will be heightened pressure on agriculture for crops as input into ethanol production. This will trigger massive increase in the price of staples and food, and again the likelihood of regional instability will be heightened.

Hence with the anticipated addition of 300 to 400 million people to the global retail game, the development path that India pursues can have a significant impact on how future global business and economic activity is pursued. If India proceeds along a paradigm of business-as-usual, instabilities of the type mentioned have a higher likelihood of coming into being. If, on the other hand, India chooses to change the rules of the game, a very different and far more sustainable shorter-term reality will come into being. It is the wisdom of the flower that must be pursued. India has the opportunity to display leadership so that the operational models strapped to the stalk level, can indeed be evolved so that concept and operation both begin to operate in consonance with the ubiquitous flower.

Business-as-usual must change. The burning of fossil fuels, the life-blood of business today, results in the tangible phenomenon of climate change (Flannery 2005). Rising temperatures due to the increase in carbon dioxide in the atmosphere result in changing weather patterns and the shifting of living ecosystems to cooler climates. In turn this decreases the earth's bio-capability – its ability to create natural capital. Rising temperatures also result in the melting of polar icecaps, the rising of sea levels, and the creation of powerful storm-systems. Melting of the icecaps will release a large amount of fresh water into the oceans, which will presumably affect the salinity and hence the flow of major global water-currents such as the Gulf Stream on which the temperatures of Europe are dependent. This in turn could cause a major drop in the temperature of Northern Europe resulting in the altering of entire eco-systems and hence economies at the local level. The rise of seal-levels also threatens coastal regions, and can result in the submergence of ports critical to the functioning of the global economy. The wrath of hurricanes such as Katrina, Wilma, and Rita have already been experienced. Multiple this type of force and occurrence multi-fold and the reality of unpredictable, uncontrollable coastal and in-land devastation, forced migration adding to or accelerating the social instability in increasingly populated areas, and increased disease due to debilitated and overburdened sanitation systems, can become overwhelming.

Further, the increase in carbon dioxide in the atmosphere also results in the increase in carbon dioxide in the oceans, which in turn become more acidic. This will alter the existing chemical balance of the waters affecting the formation of plankton. Lying at the bottom of the food-chain, any threat to the existence of this organism will certainly threaten aquatic life and all else dependent on it.

Other immediate effects due to the business-as-usual paradigm are being felt in the increasing toxicity of earth's natural systems due also to our habit of polluting the air, water, and land with non-biodegradable and often poisonous materials. The very basis of the matter from which we are made is being attacked by actions emanating from our own shortsightedness. That matter streams into us in the air that we breathe, that water that we drink, and the foods that we eat. Unable to process the poisons, our cells become overloaded and acidic. Our immunity falls, and diseases more easily appear in us. Thus the toxicity of the world incarnates as the toxicity in our bodies.

Resource shortage, energy insecurity, instability of food supply, climate change, disruption in the food chain, toxicity of the earth's natural and human systems, requires a whole different approach to being solved. It is not enough that isolated local action take place. One has to think globally, and act globally, through concerted local action. Perhaps disasters like the Tsunami are somewhat preparing the mind of humanity to act in such a manner. In other words it could be that natural disasters cause us to shift more quickly from a psychology determined by the physical-vital or seed and stalk, to a psychology determined by the progressive-mental of flower.

If we are unable to make the shift and step up to the challenge before us, it is those areas of the world most dependent on the current global business model – oil-based infrastructure, consumption of excessive resources, highly concentrated urban dwelling – that will be most affected. The

227

places where comparative simplicity and reliance on sustainable sources of energy and materials is already existent will be relatively less affected.

So the question is, what is the Indian Statesman to do? There is an intricate balance to be worked out. On the one hand, there is the practical pressure to increase GNP along commonly accepted lines of business-as-usual. Not to increase national economic activity and hence national coffers is to compromise national security, especially at a time when regional instabilities could be ignited in one of many different ways. On the other hand, the hurtling forward along existing lines of business-as-usual will expedite the environmental and climate change challenges discussed and create a more apparent urgency around the need for another equation with earth's system of natural capital. It is inevitable that there will be directional change in the earth's global economy such that reliance and the augmenting of rather than the depletion of earth's natural capital must become the modus operandi.

India will be wise to proactively innovate along lines that allow a symbiotic relationship between manufacturing process, product, business action, community development with earth's system of natural capital to come into existence. A shift in the rules of business-as-usual such that there is a thrust to develop in balance with earth's systems of natural capital is a clear demand of the hour. More has to be done beyond allowing mom-and-pop shops to remain the anchor in a retail eco-system, or imposing stipulations of back-end structural development on global players. The nations that are able to lead this shift will likely become the living centers of global developmental activity correspondingly gaining access to a vaster source of sustainable wealth.

At the same time the Statesman must never forget the apparent wisdom in the criticality of the hour, as has

228

manifested or will manifest in the challenges of resource shortage, energy insecurity, instability in food supply, disruption of the food chain, increasing global toxicity, and climate change. In the solving of these global problems is a sign that humanity must become one. For practical thought that promotes the reality of global interconnectedness, and multilevel global coordination are the master-strokes required to address these challenges. It is perhaps these devices, as opposed to that of the conquering and aggressive army, which might herald the dawn of greater human solidarity. For the first time perhaps, a vital need for international unity is being thrust upon the human race. And as with any need that is vital in nature, the effect it will have on the creation of a corresponding psychological reality, in this case to do with that of human unity, gets expedited.

The Indian Statesman hence stands at a unique window in time. Change in the economic direction, power, and way of being of the subcontinent, by virtue of its position at a critical margin, will unlock positive pathways by which future global development takes place. Grasping the high road will stabilize development in the world, strengthen the dynamics by which human unity might be more successfully worked out, and ensure that humanity maintains its place in the march of life, thereby also fortifying India's position as a just regional and global power.

Summary

In this chapter we perhaps have come face-to-face with the reality of how intricately interwoven many seemingly separate dynamics are in determining the political reality of any one region of the world. A case in point is the consideration of the Indo-China-Afghanistan-Pakistan region that is seen as the coming together of important dynamics from different parts of the world. The pacifist, peace-promoting attitude of a Gandhi, no doubt admirable and needed in the development of the world, can perhaps be considered as an anachronism that applied in its improper sequence, has resulted in the weakening of the entire Indo-Pak-Afghan region and has given license to organizations such as the Taliban and Al-Qaida to come into being. Further the wisdom and necessity of conflict can be seen as a means by which fundamentalisms are resolved. Fundamentalisms themselves can be seen as nothing other than stagnations in inevitable flower journeys.

We also consider the unique situation present-day India is in by virtue of the massive off-line population of 300 to 400 million people who are quickly going to be integrated into the global retail environment. India doe have the opportunity to change the nature of business-as-usual if it plays its cards right. But this will require an extraordinary statesmanship, the result of the flower itself. If such statesmanship does arise then India will truly emerge as a just regional and global power.

In this chapter we cast a wider net and consider political development in other areas of the world. We also look at the political situation in the European Union, another area that threatens to split apart if not properly addressed. The problem with the EU surfaces a deeper problem of management of diversity that has no doubt been made difficult to manage because of our current financial models and beliefs. We look again at the inevitable urge that was bought up in a previous chapter on democratization of markets, only made more real when we consider recent development in both the EU and South America. We also consider the ramp up in espionage and consider that as a symptom of needed underlying political development that helps change ground reality. Finally, we suggest that multipolarity as opposed to our current distribution of global power is the true answer to a sustainable global development.

Development of the European Union

"A day will come when all the nations of this continent, without losing their distinct qualities or their glorious individuality, will fuse together in a higher unity and form the European brotherhood. A day will come when the only battlefield will be the marketplace for competing ideas. A day will come when bullets and bombs will be replaced by votes." These words were spoken by Victor Hugo in 1849.

Yet today, in the continuing turmoil precipitated by the EU Sovereign Debt Crises one must ask what is to be done to move the European Union securely forward to the vision voiced by Victor Hugo almost 2 centuries ago.

Certainly, a problem is that financial investment is a global dynamic that in its current incarnation could not care for anything other than an immediate financial return. If there is a perceived hot-spot then money will flow to it. If there is a perceived problem then money will flow away from it. But as history tells us, every bubble is followed by a burst. The bubble enriches the few. The burst impoverishes the many. Culture, civilization, brotherhood, individuality are tossed aside, in the fervor of speculation

Global financial investment hence, appears to be at odds with the very values espoused by the European Union. Here is an extract from the official website of the European Union (Europa.eu 2013):

"The EU wishes to promote humanitarian and progressive values, and ensure that mankind is the beneficiary, rather than the victim, of the great global changes that are taking place. People's needs cannot be met simply by market forces or imposed by unilateral action."

But as the continuing riots in Europe, through Greece, Sweden (Taylor 2013) and most recently Spain (Daily Mail 2013), point out this is not really the case. Humanity is unfortunately the victim of the global changes that are taking place. And yes - people's needs cannot be met simply by market forces. But what is to be done about this?

In Redesigning the Stock Market (Malik 2011) I have suggested an approach to begin to manage the vicissitudes of markets and also suggested revisions to the body of financial theory responsible for these in the first place. While these suggestions will help in disentangling the forces that currently compromise the goal the EU has set for itself, and put into focus the financial aspect responsible for the turmoil, more needs to be done.

The financial complications have been intensified by the EU rushing ahead with the creation of a single European currency, the Euro, which has replaced the local currencies in 12 of its 27 member states. But the upkeep of this currency requires some stringent conditions at the member state level. This includes criteria such as keeping the rate of inflation within a 1.5% band of the average inflation, and long-term interest rates within 2% variance of the average interest rates, of the three member states with the lowest inflation. Further, national budget deficits must be below 3 % of GDP, public debt may not exceed 60% of GDP, and exchange rates must have remained within the authorized margin of fluctuation for the previous two years.

But how are member states to manage this if they do not even have control of the money that flows into and out of their countries? I am not saying that they should have an absolute and rigid control – that is not even possible. What I do suggest however is that the emphasis on money as it is currently defined and understood has to be enhanced so that there is more subtlety and sensitivity inherent in it. But how is that to be done when a single currency replaces many diverse ones that arguably were a better reflection of local ground conditions?

Here a key principle in the formation the EU is at stake. This is the principle of subsidiarity that can be thought of as a key organizing principle of decentralization. The idea is that a matter ought to be handled by the smallest, lowest, or least centralized authority capable of addressing that matter effectively. But the opposite is happening as living standards are slashed because taxes are used to bail out governments, and austerity is forced on local populations by an ever remote Governing body.

It is no wonder that David Cameron in his speech earlier this year (Cameron 2013) clearly states that Britain will never be part of the single currency. How can she when doing so will undermine her very independence and national sovereignty? And that is the question that each of the member states really needs to ask themselves.

Has the development of the European Union proceeded so that she can really call herself a Union? Referring to the ubiquitous flower model, where the first stage is the seed or physical and the status quo tends to be maintained, the second stage is the stalk or vital and energy asserts itself often irrationally, and the third stage is the flower or mental where intent resident in the seed expresses itself (Malik 2009), that perhaps is the blueprint of all sustainable development, the question is what are the stages that the European Union has really traversed? The values of the EU, no doubt inspired by visionaries such as Victor Hugo, suggest the great goal before it. It is clearly not at that flower stage yet.

As a politician from a member state has stated, Europe has been able to reconcile its geography and its history. But has it really? The reconciliation is not at the end-point that perhaps many feel it is at, but only the starting point. Initial conditions have been put in place – the promise conceptualized, the geography outlined. But now the real journey is to begin. And there are many pitfalls along the way that at any moment may even force it to go back to the drawing board. How can the rich diversity of each of its member states be kept in tact, and yet become the bridge to a single union?

The notion of union itself has to be examined. If one thinks of union as the coming together of nations in a common declaration of purpose without achieving that, then yes, that could be a union. But as we know more and more marriages end in annulment. So it is definitely not a sustainable union. This appears to be the model that the European Union has adopted in imagining itself to be a union. But by its very definition it is fraught with instability.

Of necessity it has to move to the next working definition of Union in the flower model gradient.

If we think of union as member states sticking it out through thick and thin as per their initial vision to finally arrive at some common and workable approach to manage union in real-time, then yes, that could be a union. But as many reports indicate, even the ability of the governing body to arrive at that status is in question. One recent article from June 10, 2013, in the Financial Times (Fratzscher 2013) suggests it has a ways to go in doing this. And Britain's stance exemplifies this. So clearly if the European Union is to remain a union, it has to move to this definition in the gradient. As a result of this part of the journey hopefully the diversity inherent in each member state becomes a real difference that is cherished without compromise.

If the second or stalk-stage is successfully traversed then there is the real promise that Europe's incredible diversity will become the engine by which unity is achieved. And this means that a new equation will be worked out for investments and finance that replaces our current caricature of the promise, that the laziness is valued equally with the precision, and that equality, fraternity, liberty in all fields becomes the cornerstone of progress.

Then perhaps, the vision voiced by Victor Hugo will some day be realized, and the great European Union Odyssey fulfilled.

Leadership in Global Finance and Market Thinking

Recent global market events have so easily created a series of negative effects. The 2 events that I start with are the Fed indicating that it is going to reverse Quantitative Easing (QE) (Harding 2013) and the Chinese Central Bank similarly allowing interest rates to rise (Rabinovitch 2013). They are doing so for different reasons, but when layered on top of the already volatile financial situation in the EU (Sandbu 2013), a suggestive picture appears.

Here we have three major centers of global financial activity, each slowing down on injecting cheap money into regional markets. The last few years has seen each of these centers continuing to inject cheap money and suck up junk assets. Doing so has pushed back the examination of what is really happening globally.

But what is it that is really happening. Unfortunately Finance as it is currently configured paints an incomplete picture partly because it has failed effectively to integrate its two-sides of Behavioral with Mainstream Finance. As a result its grand market and portfolio theories are hardly practiced, even though there is a belief that they are, and some ineffective hybrid under the name of Established Wisdom takes its place.

Established Wisdom suggests that the out-of-date companies, industries, and models of business and trading have to be supported at any cost, and that is exactly what has been done. Working people around the world have contributed to the continued bailout of that which arguably should be left to die, with their hard-earned tax dollars. Established wisdom suggests that if large regional centers do not support inefficient banks, industry, and companies then that is going to have a ripple effect and cause an irreversible weakening in the global economic system. It is not that that has to happen, but because some partial financial model says that this is what will happen, that fear and anxiety kicks in, and then of course it tends to happen. So really, the arrestation of potential QE by the US, China, and possibly the EU, only has its effects because like Pavlov's dog we have been conditioned to believe that this is the case.

There has been continued lack of insight when it comes to the integration of the sides of Finance, which quite simply can be effectively brought together under the aegis of the flower model that I continue to propose as the ubiquitous model of all sustainable growth (Malik 2009). The three stages in the growth of the flower – the seed or physical that reflects the status quo, the stalk or vital that reflects assertive and even aggressive growth, the flower or mental that reflects purpose and truer curiosity resident in the seed – suggest psychological or behavioral orientations (as in Behavioral Finance) that can become the axis around which different mainstream financial models kick-in. Models such as Efficient Market Hypothesis and Portfolio Theory are relevant only when the underlying psychological orientation is at the mental stage, and different models need to be used prior to that stage. I have suggested a number of alternative models and discussed the integration of the two-side of Finance in Redesigning the Stock Market (Malik 2011).

The fact is that the often irrational injection of cheap money over the last few years, following the supposed global financial crises, as already mentioned, has pushed back the examination of what is really happening. And what is really happening is that there has been a continued shift in the democratization of markets as already suggested earlier in the book. Power is inevitably moving away from the elite to the rest of the people, and all the hue and cry about the continued global financial crises is perhaps nothing other than a Pavlovian response or even a Machiavellian play by those who want to maintain outdated monopolistic power invoking the crutch of, as suggested, blinded and partial financial and market models.

Because the bluff has not been called, these defunct financial and market models have successfully been able to cause panic, and have caused Governments such as Greece,

Italy, Ireland, Iceland, Spain, Cyprus, to mention some recent ones, to arrest their own rhythm of indigenous development by siphoning development funds through the channels of interest, debt, and other payments, and accepting irrational and curious fiscal conditions that limit ability to respond to real-time societal reactions.

Seems like a short-sighted deal, and, it is surely time to wake up. And that is exactly what has been happening. The events of the last few weeks in Brazil and Turkey point again to what is really happening – the inevitable democratization of markets. A million took to the streets in Brazil last week in an outcry against the obvious inequity between layers in society (Leahy 2013). The continued unrest in Turkey too is a demand for more democracy and prosperity (Dombey 2013), and only reinforces the movement that began with the Greek rebellions and the Occupy Movement, and continued with the Arab Spring two years ago.

Leaders around the world have to begin to see the forest through the trees. The grip that outdated financial thinking has on Governments has to be removed. Central Banks have to work to democratize local markets. Leaders have to do more to complete their own flower journeys. There is an urgent reinterpretation of markets, finance, leadership itself, which needs to take place. A process of systematic desensitization to the seed or status quo orientation that continues to plague us has to take place and a systematic resensitization as envisioned by Pavlov needs to take place about the possibilities of the ubiquitous flower blueprint.

Of course all of this is inevitable. The flower blueprint will ensure it. The only question is does it happen through a lot of reluctant kicking and screaming, or will it happen more consciously and easily.

Let us hope that it is the latter.

At some point in the future it will perhaps be true to say that the individual, a country, and the world will stand as equal powers in the scheme of things. From a fractal perspective this has to be true since the micro is as equal as the macro, and even, the micro and the macro are meaningful reflections of each other. But what might such a reality mean?

There would be an utter recognition that each of these incredible organizations is a valid and necessary reality endowed by a deep and original creative source that gives it right to be.

The individual will be the result of an eons-long process of the development of consciousness in which it is not the habitual and often meaningless patterns that we see playing themselves out in us now, but something truly unique and creative that derives its inspiration from a source that we perhaps rarely glimpse now. Such individuals will be naturally in tune with all individuals around them expressing their unique score in the music of creation. Equally, countries will be seen as organized around a theme, a deep theme, absolutely necessary to the wholeness of the world. And the world will continue to be that incredibly nurturing matrix in whose womb all other developments and compositions are forever taking place.

In such a scenario there would be no secrets, and even, no need for secrets. For individuals are world-citizens, belonging to but not bound by unique areas or countries of the world. All may roam around freely, and contribute to the development of the world by virtue of who they are, no matter where they are. The questions of espionage and of privacy do not even arise. How can they if for instance the consciousness of another individual, a country, or the world, may even be experienced in one's own consciousness as part of oneself.

This is in the future. But what it implies is that there is a journey with that as goal that we are on now. In that journey whatever else may be, one thing is for sure: at no point can the existence of any of the incredible three-fold organizational constructs be compromised to the point of disappearance. Progress of the individual has to continue, as does the progress of the country, and the world.

The recent spotlight on US espionage in Europe (McGregor 2013) bought to the surface by the Snowden disclosures, and any individual privacy concerns (Dyer 2013) about activity on the Internet should be considered in light of the larger context of the journey and the ultimate equality of the three-fold powers of individual, country, and world.

Let us begin with boundary conditions derived from some obvious threats to the world from its past. Perhaps the most recent is World War II and the prolonged confrontation between the Allied and Axis powers. The resolution of this confrontation in favor of the Allied powers was critical to continued development of civilization. Had the Axis powers won, then Hitler's destructive vision would have reigned and the world been set back by centuries.

In such a circumstance it is understood that whatever needs to be done to protect the sacred institution of the world, even if at a very high cost, is worth it. In such a circumstance any kind of espionage is perhaps warranted, and upholding the individual and even country become secondary in the balance of things. But this is only if the situation is so out of balance that great sacrifice has to be made to ensure the progressive continuance of the world. Similarly it can be argued that if the institution of country is at stake, or the institution of individual, then similar sacrifice needs to be made by the other two in order to ensure the progressive continuance of the third.

So the question now: is there a similar threat that perhaps any of the three-fold constructs face that may warrant special consideration to uphold it in the scheme of things? It is perhaps true that on a global scale the three largest known threats we face are those of climate change, terrorism, and the global financial crises. Barring arguments, let us suppose that this is true.

So if climate change were a threat as great as the Allied-Axis confrontation, what rights would that give the world, over country and individual? Certainly this may be the right to enforce GHG regulation, the right to ensure that the range of valuable ecosystem services are not compromised, the right to police countries whose business and foreign policy may compromise sustainable development, leading to the right to put in place a framework by which decisions made – at any scale - do not exasperate the problem of climate change. Assuming terrorism today is as great a threat as the Allied-Axis confrontation, then what rights would that give the world, over country and individual? In such a case the Five Eyes agreement (Wikipedia 2013b) between USA, UK, Canada, New Zealand and Australia is even not enough and should be assertively expanded to include more countries and even means. Further, surveillance of individuals focused on terrorist threats would also have more credibility. Assuming the global financial crises is as great a threat as the Allied-Axis confrontation then forced regulation on a larger scale than even the 1933 Glass-Steagall Act (Wikipedia 2013c) following the great depression of 1929 would also be warranted.

But these are all boundary conditions, and should kick in only if we have reached a situation as desperate as when Hitler threatened to successfully impose a standard to the meaning of the "perfect" individual and race. Similarly, it is easy for the powerful to impose their belief and consequence on innocent others, and in the three-fold developing scheme of things unless it is clear that the situation has become Allied-Axis like, it is ideally the balance of the three-fold anchor-points of individual, country, and world that would arbitrate the development of things, whether this be the management of climate change, terrorism, or the global financial crises. But for this to be the political structure of the world will have to change.

This may mean that it is not just the "rich" and "elite" nations, by our current definitions of rich and elite that arbitrate the development of the world. The meaning of wealth will need to expand to become multi-dimensional so that even "poorer" nations, be they the Democratic Republic of the Congo, Mozambique, or Senegal are recognized for their richness and given a seat at the table. This may mean that all individuals, not just those with a Harvard or Imperial College degree, are given the right to work and to create a proud and meaningful existence for themselves regardless of the socio-economic strata they may originate from. This may mean that work itself is not constructed to enrich just the few established paths of development, but expands out to express all the deep, creative possibility inherent in the human soul. This may mean that the very symbol of wealth be expanded beyond its current equivalence to cash, to include a range of different currencies – be they joy, peace, silence, beauty, knowledge, or industry.

But our handling of the underlying condition of which espionage is a symptom, is going to be a function of the consciousness with which we approach it. From a flower chronicles perspective, this consciousness is a function of the stage of development the potential flower is in. Hence, if it is in the seed or physical state, there will be a drive to maintain the status quo, just as the seed will continue as a seed forever unless external conditions change it. Reality will be perceived as what the eye can see, and hence the problems of climate change, terrorism, and financial crises will continue to be handled independently, and the rationale for elaborate espionage programs, be they on one's own citizens, or on other countries of the world, will continue forcefully in their own right, rather than espionage being seen as a symptom of a deeper condition, that ultimately is in process of evolving. In such a scenario Snowden will be brought to justice for a problem much larger than what he was implicated in, Morales' and other President's flights will continue to be diverted on the order of a threatened nation (Schipani 2013), and the world will continue as a very reactive place.

If it is the vital or stalk state, there will be a drive toward experimentation and even assertive experimentation. Not all experiments are equal nor fruitful, but it could be that released from the shadow of yesteryear thinking some experiments may truly set a path toward the flower. Such possibilities may include terrorism being viewed as a side effect of the global financial crises. Financial crises itself could perhaps be thought of as being the condition where development funds circle only amongst a favored elite, and its resolution, as causing it to flow wherever it is truly needed, so that even the Sierra Leones and the Sudans of the world receive funds to develop along lines that are consistent with the deep theme that animates them. If the poorest nations of the world develop, then the incentive for disenfranchised youth to join terrorist organizations is minimized, and terrorism itself diminishes in possibility. Further, if funds are distributed to a variety of groups to pursue development along their own lines of possibility, then the problem of replicating the American Dream in China will not be repeated in every country that tastes progress, and the slow down in exaggerations of consumer conspicuousness will halt the engines of climate change, as other developmental paradigms are pursued instead.

In this scenario espionage too becomes something different as the threat of targeting symbols such as the World Trade Center lose meaning. It is not then espionage driven by the instinct for survival, which is perhaps what is driving USA's supposed ramp-up in this area, but espionage to learn what other possibilities beyond one's own narrow view of world development exist. Already a spin-off of this, alluded to as the "Snowden effect" by Markus Kerber, chief executive of Federation of German Industries, is one in which cyber security creates a huge number of jobs, enhances the possibilities for growth, and helps create a more digital industry model in the EU (Kerber 2013).

In the mental or flower stage, ideas and purpose resident in the seed come to the forefront and begin to organize events. This is perhaps where the political structure of the world changes along the lines already outlined, and we are more securely propelled to that inevitable reality where individual, country, and world stand as fully free and equal powers. As a continuation of this scenario espionage perhaps becomes that willed glimpse by which a part of oneself is revealed in its truer beauty and abundance, and causes the uniting power of love to flow more freely than ever before.

Multipolarity is the Answer

In her address to the Senate Foreign Relations Committee on March 1, 2011, Secretary of State Hillary Clinton stated - "We are in a competition for influence with China; let's put aside the moral, humanitarian, do-good side of what we believe in, and let's just talk straight realpolitik," (Dombey 2011). This statement gets to the crux of our current paradigm on international relations where the world playing field is led by might, and to maintain it and its balance is the primary consideration in a nation's foreign policy. While there is obviously truth to this, that truth is a function of where we are at in the global flower journey for development. While we currently stand more in the vital level, the growing acuteness of our global problems signal that the vital level is hitting against its boundaries, and that we are potentially at the transition to a relatively more fruitful mental phase.

Power does not belong to the few nor to the mighty. It belongs to all. But each and every one must realize this, and act as if they each are empowered ambassadors of the world. Vital consciousness at the individual level has to transition to a truer mental consciousness. The continuing spate of revolution in North Africa and the Middle East perhaps puts this dynamic into focus, as citizens seek to seize back the power that truly always belonged to them. This pattern of rebellion must generalize itself on a much deeper and larger scale and become a driver of accelerating the transition from the vital to the mental.

The current bases of global power, whether American, or in Clinton's concern, Chinese, has as its heart the dysfunctional and short-sighted contract that every citizen of the world has implicitly agreed to – that their happiness and well-being will be determined by the acquisition of often meaningless product, for which they will pay a self-serving third party a sum of money that in reality does not begin to cover the costs of creating the product. In the bargain each will inadvertently pay for the product with a price much higher than they have imagined. For assuming that acquisition of meaningless product is the aim of existence, implies that the models, engines, supply-chains that enable this transaction will be upheld and supported by each and all, one way or another regardless of what it takes. This practice has been reinforced by any nation in power over the last few centuries. But its time is fast coming to an end.

This global economic and social model is seriously flawed, starting with the issuance and power over currency by a few elite institutions at one end, and ending with the continued destruction of environment and society at the other. No wonder, Ban Ki-moon, the Secretary General to the UN, in his address to the World Economic Forum on Jan 28, 2011 has called for a new world economic model (Ki-moon 2011).

The current economic model has implicitly propped up the flawed model of scarce-polarity. The rich grow richer at the expense of the poor and this is true regardless of scale of observation. The world for the last few decades has been decidedly unipolar, with the USA being the reference of all "meaningful" dynamics, and only now is transitioning to possible bipolarity with China in the ascendant (Kynge 2011), as per past definitions of power. But one way or another all past definitions have to end – and that is what transitioning from the vital to the mental means. Clinton's recommendation – to put aside the moral, humanitarian, do-good side and practice realpolitik instead is the quintessential summary of the vital-level, and quite frankly of all that has to disappear, rather than be reinforced through the bi-polar world we are fast entering into. Bi-polarity means that we just accelerate the rat race we have been a part of. So does tri-polarity or quadri-polarity, for that matter. We do not want to simply practice a foolishness on larger and larger scale. Demand then fast outpaces supply and in the accelerating battle for scarcer resources the very basis of the world economic and social order comes undone, blow by painful blow. This is not a scenario worth supporting.

Instead, people all over the world have to continue to rise, continue to take back that power, and establish true multi-polarity as the bases of the world economic and social model. While national currencies may remain, locally issued currency, down to the smallest scale has to become reality. Self-organization and increasing self-reliance at the community level has to become the bases of a world society and economy. People have to exercise their power to not allow destructive resource and market exploitation in the areas and regions they live in. This means increasingly saying "no" to the established and ascendant poles, and to cronies that support them, that may wish to continue to reinforce their short-sighted ways of being on the world. If the transaction of buying meaningless and ill-conceived product ends, established money-power gets destabilized.

Clinton would be much better advised therefore to do what it takes to end the rat race, by changing the current means and very definition of establishing global power. Then there will not be a Chinese threat to worry about.

Multi-polarity practiced at every scale is the answer.

Summary

Developmental problems such as being experienced by the European Union today can also be seen as the stagnation of a flower journey, where the notion of Union has itself to evolve to become more complete and holistic. The pursuit of Ideals of union such as voiced by Victor Hugo in the 19th century have to be examined more carefully and forces disentangled and understood more completely for such union to indeed take place. In particular is the force of Global Finance, a way of thinking that has woven itself so intricately with everything else that it is hardly recognized that in its current incarnation it is contrary to the notion of true union because it compromises the true founts of stability, that of diversity. Symptoms have to be separated from their causes, and the focus on espionage and its possible destabilizing effects put in balance in light of the underlying political development that needs to occur.

Diversity itself has truly to be put onto a pedestal and become the foundation by which truer multipolarity can establish itself in the world. Answers such as the American Way or the Chinese Way or the European Way are short-sighted and will result in sure global instability. Ultimate multipolarity will become a true force when each human-being reestablishes their contract with the world to become a true citizen, a true ambassador, aware of their power and responsibility in determining and maintaining a sustainable global playing-field.

Now that we have laid out some broad top-down, macro-level strokes in terms of global political development, let us refocus on recent some bottom-up, micro-level developments to put things in better perspective. We will look at some developments at the level of institutions such as the G20, the World Economic Forum, and policies such as tax credits. We will also some of what has been happening on the ground in movements such as the Arab Spring, amongst other such developments.

The G20 Summit: Gain or Loss?

In a typical G20 summit it had been reported that there was definite forward (Pimlott 2011). Most notable movements were the following:

1.   It was actually 20 countries that came together to address the on-going financial crisis and countries such as China and India had a real say at the table thereby reflecting real conditions in the world.

2.   Over $1T is being made available to fight the international financial crisis which will include $750B funding for the IMF.

3.   Regulation and oversight will be extended to all systematically important financial institutions, markets, and instruments, including a crack down on tax havens and regulation over large hedge funds.

Let us consider these gains in the light of what holding up a flower-journey lens would say is most important at the moment. Broadly speaking a flower model analysis of the global economic situation suggests that the world economy is currently in transition between an overarching 'vital' phase and a 'mental' phase. This is borne out by a couple of facts. First, while a centuries long movement, the predominantly agricultural economy (physical phase) has given way to a predominantly industrial economy (vital phase) which has recently given way to more of a digitally-centered economy (mental phase).

This indicates the end of a particular journey and the start of a new one. Second, the essence of a dying way of being often arises with even more fury as it realizes it is at its end. Dynamics such as climate change, the plethora of environmental problems, and the depth of global financial crisis, all caused by a business-as-usual way of being, itself indicates that we are potentially at the end of one journey that is about to cede to a new one.

Regulations and aspirations that therefore assist the starting of the inevitable new journey, driven by a greater measure of mental and intellectual powers thereby more easily promoting different ways of being, as opposed to the predominant and unrefined vital powers of the likes of greed and fear that have driven the business-as-usual paradigm, is the need of the day. The question hence is to what degree do the projected gains of the G20 Summit support the birthing of the needed and inevitable new journey?

Reviewing gain number 1 - "It was actually 20 countries that came together to address the on-going financial crisis and countries such as China and India had a real say at the table thereby reflecting real conditions in the world": This would indeed be an extraordinary gain if something of what China and India and the other members of the G20 group really stands for in their respective essences were coming to the table to recast global financial realities. In that China or India may have created their recent successes by virtue of operating from who they really are and by virtue of causing those deeper drivers of being to animate their play in the world business arena, this would indeed be commendable. In that they may be replicating established models of corporate success to establish their success on the world-stage, it is not really anything new that is being projected on the world-stage, but old wine in new bottles. In this case it is established and old ways of thinking that will reinforce old ways of being.

Reviewing gain number 2 - "Over $1T is being made available to fight the international financial crisis which will include $750B funding for the IMF": IMF has often been touted as an instrument of an elite business cartel that exacts difficult conditions on its donee nations thereby subtly extending donor nation power into the donee nation. If this is the case then such funding is hardly a gain. If this is the case then IMF has itself to go through restructuring before it is independently effective. A more triumphant use of the money may be to promote micro-finance that has had proven results on large segments of the poor, such as envisioned by institutions of the likes of Muhammad Yunus' Grameen Bank. Yunus himself has suggested the initiation of a Social Stock Market to parallel today's existing Stock Markets as a means to get needed funds into the hands of NGOs doing real work from the ground-up. Further, it is of no use throwing good money after bad. If the new money is always used in the ways old money was used any gains are questionable. $1T could be used in creative ways to seed a new approach to business development and growth that used an array of deep drivers as the seeds for unique development.

Reviewing Gain #3 - "Regulation and oversight will be extended to all systematically important financial institutions, markets, and instruments, including a crack down on tax havens and regulation over large hedge funds":

• Given the current reality of these organizations operating at the vital level, such oversight and extension of regulation is a necessity and will surely be a gain. Even better though, if these organizations could change from within to begin to operate at the mental levels. More personal crises and pain may need to be experienced before such organizations are willing to go through that level of transformation.

• Crack down on tax havens could be a positive move if it binds a corporation more concretely to the soil it is ultimately accountable to. Globalization and the establishing of corporate headquarters in tax havens has tended to create non-accountable asset bubbles free form the scrutiny of stakeholders that it is ultimately accountable to. What we need more than anything else in today's world is the development of real capital – social, community, environmental capital – where investment and development is real and tangible and results in real gains in the present and for generations to come.

• Regulation over hedge funds is a necessity. The results of years of hard work of innocent people cannot be allowed to disappear in a smoke and mirrors act to satisfy an impulse of greed or fear on the part of hedge fund managers.

These gains could therefore indeed be incremental gains under certain conditions. The real issue, however, that of birthing a different financial and business order that will truly unleash creativity because it feeds possibilities of uniqueness, thereby changing the nature of the global economic journey from one of being vitally-centered to one of being mentally-centered, has not been addressed. Doing so, now or in the near future, will be the real gain. In the final analysis, therefore, while the G20 summit has had definite positive aspects to it, it has not addressed the real issue of facilitating the birth of a new way of global economic being.

When the World Economic Forum had its 40th annual meeting in Davos in 2010, I was struck by the theme of Rethinking, Redesigning, Rebuilding the Global Economy because this requires a deeper understanding of the global economy than I believe the World Economic Forum is willing to explore. Such an understanding requires a plunge into a holistic, systems-based world-view such as the Flower Chronicles, which suggests that the global economy is a manifestation of the ubiquitous flower journey and in the scheme of things is self-organizing.

At Davos they talked about a changing model of capitalism where addressing Climate Change, Global Poverty, and Unemployment are critical. This is no doubt a huge step forward. To actively talk about one sphere of activity with the others was unthinkable a few years ago. Also in his opening comments, Klaus Schwab, the Founder of WEF, talked about the financial crises of 2008, the economic crises of 2009, a potential social crises of 2010, leading perhaps to a future inter-generational crises (Schwab 2010).

The question is - is progress happening inspite of these crises and breakdowns? One way of looking at this is that it will depend on the orientation of actors in the system. If actors have a physical orientation, then change is not progress. If actors have a vital orientation, then since this is all about self-aggrandizement, and getting rich at the expense of others, progress has happened. And perhaps this may be the more active orientation amongst a large part of the WEF membership that thus believes that progress is happening, and for this reason. If actors have a mental orientation, then this is more about free-thinking and even idealism. So progress for these actors has not really happened.

But if the few are getting rich at the expense of the many, is this progress? If people, communities, society, earth have to pay an unfair price, is that progress? This moves us to the notion of a recursive flower journeys – or flower journeys that are part of larger containing flower journey. If we imagine that the whole development through the physical-vital-mental journey has been part of an overarching vital 'phase' in its own flower journey, then we will have to conclude that progress has happened.

So let us examine if that is the case. Movement into the Digital Economy as evidenced by the last decade indicates that we are at the mental phase of some journey. If this is true, we should also be hitting limits: increasing resource shortage, widening inequalities, decreasing happiness, and a massive crises of perception. This too appears to be true. Further, if we consider the modern-day corporation, essentially the corporation has many rights of a person but with limited liability. Add to this the ability to transfer large flows of cash without accountability, and it is certain that today's corporation is essentially a vital animal. Hence putting two and two together we can say that we are at the end of an overarching vital phase, and that what is going to happen is a transformation of the modern-day corporation and economic activity into some other form. Hence, from the intuitional perspective, and in alignment with the deeper flower journey, yes, progress has happened.

However, the two kinds of progress – vital and intuitional – are different and require the ability to think and act differently in order to continue to move things progressively. So the real crises is the underlying change or shift in consciousness that must occur at the level of the person so that there is awareness of the underlying and ubiquitous flower journey, and the central part that each person holds in the build-up of a sustainable world, by virtue of being the key that exists at its very base. Flower journeys need to be completed so that the general physical-vital orientation can yield to a general mental-intuitional or flower orientation.

So long as this does not occur one crises after another will continue to arise, as a means by which the needed shift can occur at the base-level of this massively interconnected system.

The effort and thinking at Davos, which is naturally reflective of the world business and political community, is rather about acting on the surface of the economy according to physical-vital heuristics. Regulation, job creation, financial overhaul, public-private partnerships are all well and good, and even necessary in such heuristics. But it will be difficult for efforts to bear fruit, however, unless the conversation at Davos begins to focus on this system behind the system: hence leading to the flower-journey base of the economy. It is not just that lateral or horizontal thinking and interconnecting is required, but these have to re-contextualized by a penetrating vertical plunge that uncovers once and for all the intimate relationship between personal perception and behavior and the world that is created as a result of that.

Across the Skies of Tomorrow: What President Obama Needs to do Beyond Offering Tax Credits For R&D

A couple of years ago President Barack Obama asked Congress to expand and make permanent a tax credit for research and development to boost a flagging economic recovery. (Harding 2010).

The question is, is such a scheme of any use? This seems like a pretty conservative approach when what we are in reality witnessing is a remarkable and historical shift away from what has driven global development till today, to a new and completely different way of being. Failure of global leaders today is that they do not see the tremendous light that is actually causing the formidable problems whether of financial crises, climate change, overshoot, amongst other, that we are witnessing today.

Economic recovery will only become a permanent reality once these powers-that-be realize that the world economy is in reality part of a ubiquitous flower-journey that is in process of transitioning from the vital to the mental phase of the physical-vital-mental-intuitional stages.

What this means is that at the very least the powers of monopoly that have existed for the last few centuries are going to crumble whether they realize it or not. The world is done with the few controlling the many, and this is true regardless of scale. The power for this impetus is a growing and inevitable shift in consciousness from the vital to the mental at the level of the person.

The time for the ExxonMobils, Citigroups, Pfizers, ADMs, Dow Chemicals, McDonalds, Monsantos, Walmarts of the world and their clones is over. What is needed is to consciously usher in a multi-polar world in every sense of the word. The best way to do this, starting here in the USA, is not to take another $4.6 T of taxpayer money and disburse that in the form of direct loans to Wall Street companies and banks, for the purchase of toxic assets, and for the support for the mortgage and mortgage-backed securities markets through federal housing agencies (Bottari 2010) or to offer tax credits to established businesses, but to disburse incentives directly to the people.

What we need now is new centers of power emerging from the ground-up. I will bet that if the Government takes its next proposed stimulus, whether of $5T or $10T and makes this available even to people who work in established corporations who want to set up enterprise aimed at facilitating the shift from the vital to the mental, that what we will see is a mass exodus from many of the fumbling corporate entities of the past, by people who want to release themselves from the yoke of yesteryear and create something truly more sustainable and enduring in its place.

The stimulus is needed to further expedite this inevitable shift from the vital to the mental. The stimulus is needed to break-down monopolies and usher in many centers of creativity from the ground-up. The stimulus is needed to more deeply sow the seeds of tomorrow's sustainable technologies and ways of being today. The stimulus is needed to help the people break the chains that bind them to a life of imprisonment, and breathe in anew as the rising sun makes its inspired climb across the skies of tomorrow.

2011: A Watershed Year

2011 indeed seemed to be a watershed year. North Africa and the Middle East were the play-ground for a significant journey, as the pattern of rebellion against authoritarian rule repeated itself on different scale. Tunisia, Algeria, Egypt, Morocco, Libya in North Africa, and Syria, Jordan, Iraq, Bahrain, Yemen, and Iran in the Middle East (Oberlander 2010) have experienced this essential rebellion against authoritarian rule, with different results.

In one way of looking at it, rebellion is successful and authoritarian leaders yield to the power of the people when the cost of maintaining the status quo now exceeds the cost of change. The successful rebellion therefore, is one in which the country is experiencing a Burning Platform situation (Conner 2012). This notion of the cost of the status quo is well illustrated in the interview of Wael Ghonim, the Google

Executive, after his release by the Egyptian authorities (Youtube 2011) where he repeats that he did not care about any consequence to himself for his actions, but just cared for his country Egypt.

This notion of acting without any calculation involving returns to oneself is I would say the critical factor in determining a successful rebellion, and in really identifying a Burning Platform situation. It is when one is, in an instant, willing to transcend all the patterns that define normal transaction with everything one is a part of. In terms of the ubiquitous flower, it is when one is able to complete the physical-vital-mental patterns that may stall progress to thereby allow that flower which is imperative behind all facades to come forward.

Whatever else may occur, one thing is certain – the "rebellion" journey playing itself out in North Africa and Egypt is going to have inevitable repercussions the world over. And the reason is simple: instability in the region is causing and is going to continue to cause instability in the global supply of oil. This in turn is going to increase the operating costs for an array of companies and industries, which in turn is going to increase the costs of fundamental goods. This will further dampen economic growth, and increase the cost pressure on the average citizen, the world-over.

Higher inventories, regardless of type, always mask basic problems. But now that the supply of oil is going to be challenged, basic problems are going to be unmasked. Oil is the lifeblood of today's global economy and its shortage, which is manifesting almost "gently" in different ways, so as to prepare us for the inevitable shifts that need to take place is going to turn a lot of assumptions on their head. And questioning these assumptions may lead us to becoming fully aware of the high price we are currently paying in so many areas of our lives. What areas will we declare as Burning Platforms, and where will the deep inner voice submerged by common patterns reemerge in acts of glory? How far will the cost pressures, the pressures of living in an undemocratic way, the pressures of being subjected to a marginal way of being, be it in a corporation or a country, ignite this force for change? For of course there are opportunities and areas ripe with this.

Will it be in an area related to food, beverages, and agriculture where our connection with the land is so easily replaced by a callous disconnection in which our source of nutrients is progressively stripped away from us? Will it be in the area of health, healing, and pharmaceuticals where inherent health is so easily replaced by impulses of constant debilitation that destroy even our ability to self-heal at its very core? Will it appear in the search for alternative energy itself, where possibility is replaced by a dark and poisonous binding chain that has wound itself into all aspects of life, breathing its poisonous fumes as it draws us into the lures of lethargy and self-annihilation? Will it be in our use and misuse of water, where this very source of material life is more often than not polluted and bastardized and becomes a source of material death? Or will it appear in an area related to the hundreds of thousands of retail outlets where our connection with abundance is replaced by a reality of a lack of abundance, as we become slaves to objects that lure us into cycles of destruction, and our very psychology is altered so that our notion of self-worth is now dependent on the number and variety of objects we possess?

How far we are willing to ride such waves so powerfully brought into existence in North Africa and the Middle East, overcome the effects and patterns of similar authoritarian rule in all its forms and guises, and act "without consequence" in

259

the interest of a brighter, more sustainable future, is the critical question posed by the events of 2011.

Summary

Where will the world go in 2013 and beyond? Pressing developments have come to the forefront in recent years. These include the global financial crises, climate change, and crises in individual and community consciousness, amongst others. Leveraging off the flower model we can shed light on the global movements that now need to occur.

Actions of organizations such as the World Economic Forum, the G20, amongst many other has to occur in the context of the ubiquitous flower journey we are all on, and the sure transition point we are currently at. To propagate yesterday's phase in favor of tomorrow is a disservice in the scheme of things.

In the flower model we have a seed or physical stage characterized by wanting to maintain the status quo, regardless of true cost. Maintaining the status quo implies upholding facades and the semblance of stability that has apparently marked the decades that we are now emerging from. In such a reality Central Banks buy up toxic assets, and parasitic corporations continue to exist without any fundamental change in their dynamics. Bailouts are common, and large organizations are supported, for fear that their demise may create too much upheaval in society. Business continues as usual, and the destruction of critical eco-system services in all their forms continues unabated. Political and religious dictatorships too are supported for fear that not doing so will cause too much sudden instability. This is the scenario that guarantees sure death at a slower pace, and in the scheme of things has to be exited. But first it must be recognized that this is the case - that living in such a scenario is the same as slowly bleeding to death.

As consciousness of people shift, and this is inevitable, it is certain that these dynamics will not be upheld for long.

The natural progression is to the vital or stalk level where, without overarching reason, systemic debilitation will occur at a much faster pace. Freed from the bonds of a status quo, and injected by irrational capital, limits will be hit much faster. China will grow in power as it becomes the unquestioned manufacturing capital of the world. Environmental and social disaster will happen faster. Rainforests, indigenous cultures, and centuries-old capital will be wiped out in instants, and we will all be consumed by Climate Change so aggressively that we will not know what hit us.

But deeper questioning can intervene and our journey can more quickly arrive at the lower-mental stage, on the outskirts of the flower. It is clear that this has been happening in deeper and wider measure the world over. This is the pattern that is becoming more surely alive. In this stage more movements like thee Arab Spring, Occupy, Anti-Corruption come into being. This signifies a great progress that happened. And so long as anchoring is decoupled from the institutions of the past, there is the possibility that these movements will become so powerful and spring into being entirely new structures, systems, and cultures.

But to truly become sustainable such development has to be centered around a leader. The leader or leaders must become the living springs of organically developing movements that more and more are compelled to embrace because it speaks to and shifts the flower journeys toward the flower.

2011 was a water-shed year. We saw the emergence of the Arab Spring, Occupy and various Anti-Corruption movements. As we move more deeply into 2013 and beyond such movements are going to increase in number and force. India and South America will see an acceleration of such movements. True leaders are going to emerge in the Arab World and what started off as questioning and rebellion from the status quo will begin to shift the needle in the way the culture functions.

In the next few years there is going to be a fundamental change in the way the global economy functions. Democratization of markets is going to become more of a reality. Further, many new models and ways of looking at events and society will emerge. The next two chapters explore some of these possibilities in greater detail.

Part 7 – The Nth + 1 Wave of Sustainability

Sustainability has come strongly to the forefront in recent years and its inclusion in decision-making is a definite step forward. However, its current definition is incomplete and needs to be further expanded in line with the possibilities of the ubiquitous flower journey. Climate Change is the type of phenomenon that can result from this incomplete definition of sustainability. In this chapter we look at the missing piece of sustainability and explore the phenomenon of Climate Change from this expanded flower-based view. We also look at the rise of Corporate Social Responsibility from a flower-perspective, and conclude with a more complete model of Sustainability and Climate Change.

Deeper Drivers of Sustainability

Sustainability is often thought of as maintaining a process or equilibrium. A common definition made popular by the Brundtland Commission is "to meet the needs of the present without comprising the ability of future generations to meet their own needs" (Wikipedia 2013d). In practical terms this has equated to the 'triple bottom line', a phrase coined by John Elkington (Wikipedia 2013e), with its emphasis on organizational and societal development along economic, social, and environmental lines simultaneously.

This is a huge leap forward from the common business-as-usual model that has created so many externalities in its wake. When one thinks of the needs of future generations however, there is still a key aspect that remains missing. For the business-as-usual model has done such a great job in its own execution that it has made much of society and therefore a vast number of people believe that they exist often solely to support or create new business or amass huge sums of money.

Hence, the needs of the people have been simplified and often form a distant caricature of the deeper needs that truly drives individual fulfillment. Unless these deeper needs, be it the urge to serve, or a seeking after uncompromised knowledge, or a seeking after freeing adventure, or the need to create living harmonies, amongst others, can resurface and become the seeds around which development proceeds, much of human aspiration and effort has been standardized, and will surely result in completely unsustainable outcomes in the near future, let alone unsustainable outcomes of future generations.

These deeper drivers though will only surface when each individual has moved further along in their respective flower-journeys. For it is only when the smallness and selfish-aggressiveness prevalent in the seed and stalk stages can be overcome, and one is led to the possibilities inherent in the flower, that uniqueness and deeper drivers can manifest.

It is imperative, therefore, in the spirit of true sustainability, that development be de-linked from blind money making, and be reconstructed around drivers that make people whole. Such a reconstruction will through creative pressure, begin to reconstruct more complex organizations from corporations to whole societies to create truly more sustainable futures.

Climate Change As A Repeating Pattern

The growing turbulence we see on a large scale manifest as climate change is rooted in smaller instances of turbulence caused by myopic and egotistical states of personal and collective consciousness, particularly in the consumer and corporate decision-making spheres. This repeating pattern of turbulence that can in fact be traced from the micro to macro levels is part of a single and pervasive system, the Climate Change phenomenon that must be addressed by altering the micro-pattern at its very roots. For, there is a repeating reality that animates practical existence. That is, seed-states or seed-patterns at the micro-level repeat themselves on larger and larger scale. This is true not only of the material world, and of the behavioral world comprising of people, teams, corporations, and markets, but of hybrid worlds, such as characterized by phenomenon like climate change, comprising of both material and behavioral components.

States such as desire, haste, greed, fear, insecurity, anger amongst other similar states of consciousness practiced both individually and collectively often form a general destabilizing milieu that impact consumer and corporate decision-making and result in sub-optimal market and environmental outcomes. Hence, under the influence of the seed-states consumers may consume conspicuously, companies may innovate in myopic ways, and people in general may consider the physical world as their source of unending resources.

These realities each represent stagnation in respective flower-journeys. Consistent with the underlying patterns, these actions ripple out in even larger spheres thus ensuring further and inevitable destabilizing effects especially on the environmental and social fronts. The largest known outcome of such a milieu is that of Climate Change. It depicts on a global scale a pattern of destabilization the nature of which has already occurred on many levels leading up to it, from individual, to team, to company, to market levels. Hence, Climate Change is part of a pervasive and stagnated journey. It can only effectively be removed by altering the root-patterns in the stagnated journey. This means that the destabilizing seed-states of consciousness at the individual and collective consumer and corporate decision-making level have to be altered.

Viewing Climate Change as the result of a repeating pattern with behavioral roots increases the set of solutions that can be adopted to meaningfully address Climate Change. This view brings into relief an additional, important, and largely non-utilized approach in solving Climate Change. Existing behavioral-related solutions focus on altering behavior by imposition of taxes or more recently through offering of incentives through the mechanism of carbon credits. This may alter behavior but does not alter the underlying states of consciousness that inevitably ripple out in repeating-manner to have their own and pervasive destabilizing effects. It is only in building awareness of the compounded outcome of the underlying states of consciousness – such as, greed, fear, anger, haste, insecurity, pride, vanity, jealousy amongst others – and in beginning to shift consumer and corporate behavior away from these states, that a truly sustainable solution to Climate Change will come about.

Corporate Social Responsibility In Appearance Only, Or In Reality?

If the meanings of our lives have become synonymous with business, we are in essence out of balance. The degree of this loss of balance is severe, as evident by the response from Earth itself in the form of Climate Change. For in its essence, Climate Change is nothing other than a rebellion of matter. We are aware of rebellions through history, of a social nature, as means to bring development back into balance. But a rebellion of matter on the scale we are seeing today is perhaps unprecedented in recorded history.

But why shouldn't there be a rebellion of this nature, if indeed earth-system is a living being, as Lovelock and an increasing cast of characters have suggested, with a trajectory of development that is in essence being compromised by the short-sighted way of her constructs? There is perhaps no other way for the trajectory of progress to continue as it should, unless individual consciousness, the root of the world-system we see playing itself out now, were itself to progress to the next phase in its own flower journey (Malik 2009). That is the need of the hour. This change lies at the crux of the remaking of business to bring about true and meaningful sustainability.

There is no other way to promote true sustainability. In recent years we have seen the rise of the Corporate Social Responsibility (CSR) movement. In its essence CSR is about integrating more holistic environmental, social, and governance considerations and factors into the strategy and operations of business. At its best it is about pushing the Business journey from a vital to a more mental mode of operation. But at the end of the day, there is a real business case for adopting CSR, which means that business actors have a business incentive to follow through with what CSR brings to the table.

The shift from vital to mental, from operating without more holistic environmental, social and governance considerations to operating with these considerations will allow a business to generate more profit. This is because more customers and stakeholders from the public to the investment community, expect this behavior from business and therefore reward it, it is because it has also proven to minimize a variety of production and operating costs thereby increasing margins, and it is because consideration of environmental, social, and governance factors also provides stimulus to the redefinition and creation of new products thereby enhancing revenue generation.

The point is that there is a business reason to make these changes, and therefore the mode of operation will tend to be centered in the unrefined profit motive that is essentially vital in nature. Because of the business case, business actors, hence, can remain fundamentally at the vital level, while doing all the things that CSR will make them do, to give the appearance that there has been a real shift to the mental level. But, no real shift has occurred, and the base pattern at the individual level remains at the stagnated vital or stalk level continuing to have its prolonging, and negative effect on world dynamics. At best, more mental force has been drawn to the service of the central vital principle.

The dangers of Climate Change may be immediately assuaged and we may live comforted that we have successfully addressed a potential calamity. But this is an illusion. The calamity has only been pushed back into the future. The fundamental way of being remains vital, and therefore this dynamic is what will continue to ripple outward to the limit of the earth, just as in the case of Climate Change, which has rippled out to the limits of the earth.

We know, for instance, that the increase in electronics introduces a distortion to the natural electromagnetic field that surrounds each living being. We are essentially electromagnetic entities and this continued vital hunger for electronics of all kinds, in every facet of our lives, is likely to continue to compromise the basic dynamics of our individual chemical equilibriums. For all chemistry that occurs in us is a result of a subtle electromagnetic equilibrium that stimulates cellular level chemical reactions. With the increase of electronics, and even with their increasingly being implanted into our very bodies, whether through devices such as attachable cell-phones and receptors or probes that enter into the bloodstream, the possibility that we are setting ourselves up for a severe disequilibrium as catastrophic as Climate Change cannot be ignored.

But there are so many other micro-threats of this nature that compromise our very equilibrium as individual entities. There is also the infiltration of harmful chemicals that alter our body chemistry, whether through intake of industrialized and processed foods and pharmaceuticals, application of cosmetics that immediately enter into our bloodstreams, use of cleaners, washers, paints, and other materials that exist in our dwellings, regular contact with surfaces such as processed textiles, plastics, automobiles and other forms of transport that are themselves centers for the release of myriad harmful chemicals, and ingestion of non renewable energy sources such as oil and gas that again pervade every aspect of the society and life we have today created for ourselves. There are a thousand ways that we are oblivious off whereby compromising chemicals can enter into our bodily systems. And there are a thousand ways in which they also enter into the very fiber of nature, right from wastes released during manufacturing, leakages during transportation, or off-gassing during storage.

All industry that we have created – consumer products, energy, food and agriculture, transportation, information technology and electronics, have through our vital lust become means to kill our very vitality.

Climate Change is in fact a wake-up call to this vital way of being, and so long as we are able to penetrate into the true cause of it, and grapple with the root patterns of which it is the result, Climate Change will have done a great service to humankind by causing the needed shift in our way of being further along the flower journey from a vital to a more mental way of being. The root pattern at the individual level is what must be changed. If however, we reduce green house gas emissions, create clever trading schemes, even create markets for promoting services of nature, force regulation and legislation that causes business to alter action without affecting the root cause, we will no doubt have done ourselves some favor, but   will also be pushing back the inevitable catastrophe, which may incarnate in another form, whether of a fundamental poisoning of life through chemical overdose, or a destabilization of living matter through alteration of base electromagnetics, or some other way that we are not foreseeing.

The shift from the physical-vital or seed-stalk to the mental or flower level at the individual level is an imperative. The transition must be made, either willingly through sincere individual, corporate, and societal effort, or unwillingly through potential catastrophes of the nature of Climate Change. The movement from a vital to a mental way of being is at the crux of the matter, and the question is what can business do, or how must it be remade in order to promote that shift?

The Nth + 1 Wave Of Sustainability

Sustainability has progressed through different iterations. In retrospect these iterations have been like gentle waves, the 1.0, the 2.0, the 3.0, beckoning us into the future. Some organizations have heeded these calls and ridden the assisting currents to begin to some degree to re-conceptualize themselves along their flower possibilities.

I believe, however, that the context of sustainability is not about compliance (1.0), not even about integration of CSR and sustainability into business models (2.0), and not even about product innovation (3.0). These waves are the calm before the storm. I believe that the context of sustainability is nothing less than a radical call from the future, that breakpoint wave plus one ('N+1'.0), insisting on wave after wave until businesses have redefined themselves such that their very bases of operation is commitment to the deepest drivers of progress possible to human-kind.

These drivers will provide an inner freedom from the biases prevalent in today's rendering of business reality to allow development to proceed along the most sustainable lines possible. Prior to that point, all the way up to the Nth wave, the context of development is continually being missed and wave will follow wave creating a veritable storm of epidemic proportions, until the true nature of the call is heeded. After that point, the Nth + 1 wave, sustainability takes on a different meaning, and itself becomes sustainable. The Nth + 1 wave, hence, alters the equilibrium of development. The Nth + 1 wave signals a tipping awareness toward a reality marked by a progressive, conscious, fully-integrated world-system.

The beginning of the storm is already evident in the confluence of forces we are experiencing now. At the visible macro-end our very playing-field is itself in increasing danger as evident through such phenomena as Climate Change. For in reality Climate Change seems to be nothing less than a rebellion by matter to the way of being of the evolving constructs of matter. A reset, way beyond management of GHG emissions, is required to truly set this aright. At the visible micro-end these debilitating forces are manifest in such phenomena as the flow of deeply compromising products, whether of processed foods, cosmetics, pharmaceuticals, electronics, energy, or financial products, that many of us have become slaves to. This compromising flow is in fact an outcome of our power as human-beings in that what we desire and seek for is what we inevitably create at the end of the day. In that many of us have hungered for the quick and cheap product easily available at our very doorstep that is precisely what we have created, even in the face of exorbitant costs to deeper ideals and more sustainable possibilities.

With the visible macro and micro ends of our progressive, conscious, fully-integrated world-system out of balance, economies, financial markets, and corporations have to fail. This is an in-built defense mechanism of a conscious and living world-system. There is nothing surprising about this.

In the face of these growing symptoms the only path forward is recognition of the truer nature of our world-system, of our central place in it, and a truer cause-effect relationship evident in various repeating-pattern type models that link players and parts of the world-system together in more accurate ways thereby accelerating the adoption of principles inherent in the Nth + 1 wave, and the movement toward the crucial tipping point.

Change at the policy level, at the market level, at the level of the corporation is all well and good, but unless there is deep change that facilitates shifts in perceptions at the individual level so that the reality of our flower-based world-system and the right relationship to it results, and so that these and other demands implicit in the Nth + 1 wave are embraced now, these other changes will at best function as stop-gap measures only.

Organizations must begin a redefinition on many different fronts based on a more enlightened understanding of the reality of our world-system. Shocks of the nature of Climate Change and the failure of financial markets will continue until this redefinition and the reality of Sustainability 'N+1'.0, that inescapable demand from a living world-system, manifests.

The most robust approach to creating a sustainable world is to manage the patterns that are responsible for chaos on a global scale at their very roots. Of necessity this implies facilitating shifts in perception at the individual level so that our learned and often myopic habits and ways of being can flower out into an altogether different way of being and the consequent repeating-patterns responsible for negative organizational activity and impact on the global levels be positively shifted forever.

New Orleans and the Sustainability Flower

I spoke about the Sustainability Flower, a flower-model for Sustainability, at the 61st Annual Conference on Standards held in New Orleans in the latter half of 2012, and an offshoot of the ubiquitous flower model that underlies all sustainable development. The theme of the conference was "Building the Future through Standards". The Sustainability Flower therefore, chronicles that journey that all progressive organizations, whether the individual, team, organization, market, system, or our world are on. The keyword is 'progressive' to distinguish it from other and common journeys that easily stagnate or quickly become dysfunctional.

From the point of view of the Flower Chronicles, whereby the three phases of the ubiquitous journey - the seed or physical, the stalk or vital, the flower or mental - need to be integrated, with the flower-level leading, the conference theme was timely and meaningful. For at its heart it seeks to alter the physical base-pattern by integrating existing mental-level best practice into it, to thereby alter all future standards-related journeys.

The Sustainability Flower is a holistic, immanent, and an all-embracing model of sustainability and I propose it as a viable option to the currently ever-changing definition of sustainability that has failed to originate from depth or

274

embrace breadth, thereby forever having to go through redefinition with every new boundary met or dysfunction encountered.

In building the future through standards, the root pattern of all dysfunction, regardless of field, must be seen as an anchoring in the unrefined or selfish vital state, where self-referencing flows of energy, be they of the nature of irritation, fear, anger, or greed, become the bases of team, department, corporate, market, and system culture. Such an anchoring cannot but be inherently unstable and must create global problems such as Climate Change and the Global Financial Crises in its wake.

Hence standards must incorporate the basic necessity of altering the root-pattern so that individual orientation and behavior more easily moves from the physical to the vital to the mental. As a reminder, the physical can be thought of as obstinately maintaining the status quo in spite of all signs to the contrary, the vital can be thought of as experimentation though most often of an irrational and selfish nature, and the mental can be thought of as a more sincere questioning seeking to alter existing and possibly future dysfunction.

That this conference took place in New Orleans is meaningful from a couple of perspectives. As the organizers of the conference pointed out, the destruction that New Orleans experienced because of Katrina, would perhaps have been minimized had building codes adhered to relevant standards. Certainly future destruction, regardless of type or where it may occur, can be minimized if best practice and forward thinking drives the establishment of base or physical-level standards that form the base of all Standards journeys.

But further, New Orleans is an organic mix of different cultural strands. French, Spanish, African, American and Native American, amongst other influences have integrated in a place that upholds and allows these influences to remain living. A walk through the French Quarter illustrates this. As the base-pattern at the root of the New Orleans Journey this suggests the possibility of an integration of even diverse business views. Perhaps the built-up global business dysfunction as suggested earlier, and manifest as Katrina, can be positively influenced by this Jazz-loving, culturally-diverse part of the world.

Summary

The Brundtland Commission defined Sustainability as "to meet the needs of the present without comprising the ability of future generations to meet their own needs". For this to happen though, the deepest drivers of sustainability have to be invoked. And these deepest drivers are none other than that that creates individual personality and therefore diversity. As discussed earlier in this book also, these drivers can be summed as the urge for knowledge, adventure, harmony, and service. Unless these come to the surface the Brundtland Commission definition of Sustainability will never come to fruition.

But for this to happen the patterns of dysfunction at the individual level, manifest as movements such as fear, greed, anger, anxiety, and so on have to be successfully managed away. These inhibiting patterns are in fact at the root of a tremendous range of dysfunctions at many levels of organization, and even the largest level of visible dysfunction - that of Climate Change - can be solved if the root behavioral patterns at the level of the individual are better managed.

Even dynamics such as the recent Corporate Social Responsibility can be in appearance only, unless there is a genuine shift in the consciousness of the individual away from a general vital-level functioning, to a more mental-level functioning.

This then, this focus on the change in the individual consciousness, that in fact underlies all larger dynamic and even global phenomena, is the true iteration, the true wave, that Nth + 1 wave, that will securely create a sustainable world in its wake.

We have made the case that the root of all global dysfunction and lack of sustainability, however we may look at it, is the result of dysfunctional behavioral patterns at the individual level. The true question therefore, from a Human Resources (HR) perspective is what can be done about human resources, the internal resources available to the human being, to solve lack of sustainability. Unfortunately the gap between the thinking laid out in the previous chapter and the reality that HR departments are currently focused on is so large, that the apparent and operative question becomes what can the function of Human Resources do in today's world to accelerate the possibilities of a flower-based sustainability?

This chapter looks at the HR department of organizations as a force in accelerating global sustainability. It also presents a conversation with a sustainability and HR leader of a large global corporation, GAP, to highlight today's best practice in this area.

HR's Role in Sustainability

We are at a critical juncture globally, where sustainability/social responsibility as a concept and way of being has to redefine how businesses function and define themselves. This criticality is reinforced through such global phenomena as Climate Change, global overshoot, break down of the financial system, and the breakdown in the social fabric in North Africa and the Middle East, which could certainly have been caused by an old-world corporate mentality devoid of sustainability/social responsibility consciousness – in other words, devoid of the fruits and possibilities inherent in the flower-consciousness.

Regardless of corporation, to effectively execute on sustainability initiatives requires breadth and depth of connection within the corporation, and the ability to affect the right levers. HR is theoretically at least positioned to step into such a role.

As per the ubiquitous flower-journey corporations today are faced with an apparent triple choice on the sustainability front. This boils down to becoming compliant with existing and increasing regulation (status quo or seed or physical), more actively altering existing business processes to integrate sustainability into the way business is conducted (stalk or vital), or rethinking the business model altogether (flower or mental) to prepare for a world in which sustainability is inevitably and irreversibly becoming a core driver of business possibility.

These three apparent choices are in fact a manifestation of the physical-vital-mental flower-journey and hence indicate a path of progression that any and every corporation that seeks to remain progressive will have to take. For in this reality:

1. Progressive organizations have to display movement along the physical-vital-mental maturity model.
2. Failing this progression from within, circumstance from without will force the progression.
3. Failing this progression even from without, the corporation will face extinction.
4. This is so because flower journey or physical-vital-mental progression is imperative regardless of organization and regardless of scale.

Given this reality, the question is what is the best way to incorporate this inevitability into a corporation. A double design consideration is essential here. First, the real work has to begin where small-patterns come into being - in this case the individual or employee in a corporation. The trajectory of effort, hence, has to occur along the primary events that constitute the employee lifecycle: hiring an employee, developing an employee, managing an employee, and maximizing the possibilities an employee can provide. The HR function will play a key role in making this a reality.

The second design consideration is embedded in the movement from compliance, as in complying with social responsibility and sustainability related regulation (seed or physical) to integration, as in integrating sustainability and social responsibility thinking into the fibers of a company (stalk or vital) to transformation, as in rethinking business and organizational possibility based on the opportunities that social responsibility and sustainability inherently stand for (flower or mental), that is in fact not a choice, but as the Flower Chronicles indicates, a logical progression toward creating a sustainable organization. In this progression the corporation has to make a series of choices that are in fact indicated by the movement from a physical to a vital to a mental orientation.

Coupling these design considerations together, what results are suggested trajectories of organizational orientation along the key employee lifecycle events already introduced – hiring, developing, managing, and maximizing. These orientations are captured by the P (for physical), V (for vital), and M (for mental) nomenclature in the following common scenarios:

1. The organization's philosophy towards sustainability-related hiring:
   - P: Hire to ensure an organization can meet social compliance goals and environmental regulations

- V: Use in-house sustainability-initiatives as a key platform in attracting talent
- M: Hire to get ready for the next wave of business process & product breakthrough

2. Organization's practices / beliefs towards increasing sustainability-related skill-sets of employees:

- P: Sustainability-related values and principles must become an integral part of the skill-set for all employees in the quality control and compliance areas only
- V: Sustainability-related values and principles must become an integral part of the skill-set for all employees in the organization
- M: Leverage of sustainability-related values and principles must be measured at the business unit and individual levels and contribute toward compensation

3. Organization's use of sustainability-related initiatives to develop leaders in the organization:

- P: Sustainability-initiatives are not used to develop leaders
- V: Social and environmental initiatives are used as vehicles to develop leaders
- M: The next iteration of product and process driven by social and environmental issues is a key platform to develop internal leaders

4. Management's attitude toward sustainability:

- P: Sustainability has no business case and is a part of compliance and philanthropy efforts
- V: Sustainability can be strategic if business units link their success to wider societal expectations

- M: Business contributes to shifts in economic-environmental-social systems to root out underlying causes of non-sustainability

5. General attitude toward creating an environment for sustainability to succeed:

- P: Sustainability efforts are best left to their own design and efforts without any intervention or support from the rest of the organization
- V: Sustainability initiatives require creation of appropriate cross-functional management and measurement systems to succeed
- M: Functional silos need to be broken-down and a number of cultural and organizational changes need to be made for sustainability initiatives to succeed

6. Organizational approach to incorporating lessons from sustainability initiative:

- P: Lessons from sustainability initiatives remains with the part of the organization that drove the initiative
- V: Lessons are reviewed and result in changes to system-wide processes, management, and measurement systems
- M: Lessons are reviewed, integrated in a system-wide manner, and incorporated into supply chain contracts and codes of conduct

7. Management's most likely area of focus on the sustainability front during an economic down-turn:

- P: Management is not directly involved in any sustainability initiatives and does not have insight into what is happening on this front. Management focuses primarily on meeting regulations and established codes of conduct
- V: Focus is on cost-cutting driven by sustainability-related innovation

- M: Management increases investment in sustainability since this is believed to drive the next wave of product and process improvement

8. Organizational approach to addressing deep-seated behaviors, assumptions, and beliefs of employees:

- P: Behaviors, assumptions, and beliefs are the personal problem of individuals and not the concern of the organization
- V: Creation of a safe working environment in which negative behaviors, assumptions, and beliefs are managed is the responsibility of the organization
- M: Proactively assisting employees to examine the many reaction, behaviors, assumptions, and beliefs they have is a necessity, since it is such patterns that repeat themselves on different scale to animate all of organizational life

For HR to consciously cause such a shift in organizational orientation at each step of the employee life-cycle, hence, is what its true role in bringing about sustainable organizations is. Hence HR has to find a way to be at the center of any approach to sustainability, since it is the small patterns exercised at the individual level that create the macro-level sustainability outcomes.

In April 2011 a report, "Advancing Sustainability: HR's Role", was jointly released by Society of Human Resource Management (SHRM), Business for Social Responsibility, and Aurosoorya (SHRM 2011b). The report is based on a survey conducted by SHRM where 5,000 members were randomly selected from its over 250,000 membership. The report is relevant in the following respects:

- It positions sustainability leadership as a tremendous opportunity for HR
- It baselines current HR efforts in the sustainability field, which net-net leaves a lot to be desired
- It lays out a roadmap for what HR needs to do through numerous research insights, which is consistent with the model just introduced, which in fact was one of the key inputs into the report

Exploring the 'Personal Perception - Sustainability' Link: Conversation Between GAP and Author

Conversation Background: Exploring how personal perception and behavior affects and even determines corporate effectiveness in the field of sustainability through a dialog between Dan Henkle, SVP Global Responsibility – GAP, and Pravir Malik, Founder and President, Aurosoorya. This is particularly true of organizations that are seeking to set the standards in sustainability – to be the transformers. GAP has been amongst the first in many different areas in sustainability: one of the first to openly share supplier information; one of the first to create alignment between Sourcing and Global Responsibility team; one of the first to have Human Resources and Global Responsibility work closely together. The following write-up is based on extracts from an Aurosoorya Radio Show, Connecting Inner Power with Global Change, Jan 15, 2010, available at the iTunes Apple Store, #13 (iTunes 2013)

Pravir: I proposed a model, elaborated in the book "Connecting Inner Power with Global Change" which you have read, that connects the dynamics at the level of a person - perceptions, attitudes, behaviors - with success in the field of sustainability. This connection occurs through patterns that repeat themselves on different scales – fractals - so that in effect personal dynamics determines team dynamics, which in turn determines unit and then corporate dynamics, which in turn influences market and system dynamics. Dan, can you comment on this model? Is this true in your experience?

Dan: Absolutely. This has been true inside GAP and outside. As some background, I started with GAP in 1992, in the Human Resources area. In 2001 I transferred to the Corporate Responsibility area. At the time GAP was facing intense criticism for working conditions in garment factories throughout the world. We needed to look at how we were thinking of things internally and whether we were aligned in decision-making. We also needed to think about whether we were connecting enough with the external community – in particular the human rights community amongst other stakeholders. In making the journey internally we began looking at how we were communicating with suppliers. Was there one message from the Global Responsibility and Global Sourcing teams? If messages were not consistent we would not get results we wanted. Since the Sourcing team is placing orders, suppliers will listen first and foremost to them. It was really important to collectively align with a single philosophy. We did a lot of work to come together, listen to one another, and move forward together.

Pravir: This is a good illustration of the model, and it had to be difficult. The Sourcing group is usually focused on bottom-line oriented goals. Global Responsibility, on the other hand, is usually often driven by a higher level of idealism. It must have required courage to bridge that divide?

Dan: People are fundamentally good and want to do the right thing. We went into the conversation with the assumption that the person we are talking with is a good human being and that we are both trying to work in a good and ethical way. This opened up the conversation. We framed the issue by reminding people of how we have worked together for a number of years trying to improve working conditions. We then asked the questions: What do you think is working well and where do you see barriers – really trying to open up the dialog. The point is, it was not just a team like mine coming and saying here is a set of goals – this is what you must do. We were really listening to what they had to say and where they thought we were having misalignment, and what we could do about it.

Pravir: Sounds like shift in personal attitudes resulted in better team dynamics, which resulted in a better outcome for GAP. Often times what happens is that different groups can approach the same issue from an emotional point of view (vital-level) or how it has always been done in the past (physical-level), and it sounds like in solving this you took the high road to get to what the sustainable reason for the change is (mental-level). In essence this facilitates moving from a fight-or-flight approach in interactions, to coming from the heart.

Dan: Yes. And we had a similar experience as we started to engage externally with the human rights community and with the environmental community. Again, the key emphasis was did we really understand what the criticism of the company was and where they were coming from, and were we open to a new way of doing the work that we were doing. We really did a listening tour. Not just listening, but to truly understand with an open-mindedness that perhaps something would need to change. So it was a similar journey internally and externally.

Pravir: Did the internal journey help in making it externally?

Dan. Absolutely. We spent a lot of time talking to colleagues in similar positions at other companies. One of the things I believe is that you have to have internal alignment before you can make progress externally. If you are talking out of both sides of your mouth internally this is going to come out loud and clear when communicating externally. Where is it that you are not aligned, where you are sending different messages? How do you resolve these misalignments? How do you take that aligned message externally as you are talking to all your different partners outside the company?

Pravir: It sounds like that in arriving at internal alignment there was a fair amount of coming together on a common message that makes sense. But taking this a step further, going into the dynamics of the psychology of the self, did you have to bridge something in the pattern in yourself even before you could see how it would play out in the corporation?

Dan: Yes. One of the things I learned, in coming into this kind of role, was that in most challenges the business confronts, you create a solution to that challenge and then execute. And in many instances you can say, we accomplished the goal and can check it off the list. When you are talking about social and environmental changes and progress, it is not so simple. One of the biggest things I needed to look at is that we were not looking at how you make progress in the next week or month or quarter. We were really talking about how we will put things in place that will stand the test of time, and ideally will be in full operation when one leaves the company, when one retires. And I think in many respects I needed to go through my own personal journey of getting from the immediate fix, to stepping back and with patience looking at the enormity and complexity of some of these social and environmental challenges, and then further understanding how to take that complex picture and break it into pieces of a puzzle. The next step then was how do you prioritize building the puzzle so that it is digestible for people making it happen. And so, this was a pretty big thing, and the

287

first quote I used in our first social responsibility report was - "There are no simple answers to complex societal issues." And I think all of us, as human beings like simple answers. We love it when we can get to the bottom of things very, very quickly and get to a solution and be able to check something off the list. This is not what this work is about. It is truly about putting many, many issues together to try and create a better future.

Pravir: I understand what you are saying. Let alone the complexity and intricateness of the social and environmental problems, which by themselves require the creation of a whole different way to look at them - and that is just from the external point of view, but then there is the whole complexity that goes into the psychology of the person. It sounds like you had first to understand the issue and your approach internally, within yourself, then within the company, and then only how it would play out externally. The pattern you worked out in yourself was able to create a whole pattern of success for successive layers of complexity.

Drivers for GAP's Global Responsibility Success & the Flower Chronicles: Conversation II Between GAP and Aurosoorya

Conversation Background: Exploring the factors responsible for GAP's being ranked in the recent top 25 Global Responsibility players rankings by Time Magazine, through a dialog between Dan Henkle, SVP Global Responsibility – GAP, and Pravir Malik, Founder and President, Aurosoorya. The following write-up is based on extracts from a Radio Show, Connecting Inner Power with Global Change, Jan 15, 2010, available at the Apple Store (iTunes 2013).

Pravir: GAP recently appeared in Time Magazine's top 25 Global Responsibility Players. Can you summarize some of GAP's achievements in Corporate Responsibility (CR) and also comment on some of the drivers of success?

Dan: When I look at the journey we have been on, I'll speak very quickly on some of the programmatic things we have done, and then spend more time about the components that have created the journey for us. We have a very comprehensive and sophisticated program in place. We have a team of over 120 people in 20 different countries throughout the world that are focused on improving working conditions in factories that we are placing business in. This is one component of our program and I think that the biggest thing that has happened over the years is that when you are at this work and trying a number of different approaches, you learn a lot along the way, and sometime you try things that don't work and you learn from them and you retool your program.

So we have been in this for 15 years and we have learned a lot along the way and I think we have a program that is very successful. This is true of our environmental program as well. The basic 5 components of our journey have been:

• Importance of internal alignment, and really having the support of the leadership team and the Board of Directors. And we have been very fortunate to have that.

• You have to have a strategy when you are looking at this type of work. There are limitless opportunities for progress on the social and environmental fronts. And you have to really understand what is the best use of resources as a company. And so I cannot emphasize enough the importance of strategy.

• And then is the importance of really staying connected with the external community – the human rights and the environmental communities. They truly are the experts on the ground. They have a lot more information than we have and we should be listening to guidance they are giving us on an on-going basis.

• It is critically important for companies to share their learning and not in a public-relations kind of way, but in a social reporting kind of way, so that you can say here are some of the things we have challenges with, here is the progress we are making. But also here are the challenges that we continue to encounter.

• And then finally it is critically important to be self-reflective and not ever believe that you have stumbled upon the formula for success. There is no such thing in this kind of work. There are things that can get you to a better place. But you have to constantly be evaluating if the way you are going about the work is exactly the way it needs to happen, given all of the different complexities you are encountering and the way the world is shifting on a day-in day-out basis.

Pravir: That approach sounds very comprehensive. I know that it is so easy for a company to continue to view the world in the way it has always viewed it (physical-level). So the whole exercise of playing around with possibilities and viewing many different options is in itself a very progressive step (vital-level). And then if one can even cap that off with phases of self-reflection (mental-level) and with a strategy that really does address the complexity as it is uncovered (mental-level), it really sets up a company for a whole different level and way of success. It sounds like that is some of what you have been doing in your leadership role – setting that environment and culture so that in the terminology of Aurosoorya's Model the company has been moving through the physical-vital-mental pattern or fractal. I would be curious though, as to what the active orientation was as you moved through these 5 components – was it to be experimental, or was it to operate from a space of doing the right thing?

Dan: Fundamentally there has to be an overall cultural value around trying to do the right thing. I am the first one to say that almost every company is going to say that. But that has to be there. I think that if you take that as something that must be there, then take a close look at our experience – what was happening when I started in this role in 2001 – we were getting a lot of criticism. And when you are being criticized and there are campaigns against your company, you are in more of a reactive mode. You are basically defending and reacting. It is not an incredibly powerful place to be. You are in a reactive place. We actually – if I look back a decade ago - I think we were in this mode of being defensive and being reactive. And what was incredibly clear was that we needed to move to a much more proactive place. If we could re-channel all that energy that was going into defending and reacting and so forth – channel that into proactive stuff, we could begin to actually improve working conditions. It would be less about defend and react and how do you actually move things in the field. That was the journey we were in. And I think we have gone from being defensive and reactive, as we became more open to what external community was saying and have become more aligned, to being much more proactive. And we have also gone into a place of saying that we will never have all the answers, and we have to continually be soul-searching to determine what the next 5-10-15 years look like for the company.

Pravir: That is a powerful progression consistent with what I am suggesting to be the fractal for progress, because in this fractal for progress there are three phases. The first can be thought of having a higher degree of defensiveness and reactiveness, mainly because an organization is trying to defend its fixed view of things. That is the physical view. And then as you describe the journey of GAP there is a migration to the second-level of the journey, the vital-level, in which you become much more open to external comments and communities, and enter into relationship with external stakeholders and there is more pro-activeness. The journey could be ended here and if you had ended the journey there you would not have achieved the results that you have. But what is apparent is that you have gone through to the next step, which I call the mental phase, because you have had a culture of soul-searching. So asking yourself the question of whether what you are doing is right, and whether you were really answering all that complexity in the way that it should be answered really created newer possibility for you.

Dan: Another framing of it is as a journey from risk-mitigation to value-creation. Taking a challenge and turning it into an opportunity. And if you think about it, even the frame of mind, of looking at something as a risk or challenge – it is a negative framing of the issue. If looking at it is something that can add value to the corporation it changes the dynamic and discussion and that is what we have been trying to do in a much more significant way.

Pravir: Yes, that framing is very consistent with the sustainability model presented, that dynamics at the personal level will ripple out to create the dynamics at the corporate level.

Summary

Given that the true root in bringing about sustainability at any scale are the drivers at the individual level, HR can play a key place in helping corporations and therefore the world in becoming truly sustainable. This can happen in several ways and these are illustrated in the notion of influencing events along an employee's lifecycle. In a study led by Society for Human Resource Management, however, the lack of involvement by HR in the field of sustainability, let alone in the managing of the root patterns on which all sustainability depends, is apparent.

Best practice though is illustrated through a conversation with the Senior Vice President of Global Responsibility at GAP, where the dynamics that GAP went through in becoming a leader in the corporate responsibility space, was consistent with the ubiquitous flower mode of sustainable development.

Part 8 – Paradigms For The Future

In assessing future development it becomes necessary to first have an insightful model against which to do so. The Flower Chronicles model is used for this purpose. In the chapter we first look at what the world may become were different stages inherent in the flower's journey, were to be the arbiter of possibility. Such consideration provides a useful framework to then assess where the world has been, where it is going, and where it needs to go in the future.

The Physical or Seed Scenario

A physical or seed orientation would imply a reality dictated primarily by what the eye can see. The notion of a single, purposeful, conscious, and fully integrated world-system, more common perhaps to a flower or intuitional way of seeing, would be an outright chimera or even blasphemy to the established way of seeing. The established way of seeing will be the unerring anchor-point and the filter through which all decisions need to be made. Climate Change, slow global poisoning, destabilization of all forms of magneto-chemical systems, destruction of environments and the resource base, common issues increasingly being discussed today, will likely be consigned to the category of hogwash and will definitely not be perceived as signs of rebellion from a conscious and progress-driven system.

At most these will be thought of as natural occurrences in a cycle that has existed from time immemorial. People and society will continue to be thought of as existing to lubricate the unerring business engine that has proven its value just the way it is, time and time again. There will be no time nor need for searching for another way of being, because the one in existence now will be perceived as being perfcct and in no want of change.

In this scenario major catastrophes and upheavals are likely to loom up suddenly. Obviously people will be utterly unprepared for what hits them. This scenario will be like that of the frog in slowly heating water. As the temperature of the water increases, rather than jumping out, the frog gets more and more used to it and does not even realize that something is amiss until it is too late and the water has begun to boil. At this point it is not possible for the frog to escape and it too boils with the boiling water. In this scenario, systemic weakness is not addressed but simply covered up. This is the scenario of financial bailouts and stark denial. Leading countries maintain global economic power by the application of military might. Currencies are artificially propped up to maintain the semblance of strength. Religious institutions intervene to promote yesteryear's leaders. The American Dream and way of life continue to be propagated as the best and strongest until it is too late. And all the while what really needs to be changed remains unaddressed.

The Vital or Stalk Scenario

In the scenario marked by vital or stalk orientation the frenzies of today continue until exhaustion. This means that the pace of systemic debilitation will proceed faster than in the scenario marked by physical-orientation. In the **physical-orientation scenario** we live with the denial for longer. Facades are kept up and we live in a space within ourselves trapped in from any hints of air or sunlight from greater possibilities. In the vital-orientation scenario we hit the limits of the system far more quickly and comprehensively. This is because vital-orientation is driven by aggressiveness and a desire to aggrandize the sense of self. Self, however, is defined narrowly without including impacts that actions by the self have on the world and people around. This quickly brings us up against the limits of our view.

Hence, driven by the vital desire of the consumer, conspicuous consumption sets in motion disastrous ripple effects on the physical and psychological health of the people and the health of the world. On the psychological side people come to equate happiness and self-worth with products and 'things' out there. The sense of possibility, of creativeness, of true as opposed to surface self-power, engendered by a world-view marked by a conscious, purposeful, integrated world-system is all but absent.

As a race we lose subjective power and become slaves of an objective and often, heartless world. The causal relationship between subjectivity and objectivity is reversed and instead of the landscape within determining the landscape without, it is the landscape without that determines the landscape within. This is a poverty-stricken deal in which we have literally surrendered our source of power to a fleeting and meaningless dance toward the bottomless darkness of the abyss. Consider, for example, that in this orientation all people are relegated to the stature of a business asset. Hence, business executives may be thought of as 'more' valuable assets and may be treated more carefully as a result of that, factory workers are thought of as 'less' valuable assets and correspondingly treated with relatively less care, and defenseless women and children are treated as 'least' valuable assets and as a result even traded as commodities in various markets.

But that is not all, the customer, who is perceived as the source of money is often treated as a god – not because god-like qualities may reside within their breasts, but because they

297

temporarily provide the lubrication for this heartless business engine to continue. If a product or service is exchanged for money, then that exchange should indicate the equality of the transaction. Yet those who provide the service or product often continue to place the buyer on a pedestal, and the buyer himself believes that he should be placed on a pedestal. This again indicates the inherent and disproportionate value ascribed to money.

This is a tragedy of epic proportions. The means has become the end. Yet money is only the symbol of a force or an energy that is needed to move things in different and hopefully progressive directions. In the vaster scheme of things it is the direction of movement in various circumstances that is of importance. In the vital scheme of things, however, it is money with its immediate power to satisfy the urge of a narrowly defined self-seeking assertiveness that is of importance.

On the tangible impacts to physical health, the stark compromise of consuming hurriedly and imperfectly thought-through products consequently replete with different sources and degrees of toxicity will take its toll on the very basis of our lives. While we have established that tobacco based products, for instance, consumed over decades result in cancers, what we have not as meaningfully established is how a vast array of other seemingly 'safe' products may similarly result in as debilitating conditions when consumed over an equal length of time. The smoke from tobacco is visible and hence more quickly has resulted in a cause-effect relationship between its consumption and ill-health. Equally debilitating toxins present in other products are however 'invisible', and therefore do not as easily lend themselves to a similar cause-and-effect analyses.

The point is that given the underlying hurriedness and lack of comprehensiveness in thought and action that marks the vital-orientation, it is inevitable that this vaster array of products, regardless of industry considered, will emerge as unsafe. A little more research on nutritional value in processed foods, for instance, will more broadly reveal that all enzymes are destroyed through processing and that perhaps a different kind of processing and distribution needs to be undergone in order that nutrition retain its value.

Weston Price's 'Physical Nutrition and Degeneration' stands as a classic in this area. Similarly a little more research on drug formulation may reveal, as Andrew Weil's work has pointed out, that active ingredients in pharmaceuticals when removed from their naturally occurring environments and array of accompanying chemicals have a compromising effect on cells that they come into contact with, precisely because the array and relative proportions of accompanying chemicals that existed to bring about more holistic interaction with cells has now been removed. The underlying aggression of the vital-orientation does not allow for this extra time and comprehensiveness in research and development and thus of necessity must result in compromises of all sorts.

As far as negative impact on the scale of the world, we have already begun to witness the tremendous price we must pay for this orientation as evidenced by accelerated resource depletion, water and air pollution, greenhouse gas emissions, biodiversity destruction, and compromise to ecosystem services.

What we have not adequately considered however is the effect on global political stability. Fueled by the twin thrusts of consumer demand on the one side, which stimulates investment in new manufacturing capacity, and business desire to increase margins on the other, which stimulates outsourcing of manufacturing to 'cheaper' countries, it is the 'cheaper' countries that stand poised to emerge as the new global leaders as more capital flows into their regions.

This is not always a good thing especially if ideology of the new global leaders is unknown or controversial or untested in the global playing field. For, it provides the country with the resources to potentially fulfill whatever agenda may exist amongst its leadership. However, from a cause and effect point of view and in that we must reap what we sow the continued vital orientation at the level of individual has to create a world that is effectively vital in response.

In such a world there is little place for idealism and balanced development. There is only place for immediate fulfillment of desire to the detriment of any deeper and more holistic ideology. USA's aspiration for relative liberty, freedom, equality, and democracy, all high ideals that belong in their nature to the mental sphere must erode when the citizens of the country are in fact not in reality practicing that, but have abandoned themselves to the petty desires and satisfactions that animate the vital sphere. If at the end of the day citizens are most concerned with bringing home a quick profit, and with convenience of access to products of all kinds, and with having plenty of toys to entertain themselves with, then this is the world that is going to result, and the question of how the profit is made, what the costs to the earth, people, and communities are, or what loss of self-power or of ideals results, will recede into the background to be overtaken by whatever it takes to fulfill the vital-based pattern in its play across the earth.

When China arises as the world's manufacturing center to stock the inventories of the Wal-Marts of the world people then fulfill their desires for cheaper, more easily accessible goods aimed at a portfolio of vital-level desires. That is what the seed-pattern had initiated. The seed-pattern had nothing imprinted in it about the upholding of the generative capacity of the earth, or of the peoples and communities of the earth, or of the high ideals that signal progress in the broadest sense.

In its vitalistic rise China, so it has been reported, has converted productive land into desert, polluted running and still bodies of water, compromised biodiversity, reinforced the notion that people exist for State, not only in China, but in Africa too, where it has entered into vital-level contracts with country governments. The short-sighted hunger of citizens in USA and in other rapidly growing parts of the world has fueled this rise of vitalistic dynamics and large tracts of the world are now fast becoming either centers of needless and wasteful consumption, centers of needless and wasteful manufacturing, and centers of needless and wasteful resource extraction.

The supply chains that span the world now exist to fuel this hunger and madness and in its essence signals the organization of an inevitable destruction so long as the vital-orientation persists. No amount of Corporate Social Responsibility (CSR) is going to make any difference at the end of the day, unless the base consciousness of citizens the world-over, and this includes employees of companies that practice CSR and communities impacted by the operations of these companies, amongst many other stakeholder groups, completes their respective journeys through their flower journeys.

CSR is practiced by large corporations that do not exist for CSR but to make money. If corporations make less money CSR programs receive less funds and CSR diminishes, unless it has become part and parcel of the way a business operates, and this can only happen if even in the absence of any calculated returns on investment, employees still practice CSR because their own journeys have advanced to the generally more holistic mental-level and they genuinely see the need for such holistic business action as represented by CSR on its own merit.

But such conversion of the world into a large supply chain, where 'cheaper' countries become leaders on the world stage and more actively dictate a newer and perhaps even crasser culture for the earth, is only the beginning of the end of the vital-orientation scenario. For as resources get scarcer, and this includes the all-important water, then likely a heightened irrationality will begin to dictate the politics of regions and countries and resource wars will become more prevalent. Then all manner of idealism gets dethroned as people enter into a phase of base survival. In such a scenario all assumptions are hopefully questioned and the seeds for a shift to the mental level are more powerfully bought into being.

The Lower-Mental Scenario

In the mental-orientation scenario, questioning comes alive. This signals a significant progress, for now all existing assumptions, many of which are of an irrational kind, can be questioned and the bases for our living consequently has a more likely chance to begin to be altered. In this scenario raison d'etre has the opportunity to come to the surface. Uniqueness and holism can begin to arise. Hence, the bases for business, amongst other modern-day institutions, can begin to be questioned, and if the questioning proceeds long enough and comprehensively enough, then more enlightened models of business and other institutions can begin to come into being.

Models in which business exists for and is accountable to a variety of stakeholders as opposed to just shareholders can come into being. Hence business would naturally begin to alter the way in which it generates profit to begin to address all costs of its transactions on the individual, social, cultural, and environmental fronts. Similarly other major institutions of the modern-day world can also be questioned and potentially altered to arrive at more enlightened versions of themselves. The often blindly-accepted tenets of religion, usually the creation of the fountainhead prophet or an ensuing circle of disciples can be questioned and affirmed through individual self-discovery. In such a manner the value of religion can be more truly affirmed and become more of a living force in the affairs of life. This same trajectory of questioning can then confirm the possible similarities, synergies, and complementarities of different world-religions. In such a way a more enlightened institution of religion that is also a more living part of life can come into being. Education itself can be similarly questioned, and the value of spawning cogs in a pre-arranged view of life questioned, to perhaps more truly make children and youth develop along lines driven by their own natural curiosities and uniqueness.

The question of course, is at what end of the mental-orientation spectrum will all this questioning proceed at? If it proceeds at the end closer to the vital region, then in many respects it will have the characteristic thrusts that marked the vital-orientation as its accompaniment and context. Then the questioning will likely not proceed comprehensively enough and what will result is a number of biased "isms" that are still anchored to the primary institution that may have characterized the recent vital milieu. Hence, even though there will be greater questioning in each of the institutions of our lives, whether of art, education, science, government, business, military, or sport, each will tend to be interpreted in terms of the recent reigning institution. In our modern-times many will continue to interpret their value in terms of business hence. This same logic will also apply to independence and definition of countries. If USA has been perceived as being the most successful country then its culture and driving institutions will tend to become the standard by which each country interprets its success. The degree to which McDonalds, MTV, and Levis replaces age-old institutions whether of tea drinking, tabla-playing, and dhotis, will be the measure of success of a country.

The Higher-Mental Scenario

At the other end of the mental-orientation spectrum questioning will proceed more independently, and may even at its highest be aligned with deeper drivers that animate a higher intuitional level beyond it. In this scenario each of the "isms" will tend to be truly more enlightened. Having been created through a basis of questioning though, as opposed to a deeper sense of who one is, the questioning will have its limits because it will be all about logic rather than penetrating through experience into the inner uniqueness that animates each person. When that experience becomes the center around which activity is organized, then creation will proceed in a more living, organic and sustainable way. This is the stuff of intuition. In the meanwhile, what will result is a number of parts of society that still function in silos or independently of each other, and not as they should, as integral parts of a single whole.

Society, hence, while objectively surfacing more of the problems that plague life, and even surfacing more of the assumptions that may have led to these problems, will likely still be impotent to solve them, because it has still not penetrated into the heart of the Flower so long as it remains stuck in questioning without following or opening to where the questioning leads. Questioning is of course powerful, but still there needs to be a receptivity to something that is beyond the mind, for true change to happen. In the mental-orientation scenario, forms and processes may change as a result of what seems like the logical solution following the questioning. The United Nations Organization and other forms that are new and different may come into being. The extent to which they successfully achieve their missions will still remain in the balance however, so long as there are no true personalities who organize themselves not based on questioning but on what they creatively and uniquely stand for in the scheme of things.

Hence, in this scenario, the world will likely have a burst of apparent creativity where new technology infrastructures, new types of organizations, new processes and ways of connecting people together, new regional and global alliances at least in name, will come into being. This scenario will also result in frustration when it is discovered that all the new structures and processes and organizations have really not made the difference they intended to make. For the difference to manifest, we of necessity must enter into the higher possibilities inherent in the heart of the flower, the intuitional-orientation.

At the Heart of the Flower: The Intuitional Scenario

In the intuitional-orientation scenario, deeper questioning and completion of many personal stagnated journeys open one to the reality of the ubiquitous Flower. It is in the opening to this reality that help beyond the present-day physical, vital, and mental capabilities comes to the surface. In the disassociation from these persistent and ever-present dynamics one becomes more of a witness to one's operations. A freedom from the ordinary allows one to penetrate that which stands behind surfaces and the essence of what one is,

305

in the vaster scheme of things that the Flower conceivably holds in its heart, is allowed to come to the surface.

Then one may find that what truly drives one is the essential reality of service and perfection, or adventure and courage, or knowledge and wisdom, or harmony and mutuality. In this state, if one turns one ear toward the heart of the Flower, and the other toward opportunities that present themselves in the various fields of practical organization, then spontaneous, organic, living, and uniqueness-based manifestations in each of the fields of practical organization can begin to emerge.

It is then that structure and technology and process and organization will have meaning, and it is then that society will begin to work in the manner intended. When the forms one creates are expressions of who one is, then there is a living and sustainable quality to them that becomes the basis for a progressive society. In this society citizens are heroes because they have stood up for what they are at their cores and they continue to take actions that are consistent with that core. Since their cores are part of the heart of the Flower there is also a more spontaneous and integral interaction and harmony between all the various parts of society. Religion, business, art, sport, education, military, science, and country relation with country, no longer exist at loggerheads with each other. Each of the institutions remakes itself from within so that each becomes an expression of the deeper drivers at the heart of the Flower. With true leaders at their respective helms it is the Flower itself that really guides things.

Summary

Development can proceed along several lines. This has been illustrated throughout this book, and is true at the individual, team, corporate, market, country, or system level.

Further, the possibilities of this development proceed along similar lines regardless of the scale of the organization. In this chapter we have considered the same phases of development that have been applied at each subsequent level of complexity, starting from the individual, to the level of the system. That is the broad encasement in which country, market, corporation, team, and individual sit. These phases are of course those of the growth of the flower form the seed to the flower. Hence, we consider a seed or physical phase, a stalk or vital phase, and three sub-phases of the flower - the lower-mental, a higher-mental, and an intuitional phase. As expected the possibilities and level of true sustainability increases as we move progressively away from the seed phase, and more into the heart of the flower or intuitional phase.

In this chapter some new and different ways to perceive circumstance are explored. In their essence these ways have to do with further integrating that which is separated. Thus we look at new ways to think about quality, the purpose of business, architecting change, and describing business within our complex and integrated system. We also look at a new basis for identifying bubbles of many different kinds, and look at the real basis for an imminent business revolution. Perhaps these can all be thought of as the hints of the flowers that will manifest were we to complete our current flower-journeys.

Emerging Micro and Macro Levers of Quality

Recently I made a presentation at the East Bay Section of American Society of Quality (ASQ) on emerging micro and macro levers of quality.

My summary thesis was:

1. We are going through a fundamental change in the business environment. Small, local actions, whether by business or banks, that for centuries could be ignored, can no longer be ignored. The micro and the macro are now intimately connected. This is evident in macro-phenomenon such as Climate Change and the Financial Crises that have been created by numerous micro-actions, and therefore indicate the changed nature of our business playing-field.

2. Old paradigms are being challenged and even failing as a result of not accurately seeing the intimate connection between the micro and the macro. A new language to connect the micro and the macro is essential. While I provide the

details of such a new language in my book Connecting Inner Power with Global Change (Malik, 2009), the essence of the most sustainable pattern of progress at either the micro or the macro level is summarized by the journey a seed makes in becoming a flower.

3. The ubiquitous flower journey brings to light a dynamic pattern that repeats itself on different scales, the constituents of which are the physical or seed, the vital or stalk, and the flower or mental-intuitional modes of being.

4. In the surfacing of this, additional levers by which quality is achieved are emerging. For it is evident that the global economy is transitioning from the vital to the mental phase of this macro-pattern. Quality has "grown up" in the vital milieu. Its very basis has to be enhanced by the fact that a new paradigm of envisioning quality that is representative of the mental phase has to come into being.

5. The fundamental issue is still that of removing waste from the system. Only, the limits and the nature of the system are redefined, to in effect allow for the removal of waste for the long-term, as opposed to the current focus on the narrowly-defined immediate and short-term.

6. In this reconsideration an important micro-lever that emerges is that of managing individual stress or stress at the personal level. A resultant macro-lever is that of sustainability or corporate social responsibility (CSR), which can be thought of as an index of dysfunction that does not need to be. These are immediate practical levers, and others will be considered at a later time.

7. The reality of replication of patterns on different scale, suggests that lack of management of stress at the individual level ripples out to create major dysfunction at subsequent levels of complexity, leading all the way up to the global macro-level. Externalities are minimized when thinking and

decision-making emanate from the mental as opposed to the vital level.

8. This gives rise to implications for management of quality, and even the central place that quality will hold in creating a more sustainable world.

Architect Change, One Pattern at a Time...

The root of many of our problems - whether globally, nationally, regionally, or locally - is that there is a disconnect between the common meanings and purpose we ascribe to key components of our lives, and the meaning and purpose that the truth of our reality demands. And these common meanings are embedded in dysfunctional patterns that keep us viewing and interpreting ourselves and the world in limiting ways.

Such limiting patterns mean that as individuals we end up supporting efforts that are counter to our own health and sustainability. Many examples exist, ranging from destruction of rainforest and other vastly rich ecosystems, to exploitation of people and resources the world over, to a simplified asset view of life where all exists to prop up the often self-destructive engines of business.

Architecting change one pattern at a time is an approach to manage such patterns and allow more powerful and sustainable patterns to emerge in their place. Such re-patterning will allow individuals, teams and organizations to more fully mirror the truth of reality, and ascribe a more accurate meaning and purpose to their efforts and framing contexts.

This means we will live a more meaningful life using our energies to support things that matter.

There are many individuals the world over who are part of a dysfunctional or a misdirected organization. Many of these individuals feel locked into their way of life because they are bound by financial constraints. They support or do work that in reality often destroys the very foundation on which all work depends. But the only way the dysfunctional or misdirected organization will change is if these individual people begin to subscribe to new patterns of perception and ways of being that gives them power to alter their circumstance.

The ExxonMobils, Citigroups, Pfizers, ADMs, Dow Chemicals, McDonalds, Monsantos, Walmarts of the world are part of a global system that compels them to act they way they do. It is only if another voice becomes active from within, only if there is change from the inside-out, that the balance of decision-making focused on short-term profit, often at any cost, will change. This will benefit not only the individuals, but the misdirected organizations they are a part of.

It is in this context that architecting change, one pattern at a time becomes important.

A New Business Lexicon

Several simultaneous and global shifts signal that we are at a transition point necessitating a different way of being. A new way of being requires a new language to both facilitate its emergence and to fortify its way forward. A quick examination of some leading problems sheds insight into some key components that such an emerging language must contain.

Unlike local, bounded problems, two of the most recent problems are global in scope. Climate Change, though caused by numerous local actions, is now a global problem. It has extended out to the limits of our playing field, and in that regard signals that a new language that connects local action to global, or the micro to the macro, is what must emerge in

311

the business lexicon. The on-going financial debacle, also the result of numerous local actions, now has a massive global effect, far beyond anything local actors would ever have assumed possible. This too requires a new language that connects the local with the global, or the micro with the macro.

Such connection between the micro and the macro or the local and the global, cannot be a loose metaphorical language, but one that ultimately upholds standards of actual experience. It is here that the Flower Chronicles can play a role. For the key features of the Flower Chronicles are that it isolates building blocks common to different structures from the micro to the macro or the local to the global, and shows how patterns created from these common building blocks tend to emanate out in repeating manner such that there is a tight correlation between the observed dynamics at the micro level and the resultant dynamics at the macro level. There is nothing metaphorical about these connections. They are tight, defined, and consistent across different instances of more and more complex organization.

Such a new language or business lexicon is necessary in today's business world for the precise reason that local action has to begin to be perceived as not just local, but as having its real global effects. The very bases of business operation has to alter so that these real and underlying dynamics that connect the micro to the macro will be given real consideration in the creation and the execution of business strategy.

Business, after all, even though it has been viewed from the physical-vital lens thereby optimizing dynamics of isolation and self-aggrandizement, is in reality like everything else around it, a construct of the underlying system, and in its final analyses a flower in process of growth that is seeking to manifest something of the harmonious splendor resident in the underlying system. Such a view requires a mental-intuitional orientation, and is the whole point of the necessity of a new language and business lexicon more attuned to the emerging requirements of the time.

In the physical-vital view, constructs, be they business corporations, non-profits, or individual people, want things delivered to them on a plate in a form that is easily palatable and ultimately reinforces their small view of the world. A new language, on the other hand, can often be anything but straightforward and easily palatable, and further, working through it begins to create the bridges that can accelerate the shift from the self-serving, self-destructive physical-vital view, and the system-aligned and ultimately freeing mental-intuitional orientation.

The Flower Chronicles offers such a bridge-language and means by which business and other constructs can ultimately find release from the paucity of their own world-views.

The Unconsidered Bubbles of Modern-Day Life

Around the 1950 – 60s, as the business paradigm began to get universalized and commonly accepted as the context for living, it was naturally found that all was not well. Social costs and externalities had already been alive for as long as the institution of business has been around. But now environmental costs and externalities were also rapidly coming into focus. At one end, the hard facts were captured in significant works such as Rachel Carson's Silent Spring (Carson 2002), which documented detrimental effects of pesticides on the environment. At the other end, new systemic frameworks that suggested a different interpretation for the concept of environment, and captured in works such as James Lovelock's Gaia hypothesis (Lovelock 2001), began to appear at the same time in the 1960s & early 1970s. These seminal

313

works heralded the start of the modern-day environmental movement.

But this has to be the case since business has proceeded along an artificially created trajectory that does not sync with the reality of life. In life everything is integrated. In Business, under the aegis of the vital-orientation there are artificial boundaries setup which define rules of business. The primary rule is profit-maximization, regardless of total cost. Such a construction cannot but run into increasing problems as the trajectory continues. Markets, being the playing-field of business, are also therefore artificial constructions and cannot but create huge problems as they continue to 'develop'.

These are the huge unconsidered bubbles of modern-day life. We have paid attention to bubbles of the financial kind - whether as far back as the Great Depression, or the more recent Dot-Com, Housing, or Global Financial Crises of 2008 - 2009. The bursting of these has created a lot of heartache. But these are only bubbles within bubbles. Their bursting gives us a small taste of pain. This is nothing compared to the heartache that will be unleashed if we do not quickly address the larger, contextual, systemic bubbles that we live in now.

The business bubble has cut itself off from deep realities, and it is developments such as SRI, GRI, PRI, DJSI, that are like projectiles being thrown from these bubbles to reality to help ground the bubbles and ease their decompression. Some of these deeper principles that these projectiles seem to be aiming at are at the very least seeking to reverse harm done to natural ecosystem services, and are captured in frameworks such as the Earth Charter Principles (The Earth Charter Initiative 2013), Cradle to Cradle Principles (C2C Framework 2013), Natural Step Principles (The Natural Step 2013), amongst others.

But further yet, and deeper still, we need to explore the other systemic bubbles we are entrapped in, for it is only with the bursting of these that we will more truly be able to get to the deepest principles of sustainability that must be considered in our attempt to meaningfully integrate any future business development with reality. There is one such bubble we continually live in and which has ben referred to many times in this book- the vital-physical bubble that seems to define much of who we are, and through pressure of repetition, the nature of many common institutions of our lives. This bubble is the result of stagnation in the underlying flower journey.

In fact a deeper understanding of a range of bubbles can be understood by considering the following principles that arise from consideration of the underlying and ubiquitous flower journey:

• There is a ubiquitous journey of progress summarized by the journey of a flower.
• The stages of the ubiquitous journey are like DNA or the building blocks that animate all organizations. These building-blocks can be seed or physical, stalk or vital, or flower or mental in nature.
• Dynamics of a particular organization are entirely determined by which of these building-blocks are active at that level of organization.
• Like DNA, the stringing together of building-blocks in a particular sequence or with particular dominance, determines that active dynamics of that level of organization.
• There is only one particular sequence of stringing together building-blocks that allows an organization to progress sustainably – that is the physical-vital-mental flower sequence with the mental orientation leading.

- This particular sequence exists in all progressive organizations, regardless of level of complexity.
- When organizations embrace sequences other than that of the progressive journey, they become a part of an 'as-usual' as opposed to progressive life.
- These unprogressive or 'as-usual' journeys are the bases of bubbles, because at its heart it is something other than the requirement of the time or space that is being artificially 'developed'.
- The requirement of the time or the space can be connected to only by continuing on the underlying flower journey.
- When a flower-journey encounters as-usual journeys a rite of passage is created by which deeper identity that defines the flower can emerge.

These emerging principles ground development concretely, because it always connects to the bias or direction of the system behind the apparent system. In this regard there is a natural instinct to break all bubbles and for development to proceed most sustainably.

The Imminent Business Revolution

Business as a way of life has become so embedded in our ways of being that we often relate success to be synonymous with success in business. The size of one's bank account and accumulated assets often offers one more prestige in life than those without these coveted possessions. Progress itself, be it at the personal, local, national, or international levels is often equated to business development and growth. Even in relations between one person and another there is often an air tainted by closing a business deal or getting some business benefit from the contact.

All this is like a subtle poison that has veiled the heart and deeper possibility. The rending of this veil from oneself, from contact between oneself and another, and from all manner of interaction in society is imperative if we are to become free as a species. For right now so much of operation, even at the seemingly most innocent levels is masked by this gray veil of needing to make money for oneself or for who one serves in the pervasive ways of business bondage.

There are crucial questions that arise. Why have we collectively allowed money to become the arbiter of all of life? In many respects money is like oxygen. We need oxygen to live, but the accumulation of oxygen is hardly the purpose of life. In fact it is only in times of dire stress that we begin to gasp and wonder where the next breath is going to come from. It is only when we are on our death-beds that oxygen becomes an issue. Money too is an energy, and orientation toward it should be of a similar nature to the orientation toward oxygen. Our constant need for it now, in our current ways of life, perhaps signals that we are collectively on a death-bed, and it is only when we recast our relationship with money that we will have the opportunity for resurrection.

For it is only when money is perceived as an impersonal force that must be managed so that the greatest good for all can emerge, that who we are within, in the depths of our hearts, will have a chance to surface. Right now we are all cogs in a machine set in motion to increase blind business activity. Such short-sightedness must create major dysfunction, and this is indeed the case as we see now with the surfacing of recent phenomenon such as the global financial crises and Climate Change. These phenomenon are our opportunity to pause and reconsider our relationship with ourselves and with what we have myopically decided is of most import to our lives.

Our reality, set in motion by a flower journey much, much larger than ourselves has to fulfill itself through the march of time, and that it will, regardless of our temporary and childish grappling with the facts of life. No shortsightedness can ever change who we are in our depths, and the sooner we grasp that possibility, the more fulfilled will we all be for it. Ask yourself therefore who you are currently a slave to? Where is your power? Who have you given that power to? Are you part of a dysfunctional organization that under the pretext of doing good things has chained you with a thousand bounds? Are you slave to a contract, business or other, where the supplier of money, whether a boss or a customer, feels they own you and that you need to be subservient to them? Because some arbitrary laws have slotted you as bankrupt or without assets does that mean that you must lose your home and prestige amongst others? Why have you lost your sight so that the money that is meant to be impersonal and belong to no one now belongs to someone who therefore has power over you? What can you do to take back your power? What can be done as a collectivity or as a community so that development can proceed in a more balanced way and one's right to remain human upheld regardless of outer circumstance?

These are the questions that must be answered now. This is the critical need of the hour. This is the basis of the imminent business revolution.

Summary

In this chapter we consider some reflections of the shift to the future, based on integration of some kind. From a perspective of the quality movement, removal of waste will still be the focus; though the means by which waste is defined will change and the drivers of waste be expanded to include the inner orientation along with assumptions, beliefs, and patterns of behavior. We also consider the necessity of a new language which more intimately connects the micro with the macro and, and which illustrates easily the fundamental pattern of progress at both the micro and the macro. In fact this book explores this fundamental pattern in the metaphor of the flower in detail. Such a new language is a sign of the bridge between the past and the future, and makes it more possible to architect change one pattern at a time. There has been an artificial segregation of life in the field of business – something that has severed the wholes along several dimensions. Such severing results in stagnation in the flower journey, and therefore in the creation of bubbles. The language of bubbles is something we can relate to because it is common in market crises. However, we live in larger bubbles that are a result of our stagnations and sooner or later we have to address these, or will be forced to of necessity. There is an imminent revolution at hand, in the field of business, and this has to be given the underlying flower of progress, and the fact that today we have stagnated in our journey.

These then – a new language, the bursting of bubbles, the urge to architect change one pattern at a time – indicate some of the integrating bridges that help us complete our flower journeys and move us into that future.

In Chapter 17 we considered a framework for future development. This framework explored reality as it could unfold along different phases of the flower journey. In Chapter 18 we considered some paradigms that lead toward the future. In this chapter we consider a possible future that may manifest if we were to successfully leverage the paradigms introduced to get to the heart of the flower (Malik 2011).

New Delhi, India, 2040

There is no haze, there are no whiffs of diesel or other petroleum-based products in the air. In fact, quite the contrary, you smell the sweetness of a variety of flowers and ripe fruit from the luxuriantly growing plants and trees in all the small community gardens and along every street of the city. You hear the beautiful chirping of birds producing unheard of ragas for the different times of the day, the different days of the week, and the different months of the year. The plumage is itself magnificent and competes with the colors and variety of flower and plant.

It is June, and you do not feel the hot loos and once oppressive heat of the summer. The numerous water-ways running through the city and the variety of trees, including pine and fir, have forever altered the climate to make it much more temperate. You are struck too by the beauty of the architecture and the buildings. All melds into all, and the human-made structures could very well be an extension of Mother Nature. It as though numerous micro-ecosystems have sprouted up where earlier were jagged concrete structures. In fact these almost self-contained micro-ecosystem communities have become the living and working quarters for people.

One does not see homeless people begging on the streets anymore. Poverty has been removed forever, and all people are part of communities that have become their real and extended families. You can see the glint in the eye, and the confidence in bodies of health. There is richness apparent in the walk and posture of all people. It is as though something gave them permission to be, and people are living a life that is attuned to their souls and more and more becoming the possibility resident deep within their breasts.

Highly efficient micro solar panels, leveraging a wave of cutting-edge technology, now provides all power for all the communities and the entire city. Vehicles, on the road-ways and the water-ways, are solar-powered and silent. The road-ways themselves are made from a material that seems to re-organize itself to maintain an essential solidity and harmony with the environment based on the temperature, pressure, and demands of traffic. There is much less traffic, and fewer larger vehicles of various kinds that carry more people. There are a variety of essentially mechanical mono-passenger vehicles designed to exercise different muscle-groups of the body. Such traveling has itself become a sophisticated means to continually develop the flexibility, durability, strength, endurance, resilience, lightness, and plasticity of the body, by also allowing an orchestrated flow of wind, light, and other electro-magnetic energy to pass over the appropriate meridians and even penetrate selected areas of the body. Such interactions have itself become an advanced means of healing and maintaining the body, and even reversing the cycle of degeneration. People now live much longer, healthier lives.

The practice of health-care has completely altered. Community gardens now double as a natural, real-time, ever-available home pharmacy. The once rapidly growing pharmaceuticals industry is no more. Hospitals have been converted into health and expo centers for the display and use of a variety of advanced natural healing devices.

Money & Power

There are no loud advertisements and signs along the roads, for there has been an essential shift from a push-the-consumer to a pulled-by-consumer model of business. Business itself has altered radically. More comprehensive, holistic, society- and community-aligned models for running business have come into being. The essential meaning of business has altered, and now implies an organization or enterprise focused on providing goods and services to people. Business is run by stewards responsible to their communities and society to mobilize and convert resources to create goods and services that capture beauty and splendor in its various forms, while increasing the overall wealth of those communities, society, planet earth, and every person involved. It is a noble profession that draws from inspired founts of creativity. And those founts of creativity find their very bases in a redefined society.

In this redefined society there are multiple and independent sources of strength. No more does all exist for an unrefined business profit-motive. Business has discovered its true engine of being, as have other great institutions – education, art, sport, service, research, engineering – amongst others. There was a time when all existed to prop up the unrefined engines of global business. This short-sighted global motive force has now been corrected and other institutions too, have found their real reason for being. All is organically organized around unique personalities who breathe and live their truth into the organizations that are growing around them. Business is not a context in itself. It exists to further the broader context of progress for society, humanity, community, person. But progress is not measured in narrow monetary and profit terms. It is measured in terms of deeper and authentic development.

Money moves, almost automatically, to support the development and creative expression of these unique personalities. There are no favored elite who control the issuance and flow of money. To build up personal wealth in terms of big bank balances or personal balance sheets of various asset-classes no more has meaning. If one is powerful, it is because they have begun to express the true power that defines who they uniquely are. If one has built up capital, it is because they have served community and society by exercising who they are. And that capital is not monetary capital. It is capital of knowledge, or capital of courage, or capital of industry, or capital of service, amongst many different capitals. There is a place for all to be who they are.

No more does one need to learn a trade, or learn to do business, or learn to be an engineer because one is compelled, monetarily, to do so. There was a time when one had to earn money by doing something even, that was completely out-of-sync with who one was as a person and a possibility. But no more is this the case. Now if one pursues a field, it is because one's nature compels one to do so. And in the act of pursuing that which one's nature demands of him or her, the field of the act is enhanced in an extraordinary way. There is not the short-term reward that is the motive of the action. The motive is knowledge-fulfillment, service-fulfillment, amongst myriad other fulfillments, leading to self-fulfillment, community-fulfillment, and society-fulfillment.

Money is not the ends. It is the means. To accumulate money means nothing. What really matters is the level of productivity of a person. And there are many, many currencies in which this is evaluated. The peace around a person, the joy, the harmony they create, the knowledge about a specific field, the perfection in art, the ability to diagnose a problem and suggest a meaningful solution, the care-free laugh, and so on. Each of these is the currency. They are not exchanged for money. They have value in and of themselves. Being who one is, is what defines richness. Money is mobilized to facilitate the emergence of this richness. It has no value in being stored.

Innovation & Community

Following the sustained global financial crises that continued for a decade, inspite of what seemed like several trends reversals and turn-arounds, there was massive introspection on multiple-levels. Many changes were made to the way money is issued, is distributed and flows. The essential monopolistic control of money, paradoxically upheld in the name of globalization and establishing fairness, was found to be a major cause of the financial crises. For it was always the few who wished to control its issuance, its flow, its valuation, at the expense of the many. As a result unsubstantiated issuance and valuation of money, not backed by an equal foundation of potential industry and activity, continued to dilute its purchasing power and continued to sow the seeds of global inflation. It was also found that the demonopolization of this critical symbol of energy needed to take place. Hence the nature of its issuance has now changed. Communities create their own currencies that are managed and monitored locally by local leaders. At the same time there are independent regional agencies that exist to monitor the value of community currencies and link them to each other in an equitable way to form an essentially regional network. There are similar national agencies that exist to monitor and link regional currencies together in a national network. There

324

are similar international agencies that exist to monitor and link national currencies together in an international network.

Guidelines for the creation of such currencies involved representatives from all levels of society and all around the world on an essentially Internet-based collaborative platform. Such global communities for all interest groups have continued to flourish and have become technically more savvy integrating all senses in the interaction. Sophisticated nano-sized sensors see, touch, smell, hear differently so that a variety of additional information becomes the norm. Keypads are thing of the past so that a whole new generation of mobile devices allows more detailed aspects of the world to be experienced by remote social-platformers in far-parts of the globe. Such sensing also allows sophisticated analyses to understand the quality, make-up, of all manner of remote communities. This further allows real-time, objective and technical bases for guideline-aligned calibration and adjustment between the many currencies from around the world.

The need for business travel has obviously been reduced tremendously, given the embedding of more sophisticated information technology and telecommunications devices around the world. Aircraft are light and strong, and covered with a material whose properties can change in real-time to become unbreakable, unsinkable, bounceable, amongst other properties so that safety of passengers is never compromised, regardless of situation.

Focused R&D efforts that require major resources are now, based on estimated efforts, either allocated to the regional, national, or international efforts respectively. Oftentimes breakthrough ideas are conceived by small communities. To make that real they are allocated to the appropriate level of organization so that the appropriate level of effort and resources are automatically leveraged.

Short-sighted competition that was once the driver of innovation has been replaced by a sustainable multi-pillared foundation in which innovation flourishes organically. The pursuit of knowledge, now not tied up with the notion of rewards, but existing to break the very barriers of knowledge has engendered a whole other level of scientific discovery and engineering break-through. Further, it was found that where the pursuit of such knowledge is seamlessly supported by the similar pursuit of other deep and primal drivers, such as the pursuit of service, perfection, courage, harmony, art, adventure, amongst many other possibilities, provides for a naturally progressive and sustainable foundation. Such rich human-systems aimed at the realization of the deepest human possibilities were found to be the magic key to unlocking a variety of wealth at every possible level imaginable – from the person, to the family, the community, to the ecosystem, to the region, to the nation, to the world. Such human-systems have become the basis of organizational building.

Terrorism and war have no need to be, since the basis of wealth has now been diversified and all are able to live a full-life on the basis of who they are, rather than what they have to do to support a once narrow and biased machinery of business. International relations have completely changed. Countries interact with countries, not based on exploitation or essential self-promotion, but because of the uniqueness that each country represents. There is something truer and deeper to be learned in the interchange, in which all genuinely profit and the whole becomes greater than the parts. In that interchange uniqueness is strengthened. And so too is diversity. In that interchange the bases of Peace is further strengthened, since each affirms the difference represented by the other.

There are far more Einsteins, Gandhis, Beethovens, & Tatas in the world, than ever before. The world has become a rich place in which to encounter a person is to encounter a mystery of beauty.

1. Amabile, Teresa, Steven Kramer, The Progress Principle: Using Small Wins to Ignite Joy, Engagement, and Creativity at Work, Boston: Harvard Business Review Press, 2011
2. Aurobindo, Sri, Savitri, Pondicherry: Sri Aurobindo Ashram Press, 1950
3. Aurobindo, Sri, Isha Upanishad, Twin Lakes: Lotus Press, 1986
4. Aurosoorya 2013a, PowersWithin, http://www.aurosoorya.com/powerwithin.html (downloaded 11.07.2013)
5. Aurosoorya 2013b, EmotionalIntelligenceBuilder, http://www.aurosoorya.com/emotional.html (downloaded 11.07.2013)
6. Aurosoorya 2013c, Leveraging Fractal Technology to Scale Change Initiatives, http://www.slideshare.net/SBODN/leveraging-fractal-technology-to-scale-change-initiatives (downloaded 11.07.2013)
7. Aurosoorya 2013d, StressManager, http://www.aurosoorya.com/stressmanager.html (downloaded 11.07.2013)
8. Authers, John, The Fearful Rise of Markets: Global Bubbles, Synchronized Meltdowns, and How To Prevent Them in the Future, Upper Saddle River: FT Press, 2010
9. Bottari, Mary, CMD Releases Bailout Tally, $4.6 Trillion in Federal Funds Disbursed, http://www.prwatch.org/node/8987, 2010 (downloaded 11.07.2013)

10. C2C Framework, http://www.mbdc.com/cradle-to-cradle/c2c-framework/, 2013 (downloaded 11.07.2013)

11. Cameron, David, David Cameron's Europe speech in full, http://www.telegraph.co.uk/news/newsvideo/uk-politics-video/9820375/David-Camerons-Europe-speech-in-full.html, 2013 (downloaded 11.07.2013)

12. Carson, Rachel, Silent Spring, Boston: Houghton Mifflin Company, 2002

13. CBS News, 2012 Presidential Debate Part 2, http://www.cbsnews.com/8301-250_162-57533848/transcript-second-2012-presidential-debate-part-2/?pageNum=7&tag=page, 2012 (downloaded 11.07.2013)

14. Chilkoti, Avantika, India Retail: Franchise catching on fast, http://blogs.ft.com/beyond-brics/2013/07/09/india-retail-franchise-catching-on-fast/#axzz2YvqKsm00 2013 (downloaded 11.07.2013)

15. Conner, Daryl, The Real Story of the Burning Platform, http://www.connerpartners.com/frameworks-and-processes/the-real-story-of-the-burning-platform, 2012 (downloaded 11.07.2013)

16. CPP Inc. 2013, https://www.cpp.com/company/index.aspx (downloaded 11.07.2013)

17. Daily Mail, Demonstrators riot in Spain, http://www.dailymail.co.uk/news/article-105333/Demonstrators-riot-Spain.html, 2013 (downloaded 11.07.2013)

18. Demos, Telis, D Börse and NYSE Euronext close to deal, http://www.ft.com/intl/cms/s/0/6ad9485a-

3610-11e0-9b3b-00144feabdc0.html#axzz2YIQFcCUR, 2011 (downloaded 11.07.2013)
19. Dirie, Waris, Desert Flower: The Extraordinary Journey of a Desert Nomad, London: William Morrow Paperbacks, 2011
20. Dombey, Daniel, US struggling to hold role as global leader Clinton says, http://www.ft.com/intl/cms/s/0/5ff5669c-4508-11e0-80e7-00144feab49a.html#axzz2YIQFcCUR, 2011 (downloaded 11.07.2013)
21. Dombey, Daniel, Erdogan woos Turks with promises of more prosperity, http://www.ft.com/intl/cms/s/0/21fa50e4-d8fb-11e2-a6cf-00144feab7de.html#axzz2YIQFcCUR, 2013 (downloaded 11.07.2013)
22. Dyer, Geoff, US intelligence denies 'unilateral' internet data collection, http://www.ft.com/intl/cms/s/0/87532b6a-d085-11e2-a050-00144feab7de.html#axzz2YIQFcCUR, 2013 (downloaded 11.07.2013)
23. Europa.Eu, http://europa.eu/abouteuropa/index_en.htm, 2013 (downloaded 11.07.2013)
24. Ferguson, Niall, The Ascent of Money: A Financial History of the World, New York: Penguin Books, 2009
25. Ferguson, Niall, A Greek crisis is coming to America, http://www.ft.com/intl/cms/s/0/f90bca10-1679-11df-bf44-00144feab49a.html#axzz2YIQFcCUR, 2010 (downloaded 11.07.2013)
26. Flannery, Tim, The Weather Makers, New York: Atlantic Monthly Press, 2005

27. Fuller, Buckminster, Synergetics: Explorations in the Geometry of Thinking, London: Macmillan Publishing, 1982

28. Fratzscher, Marcel, The ECB must open itself up, http://www.ft.com/intl/cms/s/0/7e58a3ea-d1bc-11e2-9336-00144feab7de.html#axzz2YIQFcCUR, 2013 (downloaded 11.07.2013)

29. FT.com Lex, The US Recovery, http://www.ft.com/intl/cms/s/3/13d1e4fa-7562-11df-a7e2-00144feabdc0.html#axzz2YIQFcCUR, 2010 (downloaded 11.07.2013)

30. Gallagher, James, Antibiotic 'apocalypse' warning, http://www.bbc.co.uk/news/health-21178718, 2013 (downloaded 11.07.2013)

31. Giles, Chris, IMF floats plan to raise targets for inflation http://www.ft.com/intl/cms/s/0/46c20458-1775-11df-87f6-00144feab49a.html#axzz2YIQFcCUR, 2010 (downloaded 11.07.2013)

32. Gorst, Isabel, Investors fear re-run of great grain robbery http://www.ft.com/intl/cms/s/0/2d8599c8-a177-11df-9656-00144feabdc0.html#axzz2YIQFcCUR, 2010 (downloaded 11.07.2013)

33. Glickstein, Lee, Be Heard Now, New York: Crown Business, 1999

34. Gupta, Amitabh, Book Review of Redesigning the Stock Market, Vision: The Journal of Business Perspective, 16: 142-144, 2012

35. Haramein, Nassim, Rauscher, E.A., and Hyson, M, 'Scale unification: a universal scaling law', Proceedings of the Unified Theories Conference, 2008

36. Harding, Robin, Obama seeks to retain R&D tax credit, http://www.ft.com/intl/cms/s/0/91a6cad2-

b912-11df-99be-00144feabdc0.html#axzz2YIQFcCUR, 2010 (downloaded 11.07.2013)

37. Harding, Robin, Bernanke sees 2014 end for QE3, http://www.ft.com/intl/cms/s/0/17078b02-d905-11e2-84fa-00144feab7de.html#axzz2YIQFcCUR, 2013 (downloaded 11.07.2013)

38. HealthAffairs, Health Spending Projections Through 2017: The Baby-Boom Generation Is Coming To Medicare, http://content.healthaffairs.org/content/early/2008/02/26/hlthaff.27.2.w145.full.pdf+html, 2008 (downloaded 11.07.2013)

39. iTunes 2013, Connecting Inner Power with Global Change, https://itunes.apple.com/podcast/connecting-inner-power-with/id364899923, 2013 (downloaded 11.07.2013)

40. Kanwal, Gurmeet, China preparing Tibet as future war zone, http://www.deccanherald.com/content/165996/china-preparing-tibet-future-war.html, 2012 (downloaded 11.07.2013)

41. Kazmin, Amy, Indian retailing remains a huge challenge, http://www.ft.com/intl/cms/s/0/bf7d2fc4-11cf-11e2-b9fd-00144feabdc0.html#axzz2YrE3G5mz, 2012 (downloaded 11.07.2013)

42. Kerber, Markus, Europe should turn itself into a cyber war fortress, http://www.ft.com/intl/cms/s/0/71a9eb00-e3d1-11e2-91a3-00144feabdc0.html#axzz2YIQFcCUR, 2013 (downloaded 11.07.2013)

43. Ki-moon, Ban, Secretary-General's remarks to the World Economic Forum Session on Redefining

Sustainable Development,
http://www.un.org/sg/statements/?nid=5056, 2011
(downloaded 11.07.2013)

44. Kynge, James, The China Syndrome,
http://www.ft.com/intl/cms/s/0/2ab8c5a8-45e1-
11e0-acd8-00144feab49a.html#axzz2YIQFcCUR, 2011
(downloaded 11.07.2013)

45. Leahy, Joe, Brazil: The power of the streets,
http://www.ft.com/intl/cms/s/0/5e79204e-da5a-
11e2-a237-00144feab7de.html#axzz2YIQFcCUR, 2013
(downloaded 06.06.13)

46. Lesmoir-Gordon, Nigel, Arthur Clarke, The Colours
of Infinity, Bath: Clear Press Ltd, 2004

47. Lovelock, James, Gaia, Oxford: Oxford University
Press, 2001

48. Mackenzie, Michael, Breaking circuit to halt repeat of
'flash crash',
http://www.ft.com/intl/cms/s/0/673b7bae-6e6b-
11df-ad16-00144feabdc0.html#axzz2YIQFcCUR, 2010
(downloaded 11.07.2013)

49. Malik, Pravir, Fractal Dynamics & CSR,
http://www.bsr.org/reports/BSR_Fractal_Dynamics
_CSR.pdf, 2007 (downloaded 11.07.2013)

50. Malik, Pravir, Connecting Inner Power with Global
Change: The Fractal Ladder, New Delhi: Sage, 2009

51. Malik, Pravir, Redesigning the Stock Market: A
Fractal Approach, New Delhi: Sage 2011

52. Mandelbrot, Benoit, The Fractal Geometry of Nature,
New York: W.H.Freeman and Company, 1982

53. Mandelbrot, Benoit, The (Mis)Behavior of Markets,
New York: Basic Books, 2004

54. Morris, Harvey, BP abandons 'top kill' efforts on oil
spill, http://www.ft.com/intl/cms/s/0/832b7b5e-

6a4a-11df-b268-00144feab49a.html#axzz2YIQFcCUR, 2010 (downloaded 11.07.2013)

55. McGregor, Richard, For US spies, Europe is both partner and fair game, http://www.ft.com/intl/cms/s/0/20d985f2-e3f7-11e2-91a3-00144feabdc0.html#axzz2YIQFcCUR, 2013 (downloaded 11.07.2013)

56. Oberlander, Marissa, Mapping the Middle East unrest, http://www.ft.com/intl/cms/s/0/4c5117a6-2eda-11e0-9877-00144feabdc0.html#axzz2YIQFcCUR, 2010 (downloaded 11.07.2013)

57. Pimlott, Daniel, G20 agrees $1100bn to fight crisis, http://www.ft.com/intl/cms/s/0/5c541a18-1eec-11de-a748-00144feabdc0.html#axzz2YIQFcCUR, 2011 (downloaded 11.07.2013)

58. Politico, October 22 2012 Presidential Debate Transcript, http://www.politico.com/news/stories/1012/82712.html, 2012 (downloaded 11.07.2013)

59. Prechter, Robert, Conquer the Crash: You Can Survive and Prosper in a Deflationary Depression, Hoboken: Wiley, 2009

60. Rabinovitch, Simon, PBoC dashes hopes of China liquidity boost, http://www.ft.com/intl/cms/s/0/d244210c-d8ae-11e2-a6cf-00144feab7de.html#axzz2YIQFcCUR, 2013 (downloaded 11.07.2013)

61. Rand, Ayn, Atlas Shrugged, New York: Signet, 1996

62. Sandbu, Martin, Forget the Fed – it's the ECB that should worry investors, http://www.ft.com/intl/cms/s/0/03858014-d993-11e2-98fa-00144feab7de.html#axzz2YIQFcCUR, 2013 (downloaded 11.07.2013)

63. Schipani, Andres, Brazil condemns Europe for Bolivian aircraft diversion, http://www.ft.com/intl/cms/s/0/c97c044e-e3db-11e2-91a3-00144feabdc0.html#axzz2YIQFcCUR, 2013 (downloaded 11.07.2013)

64. Schwab, Klaus, World Economic Forum Annual Meeting 2010, http://www3.weforum.org/docs/AM10/WEF_AM10_Report.pdf, 2010 (downloaded 11.07.2013)

65. SHRM 2011a, SHRM 2011 Employee Job Satisfaction and Engagement Survey Report, http://www.shrm.org/research/surveyfindings/articles/documents/11-0618%20job_satisfaction_fnl.pdf, 2011 (downloaded 11.07.2013)

66. SHRM 2011b, SHRM Report: HR Central to Organizations' Sustainability Efforts, http://www.shrm.org/about/pressroom/PressReleases/Pages/SustainabilityReport.aspx, 2011 (downloaded 11.07.2013)

67. Skibola, Nicole, Mindfulness as a Tool for Organizational and Social Change, http://www.forbes.com/sites/csr/2011/02/01/mindfulness-as-a-tool-for-organizational-and-social-change/ (downloaded 11.07.2013)

68. Tal, Inayat, Unveiling Machu Pichu, Amazon: Amazon Kindle, 2012

69. Taylor, Bob, Swedish riots could represent Europe's future, http://communities.washingtontimes.com/neighborhood/what-world/2013/may/29/swedish-riots-could-represent-europes-future/, 2013 (downloaded 11.07.2013)

70. The Earth Charter Initiative, http://www.earthcharterinaction.org/content/, 2013 (downloaded 11.07.2013)
71. The Hollywood Reporter, 'Social's' $23 mil solid start tops box office, http://www.hollywoodreporter.com/news/socials-23-mil-solid-start-28668 (downloaded 11.07.2013)
72. The Natural Step, http://www.naturalstep.org/, 2013 (downloaded 11.07.2013)
73. US Census Bureau News, http://www.census.gov/retail/, 2010 (downloaded 11.07.2013)
74. US Census Bureau, Top Trading Partners, http://www.census.gov/foreign-trade/statistics/highlights/top/top1208yr.html, 2012 (downloaded 11.07.2013)
75. Vital, Joe, Zero Limits: The Secret Hawaiian System for Wealth, Health, Peace, and More, Hoboken: Wiley, 2008
76. Waters, Richard, Silicon Valley questions Google stance, http://www.ft.com/intl/cms/s/0/c0eb89e4-0207-11df-8b56-00144feabdc0.html#axzz2YIQFcCUR (downloaded 11.07.2013)
77. Wikipedia 2013a, Fractal Geometry, http://en.wikipedia.org/wiki/Fractal_geometry (downloaded 11.07.2013)
78. Wikipedia 2013b, UKUSA Agreement, http://en.wikipedia.org/wiki/UKUSA_Agreement (downloaded 11.07.2013)
79. Wikipedia 2013c, Glass-Steagall Act, http://en.wikipedia.org/wiki/Glass%E2%80%93Steagall_Act (downloaded 11.07.2013)

80. Wikipedia 2013d, Brundtland Commission, http://en.wikipedia.org/wiki/Brundtland_Commission (downloaded 11.07.2013)
81. Wikipedia 2013e, Triple Bottom Line, http://en.wikipedia.org/wiki/Triple_bottom_line (downloaded 11.07.2013)
82. Wikipedia 2013f, Retailing in India http://en.wikipedia.org/wiki/Retailing_in_India (downloaded 11.07.2013)
83. Wikipedia 2013g, Peak Oil
84. http://en.wikipedia.org/wiki/Peak_oil (downloaded 11.07.2013)
85. Wikiquote 2013, The Last Samurai, http://en.wikiquote.org/wiki/The_Last_Samurai (downloaded 11.07.2013)
86. World Federation of Exchanges, Time-Series Share Trading Volume, http://www.world-exchanges.org/statistics/time-series/value-share-trading, 2010 (downloaded 11.07.2013)
87. WWF Global, What does ecological overshoot mean?
88. http://wwf.panda.org/about_our_earth/all_publications/living_planet_report/demands_on_our_planet/overshoot/ (downloaded 11.07.2013)
89. Youtube 2011, Wael Ghonim's Dream Interview - Part 1, http://www.youtube.com/watch?v=SjimpQPQDuU (downloaded 11.07.2013)
90. Youtube 2013, Interview with Dr. Hew Len, http://www.youtube.com/watch?v=OL972JihAmg (downloaded 11.07.2013)
91. Zuckerburg, Mark, https://www.facebook.com/zuck (downloaded 11.07.2013)

Author Background

About the Author

As Chief Technologist at Deep Order Technologies, Dr. Pravir Malik has been developing a unified theory and mathematics of organization with applications in a range of complex adaptive systems. He has written 16 books related to this, which includes a recently completed 10-book series on Cosmology of Light to elaborate mathematics with implications in quantum computing, generation of computational strata, genetics, artificial intelligence, and transhumanism.

Dr. Malik was formerly Senior Director and the Head of Organizational Sciences at Zappos.com, and in this capacity led the creation and incubation of organizational development technologies, in support of establishing a resilient organization to withstand the test of time. He also led the Pricing Operations Group at Zappos.com which was responsible for the profitable management of billions of dollars in assets on a daily basis. During his 5+ year tenure, he was an advisor to the CEO, COO, and CHRO on a range of business and organizational issues. In addition, earlier in 2020 he founded Zappos Organizational Sciences Consulting (ZOSC). His final act at ZOSC was the creation of an Organizational Sciences Certification program offered in conjunction with Forbes. Executives from approximately 150 companies participated in this program.

Dr. Malik currently serves as an advisor to several organizations around the world. In the past, he served as a Founding Member of A.T. Kearney India, a top-tier global consulting company, and served as the Managing Director Advisory Services for BSR, a leading global CSR consulting company.

He has a Ph.D. in Technology Management with a focus on Mathematics of Innovation in Complex Adaptive Systems from the University of Pretoria, an MBA from J.L. Kellogg Graduate School of Management with a focus on Marketing and Organizational Behavior, an MS in Computer Science from the University of Florida with a focus on AI, and a BSE in Computer Engineering from Case Western Reserve University.

Pravir is a global citizen who has lived, worked, and been educated in many parts of the world.

Early Books

1. The Flowering of Management
2. India's Contribution to Management

Fractal Series

1. Connecting Inner Power with Global Change: The Fractal Ladder
2. Redesigning the Stock Market: A Fractal Approach
3. The Flower Chronicles: A Radical Approach to Systems and Organizational Development
4. The Fractal Organization: Creating Enterprises of Tomorrow

Cosmology of Light Series

1. A Story of Light: A Simple Exploration of the Creation and Dynamics of this Universe and Others
2. Oceans of Innovation: The Mathematical Heart of Complex Systems
3. Emergence: A Mathematical Journey from the Big Bang to Sustainable Global Civilization
4. Quantum Certainty: A Mathematics of Natural and Sustainable Human History
5. Super-Matter: Functional Richness in an Expanding Universe
6. Cosmology of Light: A Mathematical Integration of Matter, Life, History & Civilization, Universe, and Self

Applications of Cosmology of Light Series

1. The Emperor's Quantum Computer: An Alternative Light-Centered Interpretation of Quanta, Superposition, Entanglement and the Computing that Arises from it
2. The Origins and Possibilities of Genetics: A Mathematical Exploration in a Cosmology of Light
3. The Second Singularity: A Mathematical Exploration of AI-Based and Other Singularities in a Cosmology of Light
4. Triumph of Love: A Mathematical Exploration of Being, Becoming, Life, and Transhumanism in a Cosmology of Light

- Amazon Author
Page: https://www.amazon.com/Pravir-Malik/e/B002JVAEZE
- LinkedIn
Profile: https://www.linkedin.com/in/pravirmalik/
- Forbes Page &
Articles: https://www.forbes.com/sites/forbeshumanresourcescouncil/people/pravirmalik1/#1fa1097c17be
- Forbes Profile:
https://profiles.forbes.com/members/hr/profile/Pravir-Malik-Head-Organizational-Sciences-Zappos/44463250-f2ab-434a-b1e2-0a6bdf54d970
- Google Scholar Page:
https://scholar.google.com/citations?user=7DWWWZ8AAAAJ&hl=en
- Sage Author Page: https://us.sagepub.com/en-us/nam/author/pravir-malik
- YouTube Page:
https://www.youtube.com/user/Aurosoorya
- Twitter: https://twitter.com/PravirMalik
- Research Gate Profile:
https://www.researchgate.net/profile/Pravir_Malik
- Medium: https://medium.com/@PravirMalik
- Company
website: http://www.deepordertechnologies.com/

Made in the USA
Middletown, DE
11 May 2022

65649027R00195